THE STRENGTH OF OAK

A Prequel to The Horses Know Trilogy

LYNN MANN

Coxstone Press

ISBN 978-1-9161721-4-2
Published by Coxstone Press 2020

For Dad and Fern
with love

Chapter One

I looked up at the dry, brown leaves rustling in the cold breeze, and shivered. Winter was here. I should have put on my cloak, but as was usual when I ran for the comfort of my tree, I hadn't stopped to think.

I sighed and wrapped my arms around myself as I lay back against the huge, gently curving branch that seemed to cradle me in the embrace I'd always craved from my mother, but which she'd never been willing to provide. I welcomed the feeling of calm, of strength, that always seeped through me whenever I hid in the branches of my oak tree, and wondered for the thousandth time whether I was imagining the feeling that the tree was somehow looking after me in a way my mother didn't seem able.

I found the tree by accident when I was eleven. Having spent years being ignored by my mother while watching my eight younger brothers and sisters being loved and adored by her and my step-father, Kerk, it was an unexpected and desperately needed source of peace and relief from my home life.

I was told over and over as I tried and failed to make friends, to excel at school, to complete anything to my mother's satisfaction, that I would never amount to much, that the only thing I was good at was taking after my good-for-nothing father. Apparently, it was my insistence on existing that was to blame for my father concluding that – against their agreement when they married – my mother had conceived on purpose, and leaving his wife and unborn child without a backward glance.

I tried to make myself believe that he left purely because of her; because she had lied to him, because she was cold and foul and impossible to live with. I tried, over and over, to ignore the little voice that nagged away at me, that told me that Mum's second husband loved her, and they both loved all eight of the other children they ended up having, all of whom loved them in return. I tried and failed to resist the idea that I was the only one in the Harrol household who was unlovable. That it wasn't because of my mother that my father left, but because of me.

My mother was blue-eyed and fair, Kerk brown-haired and olive-skinned, and my siblings a mixture of both their features. I didn't resemble any of them. I was tall for my age, black-haired and my eyes were so dark they appeared black on all but the brightest days. My skin was so pale, it was almost translucent. Where the rest of my family browned in the sun, I reddened. Where their eyes were bright and happy, mine were dark and miserable. I caught every glance by every single person who lived in our village whenever they looked from me to my happy, beautiful siblings, wondering how we could possibly be related. I convinced myself I could hear every time one of them thought to themselves that I didn't belong.

My brothers and sisters were all named after birds. Heron was four years younger than I, and every two years after her, another sibling was born; Finch was followed by Kestrel, Robin, Swift, Crow, Kite and Wren. When Kerk started calling me Cuckoo sometime after Robin was born, I loved it; I knew a cuckoo was a bird, and I felt more part of the family. My mother adopted the name for me too, and I wondered if, finally, she might be softening and maybe, just maybe, she would start including me in the affection she gave my siblings.

When people smiled and laughed at my new name, I loved it even more. So when months later, a boy in my class at school told me that cuckoos lay their eggs in other birds' nests, forcing them to bring up the cuckoo's offspring as their own, I was devastated.

'I HATE YOU!' I shouted at my mother as I walked in the door, slamming my school satchel to the floor.

My mother looked up from the dough she was kneading at the kitchen table, and down the hallway at me. 'How dare you shout at me,' she said coldly. 'I feed you, I clothe you and I give you a bed. Nothing is ever enough for you, is it? Just like it wasn't good enough for your father.'

'LEAVE HIM OUT OF THIS, I'M SICK OF YOU BLAMING EVERYTHING ON HIM,' I shrieked. 'I bet if he was here, he'd cuddle me, he'd love me, he'd call me by my name instead of calling me Cuckoo. Everyone is laughing at me because of you and Kerk.'

Three-year-old Kestrel, who was sitting at the table, playing with a small piece of dough, began to cry. My mother picked her up, rested her on her hip and kissed the top of her head. Then she turned back to me. 'Everyone is laughing at you because you behave like an idiot. How many other children get sent out of classes for punching other children? How many of them are kept behind, day after day, for being rude to the teachers? Cuckoos are big birds. They lay their eggs in the nests of smaller birds, and when they hatch, they're bigger than the other baby birds. They demand the most food, they grow the fastest and then they shove the other babies out of the nest. They're bullies, just like you.'

'I'm NOT a bully,' I said, my lower lip beginning to tremble. 'I punched Chessie and Mara because they wouldn't stop teasing me about my trousers being too short. Too short, because you wouldn't make me new ones. They soon stopped laughing at me when their mouths were black and blue, and then when I sewed scraps of material to the hems of all my trousers to make them longer, they were the first to copy me. Everyone wears coloured hems on their trousers and skirts now, because of me. You say I'm no good for anything, well I'm a better Tailor than you, and I'm only eleven.'

'You can sew because I taught you to sew. You're a demanding, ungrateful, rude little bully. Cuckoo suits you. If I'd thought of it at the time, I'd have made it your given name.'

'You called me Rowena after my dad, because his name was Rowan. Grandma told me.'

My mother blinked. She stroked the top of my sister's head with a trembling hand as she glared at me. 'Gwendolen was here in Clearview? I thought that interfering old woman was too old to travel now. When did you see her? She knows I don't allow it. Never mind, I don't care. She had no right to tell you anything.'

'She said you adored him, and that you chased him for years before he finally courted you. She said you would have agreed to anything so that he would marry you, but that you shouldn't have because when you agreed not to have children, it wasn't what was in your heart. She said you made out it was a mistake when you fell pregnant with me, but he knew you too well. She said that when he left, it destroyed you. She said that when I was born, you loved me to begin with. But then as I began to look more and more like him, you changed. She said...'

My mother punched her dough, then strode towards me. 'She said far too much. Now you stop talking right now, Rowena, or I'll...'

'You'll what? Grandma said you're horrible to me because it makes you feel better. My father left you, so you take it out on me, because then you feel as if you're getting back at him. You're horrible and I HATE YOU.' I turned and fled from the house.

I ran out of the village and headed for the woods. It was forbidden for children to go there alone until they were fourteen. As I ran, I tried to think of what else was forbidden, so I could do that too.

As soon as I entered the woods, a peculiar sensation stole over me. I stopped in my tracks. It was as if something were calling to me, yet without making a sound. I frowned and looked around. A little further in to the woods, just off to one side of the path that I would have taken through the trees, was a huge oak tree. It dwarfed all of the other trees as it stood majestically in its own clearing like the king of all trees, awarded the space and respect that it deserved by all of the others. Its trunk was five or six times my girth, its bark ridged and bumpy, and it was heavy with leaves.

I'd never climbed a tree before, but my eyes were drawn to an obvious route up its trunk, provided by its bulges and wrinkles. They positively invited me to climb the tree – as did something else. It felt as if the tree had somehow turned in my direction and opened its branches to me, welcoming me into its safety and protection.

I didn't hesitate. I ran to the tree and climbed and climbed, always finding a handhold or a foothold when I needed one. When I reached a branch that was wide and curved upward, I nestled against it and began to cry, something I rarely allowed myself to do. My whimpers became sobs and then wails, then finally died back to whimpers as I cried myself to sleep.

When I woke, raindrops pattered on the leaves all around me. As the leaves moved in the breeze, droplets of water splattered me. I giggled. The droplets were warm, as was the air that wafted around me, and the bark against which I lay. Everything felt warm and comfortable, as if I were nurtured, protected.

I heard my name being shouted in the distance, and sat up suddenly. No one could find me here. This was my place. I peered over the side of the branch and for the first time, realised how high up in the tree I was. I grinned. No one would ever find me up here. But what if the tree called to them as it had to me? What if they were drawn to climb into its branches as I had been? No one could know about this tree. It was my tree. I climbed down, ran to the edge of the woods, and peered around a sycamore tree. Kerk was coming up the hill towards me with my seven-year-old sister Heron and five-year-old brother Finch. Heron and Finch were both crying.

'What if she n…never comes baaaaaack?' sniffed Heron.

'She w…wouldn't l…leave us, I know she w…wouldn't,' sniffed Finch, and wiped his nose on his sleeve.

'But Mummy's h…horrid to her,' wailed Heron.

'No she isn't, she just gets angry, that's all,' said Kerk. 'We'll find her, don't worry.'

I stepped out from behind the tree.

'Cuckoo, there you are! What on earth are you doing out here? You've missed dinner and your mother's furious. See, Heron? Finch? Your sister's just been for a walk in the woods. It's very naughty, being in the woods on her own, as I'm sure she knows, but no harm done.'

'Don't call me that! I know what a cuckoo is now, I know what they do, and I know you calling me that means you don't want me,' I said as I stormed past him.

'Cuck… Rowena, wait,' my step-father said. I ignored him.

'Wait for me, Weena,' Finch called out. I turned to see him wrenching his hand from his father's. He ran to me and flung his arms around my waist. 'Me and Heron want you, and if Kestrel and Robin were big enough, they'd tell you they want you too.'

I hugged him back. Kerk's face appeared in front of mine. 'Rowena, I'm sorry. When your mother and I were thinking of more birds as possible names for the children she still wants to have, cuckoo came up and she said the name applied to you, but we were just kidding around. It slipped out by mistake when I first called you it, but you looked so happy, I carried on. I understand why you're so upset and I'm sorry.'

'Mum isn't sorry though, is she? She wishes I'd never been born.'

Heron put her arms around Finch and me. 'Don't say that, Rowena. Daddy, tell her?'

Kerk sighed. 'Your mother doesn't wish that, she's just angry with your father. It's not your fault, but there it is. Now come on, all three of you, it's way past all your bedtimes. Your mother will have got Kestrel and Robin to sleep by now, and she'll have a bath waiting for you.'

'Not for me, she won't,' I said.

'Well it's true you'll need to go in last, but you'd need to anyway, Cuck... sorry, Rowena. I mean, look at the mess you've got yourself into. Have you been climbing trees?'

'No,' I said quickly. It wasn't a lie, exactly; I'd climbed a tree, not trees – one very special oak tree that, in the years that followed, I would run to whenever I needed time alone, whenever I needed comfort and strength, whenever I needed to feel safe.

When I was told my reading was way below where it should be for my age, I took the extra reading I was given to the branches of my tree. There, I felt confident as I never did at home or at school. Within a few months, I'd caught up with my peers. When I was teased at school because my clothes were too small, too faded, or needed patching, and my mother continued to refuse to make me new ones, I would take bits of thread and scraps of material from her Tailor's shop, and the clothes that needed adjusting, to my tree.

Whenever I was there, I felt moved to try new things; new stitches, new designs, putting different fabrics, threads and colours together. I made it appear as if I had a huge collection of clothes, when in fact, my ever-changing wardrobe was the result of time spent in my tree, creating different garments from scraps and from clothes I'd worn many times before.

I began to make mock-ups from the scraps – tiny versions of my visions for new clothing designs. I found new uses for cloth; I made children's toys, festive banners, decorations for shop fronts, little ornaments that people could stitch onto their existing clothes – all in the safety and privacy of my tree.

Sewing became my passion and I began to see how it could be my salvation; I would train as a Tailor, and when I qualified, I would leave behind my home village of Clearview and start afresh somewhere else.

As the years went by, my schoolteachers all but gave up on me. No matter how they encouraged, cajoled, berated or punished me, I had absolutely no interest in anything other than the way out of Clearview I continued to picture for myself. Further, I knew how much it annoyed my mother to continually receive complaints about my lack of interest, my sullenness, and my aggression when challenged over my behaviour.

I spent as much time in my tree as the weather, school and my share of the household chores allowed. I made samplers that showed all the stitches I could do, to which I continually added more. I created more and more mock-ups of clothes out of scraps of material, all of which were smuggled out of, and then back into, the house, under my clothes.

When my mother demanded that I help her more in her Tailor's shop, I took all of the skill and knowledge I gained from her to my own work in my tree, where it combined with the inspiration that always came to me there.

I never told her what I was doing, and she was too wrapped up in the rest of our family to notice or wonder where I went when I wasn't at home. Kerk knew I went to the woods. He would watch me going sometimes, and once, I thought I saw him following me. He never passed comment, though, despite the fact that I was breaking a village rule by going to the woods alone at my age. I think he appreciated the peace my absence, and my improved mood on my return, meant for his household.

However many times I visited my tree, it always had the same effect on me. I could arrive in tears or in a temper following yet another row with my mother or one of my teachers, but as soon as I saw the huge oak, I would begin to calm down. As I climbed higher and higher, the effort required confirmed my fitness, my strength and ability, despite everyone telling me I was rubbish at everything. When I settled down to sew, to read, or sometimes just to lay back and enjoy the sound of the leaves rustling, the birds twittering and the calls of the woodland animals, a sense of peace would weave its way through me, leaving me deeply, genuinely, happy.

I often wondered whether I was mad, but in truth, I didn't care. It was strange to think that when I eventually managed to leave Clearview, the thing I would miss most apart from my brothers and sisters, was an old oak tree.

∾

When I turned fourteen, it was time to test for aptitude for the Skills. Having already decided that I would be a Tailor, I couldn't have been less interested in the lesson we all had to sit through the day before testing, as to why the Skills were so crucial to the survival of our communities. Most of my attention was on planning my next creation as my teacher droned on in the background about how the cities of The Old had imploded along with all of their machines, rules and manic need for control, and how it had been down to the brave people who managed to escape the harsh, unforgiving regime, to ensure the future of humanity. They'd had no clue how to survive without computers producing and controlling everything, and had it not been for the intervention of horses, they would have perished.

Horses? I sat up and listened intently.

My teacher told of how some horses left their wild herds and chose individuals from amongst the survivors, with whom they bonded. These horses shared a mind connection with their selected humans – known as the Horse-Bonded – which allowed them to communicate telepathically and teach the Horse-Bonded that which the people of The New needed in order to thrive. The Skills were a large part of what they taught. Through their Bond-Partners, the horses passed on information that stimulated memories long buried within the human psyche, of talents possessed by humans in ancient civilisations.

People remembered how to move rocks with a combination of their voices and intention. Where the early attempts at building shelters had repeatedly failed, Rock-Singers sang buildings of stone into existence. Tree-Singers encouraged crops to grow and flourish. Earth-Singers moved soil in such quantities that farming became easy on a large scale, especially when assisted by the Weather-Singers. Glass-Singers sang sand into windows, bottles and jars. Metal-Singers produced tools in designs and quantities beyond imagination. Bone-Singers, Tissue-Singers and Herbalists healed bodies at speeds that would have dropped the jaws of the humans of The Old.

But only certain people had aptitude for the Skills. Those who showed no aptitude at testing chose one of the Trades in which to apprentice instead, as I'd done already. I nodded to myself. I knew what I was good at, and the reason I'd become good at it was because I'd been able to practise and develop in the one place I felt supported. I wouldn't be testing for the Skills.

My heart wrenched when I thought about the Horse-Bonded. I knew they still existed today, passing on the knowledge and wisdom of their horses so that our communities of The New continued to thrive. How amazing it must be to be chosen by a horse, to share a bond with one – to share a bond with anyone. But I had my tree. That was where I would be when the Skills Testers came to our school.

I left home at dawn on the day in question, and spent the day sewing in my tree. When I arrived home that evening, my mother was furious.

'How embarrassed do you think I was, standing on my own doorstep while your teacher questioned me as to why you were absent from testing? I had no idea where you were, let alone why you would miss such an important day. Testing is important to the future of the village as a whole, you selfish little madam. Without the Skills, we'll all perish. Everyone should test to see if they show aptitude for any of them.'

I felt my temper beginning to swirl in my stomach. Now that I was settling into my teenage years, I was beginning to realise – and had already proved on many occasions – what a weapon it could be. But I was impatient to get upstairs to the room I shared with Heron and Kestrel, so that I could hide my latest creation under my bed. I swallowed and tried to remain calm. 'You, embarrassed? Me, selfish? I don't know which is more ridiculous,' I said as I headed for the stairs.

My mother put her arm across the hallway in front of me, barring my way. 'Where have you been?' she asked through gritted teeth.

'Rowena, answer your mother,' Kerk called out from the living room, where from the sound of it, he was playing with Robin and Finch.

'Shut up, berk, I mean jerk, I mean Kerk. If you're not going to tell your darling wife what a cow she is, if you're, as usual, going to take the coward's route and take her side, then do us all a favour and get lost.'

Kerk appeared in the doorway to the living room, his face flushed. 'She'll have been in the woods,' he said to my mother. 'It's where she always goes when she doesn't want to be here.'

'The woods?'

'Yep, I've been going there for the past three years. Just what sort of mother are you that it's taken three years for you to even ask where I've been? And don't pretend you're bothered I missed testing. You've told me loads of times I'll never amount to anything because of who my father is.'

'And you're proving my point, exactly,' my mother spat.

Heron came running down the stairs. 'Leave her alone,' she said to my mother, her green eyes full of tears. 'Can't you just leave her alone, please?'

My mother's face softened. 'Cuckoo's not like you, Heron, she's trouble.'

Finch appeared in the living room doorway, next to my step-father. 'No, she isn't. She looks after us when Dad's weaving and you're sewing. She plays games with us even though they're games she doesn't really want to play, and she makes us laugh. When Swift fell and hurt her knee yesterday, Weena sat her on her knee and cuddled her for ages until she stopped crying. She's nice and she's kind, and she IS like the rest of us. You should be nicer to her.'

My mother looked at me, her blue eyes flashing, her cheeks so red, they were almost purple. 'Now look what you've done,' she said under her breath.

'What is it that I've done, mother of mine?' I spat. 'Been born? According to what I learnt in school, that was as a result of something you did.'

'Right, Heron, come down here please, into the living room. Finch you come back in too, while Rowena and your mother sort this out,' Kerk said.

My heart went out to Heron and Finch as they both looked desperately at me, not wanting to leave me, but loathe to disobey their father. This wasn't their fault.

'No need,' I said. 'There's nothing to sort out. I'll be in my room, if anyone – and by that, I mean if any of my brothers or sisters – needs me.'

I smiled at Finch and pushed roughly past my mother. I blew a kiss at Heron and motioned for her to go up the stairs ahead of me.

Heron threw herself onto her bed when we reached our room, then turned to look up at me. 'Please don't keep annoying her, Ro, she could throw you out.'

Kestrel looked up from where she had been practising her reading on her own bed. 'You were shouting again.'

'I'm sorry, Kes, your mum and I get angry at each other. It's nothing for you to worry about.' I turned to Heron. 'There was no need for you to get involved, sweetie, though I love you for doing it. And don't worry, she won't throw me out, who would look after the rest of you when she and your dad are working?'

'You were looking after us when you were Kestrel's age, so if you left, she and I could both do it,' Heron said.

'Mum won't ask either of you. You need time to do your homework and have fun being kids, isn't that what she and your dad are always telling you? It's just me who isn't allowed to do that, as we all know.'

'It isn't f…fair,' Kestrel said, her lip quivering.

'No, it isn't. But it's also nothing you need to worry about. Your mum and dad love you, and I love you. Everything else is between me and them.' But of course, it wasn't that simple.

Chapter Two

I left school a year later, with no apprenticeship to go on to. It was no more than I expected. No one had ever given me a chance. I knew that many of the villagers felt sorry for me because of my home situation, but not enough to offer to take me on when my latest school report was full of accounts of "answering back with an acerbic tongue", "threatening to punch her peers and on several occasions, following through on her threat" and "absenting herself from any lesson that she doesn't deem important".

'You'd better work for me,' my mother said one morning as I came into the kitchen for breakfast.

'I already do work for you. I've been working for you since my fingers were big enough to hold a needle, and my arms strong enough to hold your babies,' I said.

As she'd taken to doing recently, she continued as if I hadn't spoken. 'I'm not going to give you an apprenticeship, because you'll never qualify and I won't have the shame of one of my household being in an indefinite apprenticeship. I can't have anyone questioning my ability to teach…'

'Why not? They already question your ability as a mother.'

'…but I've got more than enough work for both of us, so you'll start tomorrow. You can do the first three-hour shift while I look after the children. Then I'll do a six-hour shift while you have them, then we'll swap again and you can do the last three hours.'

'So I'll be working early and late, when no one comes to the shop? And I'll be working on my own? Don't get me wrong, that suits me fine, but you're saying I'm not good enough to be your apprentice, yet I'm good enough to work on my own, unsupervised? Just be honest, you don't want me as your apprentice because you know I'm a better Tailor than you. You're scared that your good-for-nothing daughter will outshine you, that people will come to me for their clothes instead of you. So, you want me working in a way that means no one will know I'm there, and then you'll take credit for my work.'

'I want you working when no one comes into the shop because you look even more strange than normal with this new insistence of yours on dressing in black, and you'll only be rude to my customers,' she said. 'If you want to continue living as part of this family, then you need to earn your keep, and that's the way you'll be doing it from now on.'

I opened my mouth to argue, but then realised I didn't really want to. I would barely have to see my mother or Kerk, I would have lots of time with my brothers and sisters, and I would be honing my sewing skills by working six hours a day for my mother. My initial concern that I would be hard pushed to find time to visit my tree, was quickly allayed when I decided that I'd take some of my work there to do, now that I was of an age that I was allowed, officially, to do what I'd already been doing for four years, and go to the woods alone.

I nodded. 'I'll start in the morning.'

I spent the next five years honing my tailoring skills. I worked faster than my mother, usually completing the work she left me to do for each three-hour shift, in around two hours, which left me time to work on my portfolio; having rooted through my mother's paperwork and found her apprentice notes and the list of that which she'd been required to make for the portfolio she'd put forward in order to gain her own qualification as a Tailor, I knew what was required.

Using offcuts from the orders I fulfilled in the shop, the tiny scale mock-ups I'd made in my tree were gradually all produced as full-size clothes. I created home decorations, ornaments, cushion covers whose openings could only be discovered once you knew the trick, table cloths whose size could be altered by the addition of tiny buttons in strategic and invisible places, blankets that could be zipped together to make coverings of different thicknesses... the list was endless. Heron and Kestrel helped me by hiding my growing portfolio under their beds when I ran out of room under mine. Since we were responsible for cleaning our own room, we weren't discovered.

Finally, I had everything I needed. Heron, now sixteen and apprenticed to the village Chandler, approached Jewner, the Master Tailor, to ask for an appointment for herself at lunchtime a few days hence; I couldn't risk my mother finding out ahead of time that the appointment was for me.

Kestrel, now twelve, was still at school but often came home for lunch. 'Let me help, Ro,' she said to me as we and Heron sat on our beds, discussing my plans. 'I can come home for lunch as normal, and then I can help you and Heron carry your portfolio.'

I looked at all of my creations bulging out from underneath each of our three beds, and grinned at her. 'Thanks, Kes, and you, Heron. I'll have Wren to look after and there's no way I can get her and all my stuff to Jewner's in one trip. You said he's going to shut up shop for your appointment, Heron?'

She nodded. 'I said I wanted to commission a very important surprise and I didn't want anyone overhearing our discussion. You know what he's like, he's a lovely old man and loves a surprise, so he said he'd close up as soon as I – but obviously, it'll be we – get there.'

'What would I do without you two?' I said, looking from one of my beautiful, brown-haired, green-eyed sisters to the other.

'Absolutely fine, as you always have,' Heron said. 'It's us who'll have a hard time without you. Are you sure you want to leave Clearview once Jewner qualifies you? You're an amazing Tailor, you know you are, he'd probably give you his shop so he can retire.'

'I'd need customers, though, wouldn't I? You may not have noticed, but I'm not exactly popular around here.'

'That's in the past, Ro,' Heron said. 'Sure, you had problems at school, but it's been years since you hit anyone, and everyone knows how hard you work, what with the shop and looking after the children for Mum and Dad. You're a lovely person, I just wish you'd let everyone else see it.'

'No one else has ever wanted to see it. I'm better off keeping myself to myself, that way, no one has to avoid me.'

'That way, you don't risk being hurt any more than you have been already, you mean,' Heron whispered. 'I love you, Ro.' She launched herself from her own bed to where I sat on mine, and hugged me.

Kestrel's arms wound around both our necks and she put her head to ours. 'I love you too. We all do. Even little Wren's first word was "Woweena".'

I chuckled. 'She's going to be a handful, that one. Promise me that when I'm gone, you'll hug her every night before she goes to sleep, in place of me?'

Heron sighed. 'I promise. I just wish you didn't have to go.'

I disentangled myself from my sisters and looked from one to the other. 'You know I have to.'

Heron bit her lip and Kestrel's eyes filled with tears, but they both nodded.

So it was that I found myself under-dressed and shivering in the cold, winter breeze as I leant back into the curve of my favourite branch, gathering strength for my appointment with Jewner that lunchtime. I'd woken before dawn in a panic that something would go wrong, so of course my first instinct had been to throw on some clothes and run for my tree.

I looked around me as the weak winter sun filtered through the branches. To my right was a conveniently placed crack in which I'd stowed my scissors, threads and smaller pieces of cloth while I was working, so that any sudden gusts of wind didn't blow them away. Tucked into it was a soft piece of bark that I'd used as a pin and needle cushion. To my left was a bump in the bark with an almost flat top, which I'd often used as a platform on which to tease knots out of threads with a pair of needles.

'I don't know what's going to happen today,' I murmured, wondering if talking out loud to the tree for the first time meant I'd reached a whole new level of insanity. 'If Jewner qualifies me, Mum will go berserk that I've gone behind her back, and I'll have to leave in a hurry. If he refuses to qualify me because I'm, well, because I'm me, she'll still go berserk. I don't think she'll throw me out – she won't want to miss the chance to gloat and she won't want to be without my help – so I guess in that case, I'll be finding my way here more than ever.' I sighed and allowed the peaceful feeling that always wove its way through me whilst in my tree, to calm my anxiety over what the day would bring. 'But if I qualify and move on, I'll never come here again. I'm scared of what life will be like without you, tree. You've been here for me all this time, I don't even know how I would have got to this point without you. You're just a tree, and yet you're not. I guess I'll never know how it is that you affect me, but however it is that you've made me feel accepted, protected, capable – I just wanted to thank you. If you can hear me. With you being a tree, that is.' I chuckled and shook my head at myself. 'Anyway, I'd better head back. I've got three hours' work to do in the shop, then it'll be time to see where my life will go from here.' I climbed back down to the ground, put my hand to the tree's trunk and whispered, 'Thank you.'

Tears streamed down my face as I ran home, even as I chuckled at the ridiculousness of crying over a tree. Once I set foot on the cobbles of Clearview, named for the view over the vast lake on whose banks the village sat, to the mountains beyond, I wiped my face and slowed to a walk. I passed many villagers on their way to work, but none of them acknowledged me. Of course they didn't. Heron had told me on numerous occasions that it was only because I looked scary in my black clothes, and scowled all the time, but I didn't see how she would know. She hadn't grown up being subjected to the disappointment and disapproval that I had, practically from the moment I was born.

My mother was helping two-year-old Wren to some porridge at the kitchen table when I got home. Judging by the plates piled by the sink, the rest of my siblings and Kerk had eaten and left for school or work. I grabbed a bread roll, spread it with butter and took it to the shop, along with a mug of tea.

'How many times do I have to tell you not to take food and drink into the shop?' my mother yelled.

I slammed the door between the house and the shop, behind me, hoping that was the last time she would ever get a chance to shout at me about anything.

My mother came into the shop three hours later with Wren on her hip. She handed my sister to me, frowning at the remains of my roll and my empty tea mug – both of which I had, until moments before, kept well away from the cloth stores and workbench – that sat atop the cloak I'd just finished. It was childish, I know, but that was what my relationship with my mother had progressed to; we spoke as little as possible while needling one another as much as we could.

I spent an hour playing with Wren, then fed her while bolting down my own lunch. When the kitchen door creaked open and Heron's and Kestrel's heads appeared around it, I beckoned them in.

'Mum's hard at it and Kerk won't be home for another half an hour, so Kes, if you could just watch Wren, Heron and I can fetch all my stuff down here.'

Kestrel nodded and picked up a small, straw doll wearing clothes I'd made for it, and began to make it walk on the table in front of two-year-old Wren, who squealed.

Heron and I shot up the stairs and pulled out the three large bags I'd made to house the components of my portfolio, from under our beds. Heron folded her bag, almost as long as she was tall, over her arms and waited for me to arrange my and Kestrel's bags over my arms in the same way. 'Careful down the stairs,' she warned me. 'This will all have been for nothing if you trip and break your neck.'

I rolled my eyes. 'You don't say.' I grinned and winked at her. 'You be careful too, you're shorter than me.'

She grinned back. 'This is exciting, isn't it?'

'It would be if we were actually going anywhere.' I indicated towards the door with my head.

She chuckled. 'Sorry, follow me then, and don't...'

'Fall. Got it.'

We fumbled our way down the stairs, neither of us able to see where we were putting our feet, then pushed through the doorway to the kitchen. Wren began to cry at the walking mounds approaching the table, but when Heron dropped her arms and said, 'Peepo,' Wren's cries turned to laughter.

Kestrel relieved me of the smallest of the three bags, then stood back and looked at me. 'I'll take Wren. You're going to need two arms for that huge bag of clothes, Ro, it's the biggest of the three by far.'

I shook my head. 'Thanks, but I'll manage. I've worked for years for this day and believe me, I'll get my stuff and my sister there if it kills me. Come on, little'un, we're going to see an old man about a Tailor's qualification.' I held my hand out to Wren, and she climbed down from her chair and took it. 'Ready you two?' Heron and Kestrel nodded.

Jewner's shop wasn't far away, but even so, walking at Wren's pace meant that it took us nearly twenty minutes to get there. I swapped her from one hand to the other several times as I shifted my bag from one arm to the other, but still my arm muscles were cramping by the time we got there.

Heron winked at me and mouthed, 'Good luck,' as she pushed

open the shop door with her foot and reversed through it. She held it open with her toe and stood back so Kestrel, Wren and I could all get through, then let it close behind us.

Two of the walls of the shop were lined with shelves filled with rolls of cloth. The glass shop front had mannequins standing in front of it, wearing Jewner's latest winter creations, and there was a rail along the fourth wall, full of orders waiting to be collected. In the centre of the shop was a large bench for measuring out cloth and laying out patterns. I was relieved that it was currently devoid of either as my sisters and I gratefully laid our bags on top of it.

'Heron, my dear, right on time, now what's this surprise you... oh!' Jewner said as he hurried into the shop from his workroom out back. 'Kestrel, Wren and, um, Rowena, this is a pleasant surprise, are you all in on the big secret too?'

Heron opened her mouth to speak, but I held a hand out to her and she closed it. She beckoned to Wren instead, who ran to her to be picked up.

My heart thumped so loudly and so fast, I was sure Jewner must be able to hear it and know how nervous I was. I thought of my tree and took a breath. 'Yes, Jewner we all are, only it's actually my secret. I'm sorry I asked Heron to deceive you as to the purpose of her, that is, our, appointment here today, but if my mother knew I was coming here, she'd have tried to stop me. She probably would have succeeded too, everyone always listens to her and believes everything she...'

'Rowena, we're not here to talk about Mum, are we?' Heron said. Kestrel squeezed my arm.

'No. We're not. We're here, Jewner, that is, I'm here, to ask if you'll look at my portfolio and, if you think it's good enough, qualify me as a Tailor. I couldn't carry it all by myself, so Heron and Kestrel have helped me, and Wren's here because

I look after her while Mum's working. I know this isn't the conventional way of doing things, and I know I'm not even an official apprentice, but I've been working in my mother's shop for years now. She's taught me everything she knows so I could do her work for her, and I've used it to make my own designs in my spare time. I know how everyone feels about me here...'

'I don't see how you can possibly know that my dear.'

'...but I'm just asking for this one chance. Please, will you have a look at everything I've made and see if you think I'm worthy of being a Tailor in my own right?'

'I'm uncomfortable going behind your mother's back, Rowena...'

'I knew it. I knew you wouldn't give me a chance.'

'...but I do see the need for it.'

'Why did I ever think... wait, you do?' My jaw was trembling so much, I could barely get the words out.

'Just turn the sign in the window from open to closed, would you, and lock the door in case anyone is feeling particularly persistent? Thank you, Kestrel, now I can concentrate.'

Jewner lifted the glasses that hung around his neck, to his small nose, and peered through them with faded blue eyes. 'This is some collection you have here, Rowena. Shall we start with the largest bag?'

With shaking hands, I began to undo the buttons hidden in the folds down one side of the bag he had indicated.

'Hidden buttons, very clever, although are they necessary on a bag, I wonder?' Jewner mused, stroking his white-stubbled chin with crooked fingers.

I silently cursed myself for a fool. Kestrel began to undo the buttons at the other end of the bag. When we reached in the middle, she grasped hold of my hand and squeezed it briefly. I pulled the bag open and stood back to allow Jewner to peruse its contents.

He lifted each item out and inspected it at arm's length and then up close. Every button was opened and closed, every stitch inspected, every colour combination examined and considered. Every now and then he would mutter to himself. 'Hidden buttons again. Very clever, and useful on this occasion.' 'Hmmm.' 'Not sure I would have... but... hmmm.' 'Aaaaaaaah, I see, but...'

I strained to hear every word that passed his lips and as time went on, my heart sank lower and lower. By the time he'd finished examining the contents of the last bag, I was convinced my work wasn't good enough.

Jewner put the last item down, smoothed a few strands of white hair back over the top of his head, and peered over his glasses at me. 'I trained your mother, you know.'

I bit my lip and nodded.

'This work is exceptional. I have to ask you, Rowena, did your mother do this?'

I should have known. Why hadn't I foreseen that he wouldn't believe it was my own work? No one had ever given me a chance. No one ever would give me a chance.

'No, you horrid old man, my mother didn't do it. Any of it.'

Kestrel took a sharp intake of breath. Heron said, 'Ro, Jewner has to ask you if it's your own work, my Master told me that's what will happen when it comes to inspection of my portfolio when I'm ready to qualify as a Chandler.'

I should have stopped to listen, to back-track and apologise, but my temper had already stepped up to protect me from the hurt and horror of rejection, as it had so often before. 'My mother makes boring stuff, the same things that Tailors like her, Tailors like you, have always made. You trained her, and you can't tell that she would never have come up with what I've made?'

Jewner straightened up, his eyes wide and eyebrows raised. 'You misunderstand me. I merely adhere to…'

'You accused me of being a fraud,' I snarled. 'A thief, even! You actually implied that I would steal my mother's work and pass it off as my own, as if I'm useless, just like she's always said. I never should have come here. I should have known what would happen.'

Wren began to cry. I couldn't bear it. I turned and ran for the door, but it was locked.

'Rowena, wait, please wait, Jewner wasn't accusing…' began Heron, but was interrupted by Jewner.

'Rowena Harrol, I pronounce you…' The lock finally freed and I flung open the shop door and tore out into the street, unable to bear whatever it was that Jewner was about to pronounce me. I could hear Heron and Kestrel shouting after me as my long legs easily out ran theirs. I couldn't bear the fact that they had witnessed my humiliation, I needed to get as far away from them, from everyone as I could.

It was no surprise when, despite being blinded by tears, I ended up at my tree. Sobbing, I climbed it as I had so many times before, and nestled into the curved branch that I'd always so badly wanted to believe was hugging me in return. Through my anger, embarrassment and despair, I felt the familiar sensation of peace, as if it were soaking into my skin from the bark of the tree and permeating through my body, calming the emotions that would otherwise pull me down and drown me.

By the time I'd cried myself out, I was exhausted. I would stay in my tree until it was dark, I decided. Let my mother have a day managing without me, because goodness knows, she would have weeks, months, years, of delight tormenting me with the fact that Jewner had confirmed what she had always told me – that like my father, I was indeed good for nothing.

When I felt my mind being eased away from thoughts of my future, I assumed to begin with that it was the tree continuing to calm me as it so often had before. But as my mind was gradually and persistently diverted from everything to do with Clearview, including my tree, I realised that this was different. The tree always flooded me with calm. With peace. Whatever this was, it was pulling at me, making me want to climb down out of the tree and travel somewhere to the west, somewhere far beyond the mountains whose slopes were already white with snow, somewhere far beyond the village just the other side of them to which I'd planned to flee for the winter before travelling further afield once the snows subsided.

What was happening to me? What was pulling at me so confidently, so surely, making me feel as if leaving everything behind and going to it was the natural thing to do? The pulling on my mind increased, and I sat bolt upright. The sensation matched exactly that which had been described to me when we learnt about the Horse-Bonded at school. A horse had chosen me as a Bond-Partner and was pulling at my mind, pulling me to go to him.

My mind raced. Was I dreaming? I pinched myself. No, I was definitely awake. Was I imagining it then? All of my hopes and dreams for the future had come crashing down around me. Most people my age were already qualified in the Trades or Skills, and contributing to their villages. While I knew I was contributing to mine, my mother had made sure I was invisible. I would never be qualified in anything, and never able to leave her to pursue a life of my own. Was this my mind conjuring up an alternate future for myself because I couldn't accept that everything for which I'd spent so many years working had come to nothing?

The pulling increased further and I lurched towards the west, almost overbalancing over the side of my branch. My heart leapt. I absolutely didn't imagine that. A horse had chosen me. Me! I scrambled towards the trunk of the tree. I might not have been deemed good enough to be a Tailor, I might not have ever been judged good enough to be anything by any of my fellow humans, but somewhere, a horse existed who thought I was good enough to be his Bond-Partner. To be one of the Horse-Bonded. I had a future after all.

I grasped the first handholds in the sequence that would allow a swift descent down the tree, but then paused. Why me? Of all the people of The New communities, why would this horse choose me? I was repellent to others of my own species. They saw me as rude, awkward and someone to either laugh at or avoid. There was nothing appealing about me, I'd been told so over and over again. I sank back onto my branch. I had to be imagining it. My mother would be delighted to be able to add delusional and crazy to all of the other things that were wrong with me. My lower lip wobbled.

A brown, brittle leaf that had been hanging on stubbornly to a branch above me, swirled down past my face and landed in my lap, where it swirled some more before being blown towards the west. I watched it go, wishing I could go with it. The calm of my tree oozed through me. The tugging on my mind increased. I was calm. And still being tugged.

I wrapped my arms around the branch and hugged it, silently thanking my tree for coming to my rescue once again. I was being tugged! By a horse! A horse who had chosen me, who actually wanted me. I would trust it, and I would go to it. Immediately, the pulling on my mind subsided to a less insistent, more… content level. Content? Yes, that was definitely it, I could feel that the horse was content at my decision. I grinned. I had some planning to do.

Chapter Three

*N*ow that the pull on my mind had subsided, I could think more clearly. I settled back to lean into the curve of the branch again, drawing my knees up to my chest in an attempt to stay warm in the gradually strengthening, bitterly cold wind. More dead leaves slapped into me, some sticking to my hair and cloak, others whipping back off as they were hurled towards the west, a constant reminder of the direction I would need to take. My long, black hair curled around my face, getting in my eyes, tickling my nose and blocking my mouth, but I ignored it. I closed my eyes and thought through how I would go about leaving Clearview.

The Horse-Bonded travelled between villages when they weren't in residence at their home, The Gathering. Any conflicts between villagers were taken to them, knowing that the advice their horses gave them to pass on in response, would keep the villages of The New on the straight and narrow, as it had since their inception. As such, they were revered and the whole village deemed it an honour when one of their own was lucky enough to be chosen by a horse, and celebrated their departure with a Quest Ceremony – a leaving ceremony where gifts and good wishes were bestowed to help the person on their quest to find their Bond-Partner.

My mother would never give me a Quest Ceremony. She would be furious I was proving her wrong and making something of myself, furious I was leaving, and she would never, ever, give me the food, and hunting and cooking gear that I would need to survive on my journey to find my horse. I wouldn't give her the satisfaction of refusing me. I wouldn't even tell her I'd been tugged. I had a way out and I would take it without giving her any chance to ruin it for me.

That meant I would need to leave tonight, when she was asleep. I felt a pang in my heart at the thought that I would have to leave without saying goodbye to my brothers and sisters, but I had no choice. If I went home while everyone was still up, there would be a massive drama over everything that had happened today, an even bigger one over the very idea that a horse was tugging me, and a point-blank refusal to give me what I would need to survive travelling in the winter. I would have to take what I needed. I would leave the presents for my siblings that I'd made for the Longest Night Festival, and come back as soon as I could to make it up to them for leaving as I knew I must.

I stayed up in my tree for as long as I could. When darkness began to fall and the tiny amount of comfort the weak, winter sun had afforded me disappeared, I climbed down my tree with numb hands, almost falling several times as they failed to grasp my well-used handholds properly, and crouched down in the lee of the trunk. My stomach rumbled. I was freezing, hungry and thirsty, but I barely noticed. My horse was out there somewhere – my horse! And he or she wanted me. The thought went around and around in my mind, accompanied by the gentle pull that my horse was exerting on my mind, making sure I never, not even for a second, forgot it. All I could feel was a sense of wonder, bolstered by the calm confidence that I'd always managed to find when in the vicinity of my tree.

Lights came on in the cottages of Clearview. Families would soon be sitting down to dinner. My heart sank again at the worry I knew would be plaguing Heron, Finch, Kestrel, and probably twelve-year-old Robin and ten-year-old Swift too. My two youngest brothers, eight-year-old Crow and six-year old Kite, would, as always, be governed by their stomachs, and Wren was happy as long as there was laughing around her; usually guaranteed when I wasn't there and surely in great supply now that my mother would have found out what happened in Jewner's shop today. I could just picture her gloating about what a fool I'd made of myself, and felt even more sorry for Heron and Finch, as I knew they would stick up for me. The Harrol household would be so much more harmonious once I'd gone, I told myself, and tried to focus on that thought as a replacement for my guilt at letting my siblings down.

I left it a further two perishing hours before I finally left my tree. 'Thank you,' I whispered, my frozen hand against its trunk. 'Thank you for being my friend, imaginary or otherwise. Now I have – at least I hope I have – a new friend to find.' The pull on my mind was consistent, reassuring me that I had.

I made my way back to the village, the moon thankfully bright in the black, star-filled sky. I crept through the paddocks that ran along the back of the cottages in our street, trying not to disturb any of the animals resident there. When I reached ours, I tiptoed past the chicken huts to which our chickens would long since have retired for the night, to the smokehouse. I eased the door open, wincing at the squeak of the hinges, lifted the lantern off its hook just inside the door and shut the door behind me as the lantern flared to life, thanking the stars above that the smokehouse had no windows. I worried that the light of my lantern might be visible from the upstairs windows of the cottage, due to the vent that allowed the smoke out of the top of the smokehouse, and shuttered the lantern so that only the tiniest amount – just enough for me to see what I was doing – escaped.

Kerk might have been a weak, cowardly excuse for a man, but he was a good hunter, and almost as good a fisherman when he had time to take his boat out onto the lake beyond the village. As always at this time of year, the smokehouse was stocked full of smoked meat and fish to last our family the winter, and the butchering table was scrubbed clean.

All of Kerk's knives and hunting gear were stowed in locked drawers so that little fingers couldn't get hold of them by accident. I took the keys from their hook above the door, opened the drawers and selected a few knives and the pieces of hunting equipment that Kerk had taught me to use in the years when hunting had been scarce and he'd needed help to fill the smokehouse with enough food for his rapidly growing brood. I lay them on the table and then began to select what I considered to be my share of the meat and fish.

I felt awful. I was only taking what I would have eaten had I been there for the winter, so I wasn't depriving anyone of anything, but I wouldn't be there to contribute to the family. I would be taking without giving anything in return, something that all children of The New had it drummed into them by parents and teachers, over and over, as completely unacceptable. Our communities worked on the basis that everyone co-operated. One didn't take without being completely, unreservedly, prepared to contribute in return.

The tugging on my mind increased, reminding me what I was about and why. I set my mouth in a line. I'd contributed plenty over the years, and would continue to do so once I was Horse-Bonded. I wasn't really stealing, I was borrowing.

When I'd sorted out my share, I took a piece of smoked fish from my pile and chewed it, followed by several pieces of meat, while I waited for the lights in the cottage to go out, one by one. As I waited, I ran through, over and over, what I would need to take with me, and whereabouts in the cottage all of those things were. I couldn't make any noise; Finch and Crow were light sleepers, and any noise would have them awake in seconds and Crow screaming that there were monsters under his bed. Then the whole house would be awake. I needed to move from room to room, silently and efficiently gathering everything that would be crucial for my survival, and in order to do that, I required a plan of action.

I peered out of the smokehouse door from time to time. Once the cottage was in darkness, I waited for what I counted in my head to be another hour, then, carrying the almost completely shuttered lantern, let myself in through the back door. I gingerly opened the hall cupboard door and pulled out my back-sack, and, with a pang, Kerk's huge one.

I went down the stone hallway and into the kitchen, where I went straight to the sink and quenched my thirst. I selected minimal crockery, cutlery and cooking gear, packing everything carefully within, or in the cases of some of the cooking equipment, hanging them on the outside of, Kerk's back-sack. Then I began to add food until the back-sack was half full; I needed to leave room for the meat and fish I'd gathered together in the smokehouse.

Guilt flooded me again, but so, immediately, did the tugging on my mind, reminding me why I was doing what I was doing. The thought also occurred to me that anyone else in my situation would be in a warm bed now, excited for their Quest

Ceremony in the morning, when their family would bestow upon them with love and best wishes, everything that I was having to sneak around and take for myself. I set my mouth, pulled the drawstring of the sack closed, and put it by the kitchen door ready to be picked up on my way out. I took a firm hold of the smaller, empty back-sack and tiptoed slowly, silently upstairs.

Once I was in my bedroom, I allowed myself to breathe a little more easily. Heron and Kestrel could, and often did, sleep through thunderstorms, so I knew that unless I dropped something really heavy, I was safe. I lowered my lantern to the floor, wondering what the huge mound of stuff was on my bed. My portfolio! Bless Heron and Kestrel, they must have lugged it all home by themselves.

I looked over to the sleeping mounds that were my sisters. If only I could wake them up to thank them, to tell them how much I loved them and to explain what had happened and where I was going, but I couldn't risk them waking Finch and Crow and then as a consequence, everyone else. I swallowed hard, blinking back tears, and opened the first bag. An envelope fell out of it. Frowning, I picked it up. In the dim light, I could just make out my name on the front of it, in handwriting I didn't recognise. I looked again at my sisters. What was this? I shook my head. I couldn't be distracted now. I stuffed it into a side pocket of my sack.

I quickly packed as many warm clothes – new ones from my portfolio, as well as old – as I could, including the cloak I'd been wearing, then drew out a new, thick, fur-lined cloak from the biggest portfolio bag, and donned it.

I dropped to my hands and knees and felt around under my bed for the bag of little presents I'd made for my sisters and brothers. I could have included them in my portfolio – they were original pieces and skilfully made – but these were personal, made with all my love for the only people who had ever loved me.

I found the bag, upended it next to the lantern, and picked out the small, thumb-sized heron, standing with wings folded, eyes looking downward as a hunting heron always did, that I'd stitched with so much love for the eldest of my sisters. When I found the kestrel in flight that I'd made for my second sister, I tiptoed over to each of them in turn, leaving their namesakes on their pillows.

Without the backward glance that I was terrified would weaken my resolve not to waken them to say goodbye, I let myself out of the room, taking my back-sack and the rest of my little birds with me. I pulled the door shut, lowered the back-sack to the floor and tiptoed along to the room shared by Finch and Robin. My heart hammered in my chest. I'd been silent so far, but here was the first place that I absolutely had to be. I stayed on the balls of my feet as I opened the door and went into their room, thankful for the balance that years of climbing and moving around within my tree had left me. I placed Finch's goldfinch as far away from his head on the pillow as I could, and then left Robin's red-chested bird above his head, resting against the headboard.

Crow and Kite shared the next room along. Their birds were left as soundlessly and quickly as their brothers'. Just Swift and Wren to go. After the four boys, they would be easy. As expected, their breathing remained deep and even as I left Swift's white-chested, red-bibbed bird in flight on her pillow, and Wren's little brown bird on her bedside table where she would see it when she woke. I left their room as I had the previous three, without looking back. I had to look forward, it was – the horse was – all I had.

I looked down to the end of the landing, to the closed door of the room my mother shared with Kerk. I'd stayed out past their bedtime and then risen and left for my tree before dawn on numerous occasions when things between us had been particularly bad, so I wondered how long it would be before they realised that I'd actually left. A sharp pang in my stomach reminded me that they would know as soon as they looked in the kitchen cupboards and saw that there were things missing. Would they accuse Heron and Kestrel of helping me as they had to know that my sisters had done, not only with regard to my visit to Jewner the previous day, but over the many years I'd accumulated my portfolio? No. Heron and Kestrel would be devastated when they realised I'd packed all my stuff and gone; there would be no mistaking that their reactions to my leaving were genuine.

With a final look at each of the bedroom doors behind which my brothers and sisters slept, I picked up my gear and went downstairs. I shouldered Kerk's back-sack and tiptoed back out to the smokehouse, where I packed the meat and fish into wrappings I'd taken from one of the kitchen drawers, then packed them and the knives into the sack with the rest of my food. I hoped it would be enough, but I had hunting gear that I hoped I remembered how to use, if my food ran out. I hung the gear on the outside of my clothes sack, blew out the lantern and hung it back on its peg. Then I stepped out into the biting night air, pulling the smokehouse door firmly shut behind me. I heaved the larger of the two sacks onto my back, and fed my arms through the arms of the smaller one, heaving it onto my front. It was a heavy load to carry, yet I felt lighter than the bitter air that had me reaching quickly for the gloves I'd stowed in a side pocket of the pack on my front.

'Where are you?' I thought out to my horse.

The pull on my mind increased steadily. I started walking west.

Chapter Four

*B*y the time dawn broke, I'd walked the length of the
north bank of the enormous lake of vivid blue water
that supplied the villagers of Clearview with a never-ending
supply of fish. The mountains from whose sides melting ice and
snow replenished the lake each spring, loomed before me. I was
relieved to see that the snow was still restricted to higher up the
slopes than the mountain pass I planned to use to reach
Highpasture, the village on the far side of the pass that was, as its
name suggested, a rare source of grazing in the mountains.

Highpasture had been my intended initial destination on
qualifying as a Tailor. When last a Herald passed through my
home village, Heron had questioned her on my behalf as to the
abundance of Tailors there, and I'd been pleased to learn that the
village currently had only a single qualified Tailor and two
apprentices in their first year of apprenticeship. Knowing how in
demand Tailors were in the winter months, I'd been hopeful that
whether or not the people of Highpasture liked me as a person,

Jewner's letter of qualification would have given them reason to give me board and lodging in exchange for my work.

I smiled to myself. I had no need to beg their goodwill now. I wouldn't even take the turning to the village, but would pass it by without a care in the world. I had no need to have to bear the frowns of disapproval at my black clothes, my attitude or my temper, ever again. I didn't need anyone's approval, or even their company. Soon, I would have a bond with a horse. If it weren't for the sack strapped to my front, I would have hugged myself.

I decided to stop and break my fast at the opening of the pass. There, I would be out of the north-easterly wind that had felt as if it were eating away at my face as I walked through the night. I would both eat and rest awhile, before continuing on my way.

As soon as the thought of being able to rest entered my mind, my burden seemed to increase in weight. I was almost bent double by the time I reached the pass, and cursing with every step at how ridiculous that was, having carried both sacks through the night without issue.

I pulled the sack off my front and let it fall to the ground. Then I stood up straight, groaning, and allowed the one on my back to slide off and land with a clunk as the cook pots hit rock. I pulled out a blanket I'd edged with delicate stitching for my portfolio, from the top of my clothing sack, folded it to make a cushion, and sat on it. Then I rummaged around in my food sack and quickly cobbled together some sandwiches from bread rolls and meat.

I leant back against the sheer rock of the pass and looked about myself. To my right was a stony track wide enough for two carts to pass one another, sloping steeply upwards and appearing to get ever narrower and darker, although I knew that was only an effect of distance; I'd been this way several times before when collecting cloth and thread from Highpasture, and I knew that I would run out of neither light nor space as I made my way up into the mountains.

Looking back the way I'd come, I noticed a tree that I hadn't long passed, yet had failed to see in my desperation to reach the pass and shed my load. It had dropped several branches which had been stripped of bark and appeared dry. Once I'd eaten, I would gather the wood and build a fire.

Looking beyond the tree, the mist that had accumulated over the lake during the night was beginning to lift. Once the sun's rays had burned off the mist, the lake would sparkle, as if covered in jewels. I sighed. That, I would miss.

I looked past the lake to where I could just about make out the grey stone buildings of Clearview. Aside from my brothers and sisters, there was nothing there I would miss. They would all be waking up now and discovering their farewell presents. I wondered how long it would be before they realised that was what their little birds were. No. I couldn't think about that. I switched my attention to the gentle but insistent pull on my mind, and looked back up the pass again. That was where I was going. I needed to collect wood, build a fire and then keep looking that way.

I groaned as I persuaded my aching body to get up and fetch the wood. It was indeed dry and also brittle, easily breaking down to smaller branches and twigs when I stamped on it. I soon had a roaring fire going in the mouth of the pass. I fed it for some time, building it up until I had a fire that burned hot enough to take the rest of the wood, and which would burn for some time. I spread out my blanket, wrapped the fur-lined cloak I'd taken from my portfolio bag tightly around myself, and settled down to sleep.

∾

I dreamt I was on Kerk's boat, sorting fish he had caught. The boat was rocking gently but then for no reason, began to rock more violently. I held on to the sides, looking around for the reason, but the lake was calm. There was pressure on one of my arms. Someone was holding on to me... My eyes blinked open. A weathered face was peering into mine.

'What the hell? Get your hand off me, or I'll break your nose.'

'Well I'm glad you're finally awake, even if that wasn't quite the reaction I was hoping for.' The face moved further away, allowing me to sit up.

'You don't have any right to hope for anything from me. No one does. What do you want?' I peered up at the man standing before me. He wore a fur-lined, brown hat with ear flaps, below which a fringe of brown hair streaked with grey met warm, brown eyes. He was wrapped in a heavy brown cloak, above which I could see the red bandanna of a Pedlar tied around his neck. I looked past him to where four donkeys in traces stood patiently waiting in front of a large cart, whose contents were covered with a brown tarpaulin.

The man lifted his hands. 'You're a prickly one, aren't you? I could have just walked on by, you know. I could have ignored the fact that you were lying on a single blanket when it takes more than double that to stop the ground taking your body heat, and that you're wearing clothes suitable for walking instead of sleeping in a mountain pass. I could have allowed the blue of your lips to spread to the rest of you, so that the next person who came by here found you dead.'

'I've slept outside lots of times,' I said. 'I just didn't realise how tired I was.'

'No one who dies of hypothermia ever does. What are you doing here, anyway, lass? You do know the snows are due any day? I'm here later than I planned to be and now I'm going to have to limit my time in Clearview to a single day. Even then, I'm going to be hard pushed to get back down south before the really bad weather hits. I hope you're just going as far as Highpasture? Do you have relatives there?'

'Not that it's any of your business, but no, I'm going well beyond Highpasture.'

'You'll never make it.'

I got to my feet, shivering, and glared at him. 'I've lost count of the times I've been told that, yet here I am, still standing. You don't know anything about me.'

The man looked at my blanket and sacks on the ground, and then back at me. 'I know you're woefully unequipped to travel through the mountains at this time of year.' He took a deep breath. 'Look, come back to Clearview now, and then you can travel with me. At least you'll have someone to look out for you and a cart to shelter under when the snows come.'

I scowled at him. How dare he assume I didn't know how to look after myself, that I was useless? I'd made a mistake, that was all, and one I wouldn't make again. 'I don't need anyone to look out for me,' I stormed. 'I've never needed anyone. I've got this far by myself, and I can find my horse by myself too. My horse. Did you hear that? I'm being tugged. My horse clearly thinks I have more than half a brain cell, otherwise I wouldn't have been chosen now, would I?'

The man stared at me, uncertainly. 'Well, I hope your horse isn't far away, and that once you find him, you find a way to be better at taking advice because otherwise, the world will soon lose its newest Horse-Bonded.'

'Do I look like I want your opinion? Didn't you say you were in a hurry?' I looked down towards Clearview and then back at the man.

He shook his head. 'Farewell, then, and good luck. You're

going to need it.' He turned to his donkeys and clicked his tongue. They pulled into their harnesses and followed him as he walked slowly away.

My stomach growled, and I noticed for the first time that my fire had gone out. How long had I been asleep? I took a step towards the opening of the pass and then stopped. I wouldn't have the Pedlar thinking I was following him back to Clearview after all. I would eat, then when he was out of sight, I would step out into the open and find the sun's position.

I cursed when I discovered that it was well into the afternoon; I'd only meant to sleep for a few hours. I'd never slept longer than that when out in the open before, it had always been as if my body just knew when it needed to wake and get somewhere warmer. But I'd always been in my tree, I realised. There, it was as if everything about my body, my senses, was fine-tuned and working optimally, as if the tree somehow gave me the energy to be everything I could be. Now I was on my own. Now, I would have to be more careful.

The pull on my mind increased slightly. When I transferred my attention to it, it seemed to envelop me and hold me still, somehow. This was different. Had the horse changed his mind? Had he seen that I'd been stupid and decided I wasn't Bond-Partner material after all? No, it wasn't that. I didn't know how I knew that, but I did. It was as if I were being perused. Inspected. I was let go, and the pulling returned with far more strength. The horse wanted me find him more quickly. He wanted me to move faster.

I hefted the large sack onto my back, and the smaller one onto my front again, then spread the remains of my fire and continued on my way.

By the time I'd trudged up to the far end of the pass, the sun was setting. When I reached the turning for Highpasture, I felt a sense of longing. The air was still and the night clear; it was going to be a cold night. A hot bath and warm bed would have been welcome – but not there. Not where I wouldn't be wanted. There was only one who wanted my company, and I needed to find him. Or her. I realised I'd taken to thinking of my horse as male, when I had no inkling one way or the other. I decided that he would be a he until I knew for certain.

I resolved to walk through the night again. The moon would give me enough light by which to see, and my horse was giving me my direction, so I would be better off walking while the temperatures were at their lowest, and then resting during the daytime when it was less cold.

I rummaged around in my clothing sack for my black, fur-lined hat with ear flaps, wrapped a scarf around my neck and face so that the rapidly cooling air felt less sharp in my lungs, and exchanged the gloves I'd been wearing for warmer ones. How dared that Pedlar accuse me of being under-prepared.

I plodded on through the night, comfortably warm even as I was uncomfortably weighed down by my packs. I didn't stop to eat, unwilling to stop generating body heat by being stationary for even a few minutes, so munched from my stores as I walked.

When a deer shot out of woodland to one side and bolted across my path, followed by the rest of its herd, I cursed myself for not having my bow and arrows to hand. Even in the moonlight, I would have been hard pushed to miss a whole herd of deer at such short range. Then I rolled my eyes and grinned to myself. What was I thinking? That I would add a butchered deer to my load? I wasn't in Clearview now, where I could take my kill home for Kerk to butcher and smoke. No, I realised with a grin, I was nowhere near Clearview now, I was further from it than I'd ever been before. I was walking along a stony ridge with trees covering the slope that descended away from me to my right, and sheer rock extending up towards the sky on my other side. I had absolutely no idea where I was, or where I was going – I was free.

I was almost disappointed when the first rays of sunshine fumbled their way weakly over the treetops; with daylight came the chance I would come across people. Unlike the people of The Old about whom I'd read at school, I had nothing to fear from other people of The New, I just didn't want their company and the disapproval that was bound to accompany it.

I looked into the trees that covered the slope below me. They would give me wood for a fire, but they would also shade me from the sun which would seep through my eyelids and stop me sleeping too long, as well as taking the edge off the cold. I could light a fire here on the ridge, and hope that no one came along, but with the snows due, if the villages of Highpasture were anything like those of Clearview, people would be visiting family and trading in other villages until the very last minute. There would likely be people converging on Highpasture from all directions over the next day or two. If I slept in the open, it was very possible that I would have an awakening every bit as rude as the one I'd had the day before.

The tugging on my mind, now pulling me steadily southwest, eased significantly and held me still, just as it had the day before, only with less insistence. I closed my eyes. Was the horse trying to communicate with me? No, from what I knew, mind to mind communication didn't happen until a horse and person had actually met and bonded. So, what was happening?

My mind was nudged firmly – sharply, even – and my eyes flashed open. What the...? Before I could finish questioning myself, my mind was held still... and then nudged sharply once more. I frowned. It was a horrible sensation. What was the horse trying to do to me? Drive me insane? My mind was held still yet again. To begin with, I tried to fight it, to move my mind around to all the thoughts I wanted to think. When I gave up, everything was still for a little while longer… and then I was nudged again. It was as if I were being lulled to sleep and then jerked awake.

My mouth twitched into a smile as understanding began to dawn. Was the horse trying to show me that he could wake me? That he wouldn't let me sleep for too long? Finally, I was left alone to think freely, which I took to be confirmation I was right.

I wasted no time selecting a path between two trees that were spaced slightly wider apart than the others. I descended until I was well out of sight of the track, then gathered tinder, sticks and small branches, and lit a fire. When it was hot enough, I positioned my metal tripod over it, from which I hung my cook pot. I made enough meat and vegetable stew for several meals, ate my fill, then put out my fire so that its smoke wouldn't advertise my whereabouts to those traversing the ridge above.

Irritated at the realisation that it was that flaming Pedlar's advice that influenced my decision to put my spare cloak atop my blanket before donning an extra layer of clothing, replacing my hat and scarf and then wrapping myself back in my new cloak, I snuggled down into all of my layers, to sleep.

I dreamt that I walked towards my horse, but in the way of some dreams, I appeared to be walking through nothingness; there was nothing beneath my feet and nothing above me, just a greyness that sometimes darkened to black and sometimes lightened to white. A mild breeze blew into my face. It was my horse, I knew it. The breeze gradually strengthened to wind. I smiled. He was moving faster. He was coming for me. The wind blew more strongly, more ferociously, until it battered my face. I had to bend over in the nothingness in order to keep my eyes open. Why did I need my eyes to be open? I wondered as I now fought to keep walking through the hurricane that would floor me – it wasn't as if there were anything to see. The wind blew even harder, lifting me off my feet and hurling me backward. I landed with a thump… and opened my eyes.

I was just about warm. I hugged myself. Finally, I had someone looking out for me.

Chapter Five

I ate the rest of my stew cold, then repacked all my gear. Judging by the ease with which I could see my way back up to the ridge, it was still light, but I had no idea what time it was. Late morning, I decided once I could see the sun. I would have a decent spell of walking in the light and then, judging by the approaching clouds, a more difficult night's walking than the previous two.

I hadn't long been on my way before I spotted movement in the distance. I sighed but kept walking. Gradually, I made out two people who were either elderly or injured, their arms around one another as they walked slowly along the ridge. Each had a stick and carried a back-sack that made them look even more hunched than they were. I hoped we were approaching a village, so that they didn't have too much further to walk.

When I was close enough for them to hear me, I called out, 'Coming past,' so as not to startle them. They both stopped and as one, slowly, painfully it seemed, manoeuvred themselves so that they were facing me. I nodded to the stooped, white-haired couple. 'Are you alright?'

They both beamed. 'Just grand, thank you dear,' said the old lady. 'We're not as fleet of foot as we used to be, but we'll get back to Tallwood before the snows come.' She looked me up and down. 'Are you in mourning? I'm so sorry.'

I rolled my eyes. How often had I been asked that? 'No, I just like wearing black. Not everyone has to look the same, you know.'

She blinked. 'Well, no of course not, it's just, well, it's just unusual, that's all. Are you on your way to Tallwood too?'

'If it's southwest from here then I imagine I'll be passing through it, but otherwise, no.'

The man shook his head. 'This ridge continues southwest, but the turning for Tallwood takes us south. See it? Just along there, where that big boulder is? We go down through the trees a way, and then we'll be in the village.'

I nodded. 'I see the turning. You'll be home soon then, that's good, I won't hold you up any further.'

'But what about you, dear?' the lady said.

If I'd had hackles, they would have been rising. 'What about me?'

'You can't carry on along the ridge, the snows are coming.'

Why did every single person I ever met have to assume I was incompetent? 'I can and I'm going to.'

The man shook his head. 'I don't think you understand, dear. When the snows come to the mountains, they come. You don't want to be outside when that happens. Surely whoever you've been visiting would have told you that if you're not used to being in the mountains?'

'I understand just fine, thank you,' I said coldly. 'Contrary to popular belief, I'm not stupid.'

The woman put her hand on my arm. 'Are you running from something? Because whatever it is, it isn't worth risking your life for. Why don't you come and stay with us for a week or so? Once the first snow has fallen, you'll be able to see how things are. It's been years since our daughter moved to live in Highpasture, you're welcome to her room for as long as you like.'

'As it happens, I'm not running from something, I'm trying to find someone and he's absolutely worth the risk. I have a brain and I know how to use it, so if you'll just let me past, I'll be on my way.'

'I'm sorry to have upset you, I only wanted…'

'To stick your nose in. Now I need to be on my way.'

The couple looked at me with sorrow in their eyes as I passed them. The woman said, 'You poor love, please let me…'

'Goodbye,' I said over my shoulder and strode away from them as fast as I could. Flipping people. The sooner I found my horse, the better. His pull on my mind increased, and I took a deep breath. I needed to keep my focus on him and keep going. Annoying as the elderly couple had been, they were also right. The snows were coming. I judged I had a day or so before they arrived – like many who grew up in or near the mountains, I'd always been able to sense when the first falls were imminent – but I didn't know how long I would be up on this ridge and I needed to make sure I was off it and preferably at a much lower altitude, by the time they came.

A slight worry arose in me that I wouldn't make it, but it was quickly replaced by the knowledge that I would; my horse wouldn't have pulled me away from the safety of my home, into danger, I just knew it. He was already helping me to rest without the worry that I would freeze to death, and he'd tugged me because we would find one another, and we would bond.

A single snowflake fluttered down in front of my face. I

looked up at the clouds. They were moving slowly, as if there were no need to hurry the inevitable. I upped my pace even so and knew, without knowing how I knew, that my horse had also upped his. Worry for him flared in me. Was he in trouble? Was he being hunted? Fleeing bad weather? Was he somewhere the snows had already hit? Did he know how to survive the winters up this way? No, he was to the southwest of me. The snows would reach me before they reached him. So why was he in such a hurry now? Was he trying to tell me to hurry even more, like when he showed me he could wake me up?

I tried to jog, but the bouncing weight of my packs ensured I only took a few steps before I had to slow to a fast walk again. I was strong, but not tough enough to tolerate the two weights lifting and slamming down on my shoulders, unbalancing and bruising me. I resolved to settle into a fast walking pace and trust that my long legs, about which I'd been teased so much and which had caused me so much grief, would get me to safety in time.

I marched on through the night, taking strength and comfort from the fact that my horse pushed on too. I could feel the distance between us steadily decreasing and when, just as the sky began to lighten, the ridge began to curve to the west, I was relieved that my sense of him to the southwest took me down amongst the trees, gradually descending the mountainside. It was difficult to see where I was going to begin with, but as the sun slowly flooded the sky with light, enough filtered down between the evergreen trees, that I could easily see my way.

I'd snacked as I walked during the night, but needed a proper meal. I didn't want to stop, but knew I needed to rest, even if only for a short while.

Immediately, my horse held my mind, then nudged it. I nodded as if he were right there in front of me and had just told me out loud that he knew of the situation and would ensure I didn't sleep too long. I smiled. I loved the fact that, while I couldn't yet hear his thoughts, he had found a way to communicate with me, and I loved even more the sense that he was continually looking out for me.

But who was looking out for him? I wondered. Horses were herd animals, but as far as I knew, when one chose a human with whom to bond, they left their herd in order to find their Bond-Partner, alone. The pulling on my mind ceased entirely for a few moments, so that I lost all sense of where my horse was. Before I could panic, it gradually increased to the level to which I'd become accustomed again, and remained steady. I shook my head and blinked. Was that a rebuke? It sure as hell felt like one. Well he could keep his reprimands to himself. If I wanted to worry about him, I damn well would.

I quickly lit a fire, enjoying the heat of its flames as I gradually added more wood until it was hot enough to cook over. I made another double helping of stew, knowing that the food I was taking from my store would give me pleasure twice over – first in my stomach and then by decreasing the weight I had to carry.

When I'd finished my first helping, I scraped the rest into an empty wrapping that had held smoked meat, and packed it away in the hope it wouldn't freeze. I built up the fire as much as I could without it being a risk to the surrounding trees, then swathed myself in extra clothes, replaced my hat, scarf and fur cloak, and curled up atop my blanket and old cloak. As I dozed off, I could feel that the distance between my horse and me stayed constant. He had stopped too. I hoped again that he was okay.

∾

I dreamt I was with Heron and Kestrel. We were walking arm in arm down the main cobbled street of Clearview, something we never did. They were trying to persuade me, as they had so many times, not to leave Clearview once I qualified as a Tailor. Every time I said why I needed to leave, one of them nudged me. As our conversation continued, they nudged me harder and harder, until Heron's nudge in the ribs left me breathless.

'OW!' I opened my eyes and sat up. My hand went to my ribs, which didn't hurt at all. My fire was still alight, so I'd only been asleep for a few hours. I nodded to myself as I came to properly. I could have done with a lot more sleep, but I'd had enough for me to be able to function. My horse was right; I needed to get going.

I kicked the fire out, took off my extra layers of clothing, repacked my back-sacks and then, with a grimace, heaved them into place and carried on my way.

I was relieved to continue descending through the trees for the remainder of the day. Judging by the speed my horse was approaching my position, I decided he had to be in open countryside. I looked forward to walking on more level ground without having to slip and trip from one tree to the next.

I exited the trees just as the light was fading. I looked up to the sky to see the clouds looking far more threatening. I sniffed the air. The first snow was almost upon me. My heart sank and my aching calf muscles began to throb as I looked down the steep, rocky mountainside before me.

There were animal droppings everywhere – goats, I thought – in amounts that suggested a very large herd had been through here recently, grazing the grass and herbs that poked up between the rocks. There must be a village not far away; no one would risk taking their animals far from shelter when snowfall was imminent. But that was immaterial. I wasn't looking for a village, I was looking for my horse and I didn't want him on this mountainside when the snow began to fall.

I was tired and I was hungry. One of those couldn't be helped. I addressed the other by taking out the packet of cold stew and scooping it into my mouth with my fingers, trying not to grimace at how greasy and chewy it was now that it was almost frozen. I ate quickly, not wanting to continue on my way until I'd finished, lest I trip and fall down the rocky slope; the pack I was carrying on my front would be enough of a hindrance to my picking my way down the mountainside in the failing light. As soon as I swallowed the last mouthful, I got going again. My horse was close now, I could feel it.

Over the past few days, I'd become used to having to memorise everything that was several paces in front of me, since the pack on my front prevented me from seeing that which was directly in front of my feet. While on the stony ridge and walking between the trees, it had been a tolerable way of walking, since the surface beneath my feet had been roughly uniform. The randomly placed rocks, stones and boulders that now lay in my way were a different prospect altogether, however.

Several times, I tripped over rocks whose size I'd misjudged in the twilight, or whose position I'd misremembered, only saving myself from tumbling headfirst by managing to either grasp or land on the boulders that also obstructed my way. When the sun's rays faded completely, the clouds allowed only slivers of moonlight through, just enough for me to make out my way, but not nearly sufficient for me to accurately see what was in front of me. I resorted to scuffing my boots along the ground, only committing my weight to each footstep once I could feel I was safely in contact with the ground. I wasn't moving quickly enough. A glimmer of panic shot through me.

I felt my horse begin to close the distance between us even

more rapidly. He shouldn't be moving at such speed, surely? He must have a thick winter coat, so he would be sweating and when he stopped, he would freeze. I tried to hold my sense of him in my mind and then push it back to him, the way he had done when he reprimanded me. 'STOP,' I shouted helplessly.

A whinny from somewhere in front of me stopped me in my tracks. Tempting as it was to look straight at where it had come from, I kept my eyes averted slightly to the side, trying to pick my horse out with my night vision. Nothing. I carried on walking as a large snowflake landed on my face, followed by another, then another.

'CURSE THE CLOUDS,' I shouted. The snows were here, my horse was probably drenched in sweat, and I could neither see where I was going, nor him. It was so tempting to try to run but silence fell around me, a sure sign that the snow was falling in earnest even if it hadn't been making its way into my eyes and mouth. As I picked my way forward, I began to slip. I breathed deeply. My survival and possibly my horse's, rested on my staying calm and slowly, carefully, feeling my way. There was no other choice.

A whinny pierced the silence of the snowstorm, still from ahead but now slightly off to my left; in turning my attention entirely to my footsteps and away from my horse, I'd gone off course.

I turned to the left and continued to feel my way, again directing all of my concentration on staying upright and keeping moving. Another whinny, now to my right, told me I'd turned too much. While I took comfort from the fact that my horse was now close enough for me to hear him as well as feel him, in the complete absence of vision I had thanks to the dark and the snow, I worried that I might walk within arm's reach of him without knowing.

I almost did. As the ground finally, blessedly, became less steep and the rocks less numerous, a whicker sounded from right beside me, followed by warm breath on my cheek. Shaking, exhausted, and desperately trying to stand on trembling legs that had been pushed way past their endurance, I reached my hand out until it came into contact with something solid. I removed my glove and touched wet fur from beneath which heat radiated, warming my hand even as the cold snow landed upon it.

We must move. Maintain your contact with me. I will lead you to where we can both rest.

I nodded, too exhausted to marvel at the fact that thoughts had just appeared in my mind that weren't mine, or to consider how to reply – it just happened. *You're sweaty, you must be, running the way you have been. And you're wet with snow, I can feel that. You'll freeze to death. I have two cloaks. I don't know how big you are but I'm sure between them, they'll cover you so you can dry off underneath.*

Maintain your contact with me, he repeated – now that I knew his thoughts, I knew for certain that he was indeed male – and I felt him move beneath my hand.

But you won't make it. Why won't you let me help you? I know what I'm talking about, you know. Everyone thinks I'm useless, but I know how to survive weather like this.

Your belief that you know how others think is one of the reasons I am here. He carried on moving away from me and I stumbled, both in shock and in my fear that he might, now that we had finally found one another, dare to leave me behind.

You're here because you chose me as your Bond-Partner. Because you tugged me.

Waiting for you in the valley would have been preferable. Had I done so you would not have survived. So I am here. We must remain in motion.

Yes I know that, but I really think you need my cloaks on you so that...

I am aware of both your thoughts and your beliefs. Neither are required or necessary at present. All of the energy you have remaining must be directed towards doing as I have instructed if we are to survive.

I stopped in my tracks as pain stabbed my heart and lanced through my gut. It was never going to stop. My whole life, I'd been treated as if I had absolutely nothing to offer. I'd thought that leaving Clearview meant leaving all that behind me, and yet I'd run straight to someone who treated me in exactly the same way.

My horse stopped beside me. *Your observation is based on your expectation and nothing more. Put your hand to my neck. I walk by your side.*

There was something about his thought that gave me pause. He wasn't angry and he wasn't scolding me, he just seemed to be stating a fact of which he was absolutely sure. Where I wanted to rage, to cry about the unfairness of my life so far and the cruel twist I believed it was playing on me now, I found myself putting my glove back on and pressing my hand against what, according to him, was his neck. When I felt him move, I walked next to him, finding myself confident that despite being completely blind in the dark and snow, I wouldn't fall.

Chapter Six

I lost all sense of time as we fought our way through the freezing snowstorm. Each of my footsteps was loaded with the same exhaustion, the same fear for myself and for my horse, who walked steadfastly down the slope beside me. Contrary to my fears for him, he didn't slip or trip, and although I could feel a weight of snow on my hand as I continued to hold it against his neck, shoulder or sometimes his leg when I couldn't hold my arm up any higher, he didn't succumb to hypothermia as a result of having sweated.

When the ground levelled beneath my feet, I stumbled. Without the slope offsetting the depth of the rapidly falling snow, I now had to lift my feet out of it in order to keep moving. My horse slowed his pace until I managed to force my legs, now screaming with the abuse I was continuing to inflict upon them, into a new rhythm. I felt his confidence that I would find the strength to stay at his side, and I believed him.

When a dim light appeared just in front of us, I thought I must be seeing things. I shook my head and blinked.

We are here. They will help us. For the first time, my horse allowed me to know of his own exhaustion. He was cold, hungry, and almost on the verge of collapse. How had he kept that from me? *They will not hear our arrival. You must continue on alone.*

Alone? I'm not leaving you.

Much depends on you following my counsel. His thought was grave, yet not a rebuke. Again, I felt as if he were stating an indisputable fact, and incredibly, could find no reason to argue.

I put both my hands out in front of me and took only four steps before I touched something that moved a little. I took hold of it and rattled it. It was a gate! I was near someone's front door! I brushed the snow away and fumbled with the latch, then swore as the gate wouldn't open due to the amount of snow on the other side.

I felt my horse's presence next to me. He gently nudged me to the side and the gate disappeared from under my hand as he pushed against it. I walked into the space he had created, towards the light. When I reached a door with a knocker made from a goat's horn, I could have cried. I lifted the knocker and bashed the door with it for all I was worth. It opened a crack and an eye peered out at me.

'Please help my horse,' I said. 'He's exhausted. Do you have anywhere he can shelter from the snow?'

'Wait there,' said a man's voice, and the door shut. A few minutes passed before it opened again and two people came out, each heavily clothed so that just their eyes showed, and carrying a lantern.

'Move off the step, love, we need to shut the door or the snow'll be in there as well as out here,' said the shorter of the two, a woman. 'Where's your horse?'

I stepped back and pointed behind me. 'Just there, by the gate.'

'Don't worry, we'll soon have him out of the snow. He can go in the barn with the goats we brought down from the mountainside yesterday. He is alright with goats?'

I didn't know. They would think I was stupid. 'How the hell should I know?'

Your insistence on assigning meaning to the words of others serves neither of us.

I spun around. *It's not insistence, it's experience. That's how people always think of me. Anyway, this isn't the time to be discussing this.*

Then I shall perish.

What? What do you mean?

It wasn't from the horse that my answer came. 'Okay fine, well we'll just turn right around and go back inside then, shall we? For all we know, there isn't even a horse out there,' said the man. He turned and opened the door, beckoning the woman to go in ahead of him. 'You can lose the attitude and come inside, or you can stay out there, it's all the same to me,' he said over his shoulder.

'But what about my horse?'

The man shut the door behind his wife and turned back to me. 'Your horse? The horse we can't see, and who you don't know anything about?'

Familiar feelings of helplessness and anger rose within me. I wanted to stalk off into the night, but a small part of my mind nagged at me. *I shall perish.*

I grabbed the man's arm desperately as he opened the door to go inside. 'He's standing right there, by your front gate. I know you can't see him, but you can't even see the gate, so that's not saying much, is it? Please, don't make my horse suffer for the way I spoke to you. I don't know whether he's okay with goats, I don't even know his name, because I only met him this evening. He tugged me, I came to find him and it was dark by the time I bumped into him. I don't even know what he looks like.'

'Well why didn't you say that to begin with?' The man opened the door again. 'Hilva, she's Horse-Bonded, come on, we're needed after all.' He turned to me again. 'Can you ask your horse not to harm our goats? Or if he has an aversion to them, my neighbours have sheep, he could go in their barn instead of ours?'

I am comfortable with the beasts of which he speaks. I will alarm them as little as possible.

'He says he's fine with goats and will do his best not to frighten them,' I told the man as his wife reappeared.

'You're Horse-Bonded?' she said.

I wanted to remind her that my horse stood freezing to death while she and her husband were being precious over helping him, and making chit-chat, but managed to say instead, 'Yes, I suppose I am. Where's the barn?'

'Follow me. Gert will go behind you to make sure you don't get left behind. Stray five strides from me in this weather and you won't be able to see my lantern light.'

I opened my mouth to tell her that I was well aware of the danger, but my horse cut in first. *You have no need to convince anyone of your knowledge or competence. Consider keeping your words to yourself until you are absolutely sure it is necessary to speak them.*

As Hilva's light picked him out of the darkness, a huge, black mound covered in snow, I felt his... what was it? Belief? No, it was more than that. It was confidence. He had confidence in me. He knew I was capable. I relaxed. If he saw me for who I really was, then who cared what these people thought?

Your decision is sound yet you have not made it from a position of strength. We will address that in time. We have more immediate concerns at present.

Hilva held her lantern up higher than the shoulder height at which she had been carrying it. 'Thunder and lightning, he's massive. Not exactly built for scrambling around on the mountainside, is he?'

Rage bubbled up inside me. It wasn't my fault he was up here, I hadn't asked him to risk himself.

Do not waste your emotions or words on insult that exists only in your perception, my horse told me.

'Come on lad, follow me, we'll soon have you tucked up warm and dry,' Hilva told him. 'There's plenty of hay and the water troughs are heated thanks to Gert's genius, so you'll have all you need.'

My horse turned to walk alongside Hilva, and I was forced to walk behind them both. Jealousy flared in me. *I walk by your side, that's what you told me, but now you're walking by hers, as well as defending her?*

I walk with her to shelter while shielding you from the storm. I do not defend her for she does not require defending. I merely highlight the pattern of thought that hinders you.

It was true. In walking behind him, a good deal of the snow that was now blowing almost horizontally was swept over my head, and he was cutting a path in which I, followed by Gert, could tread more easily. Yet I wanted to cry. An exhausting day had seamlessly merged into the night from hell, and the one good thing to have come out of it all was systematically criticising everything I said and did... and I couldn't even find it in me to disagree with anything he told me.

He stopped suddenly, and a tall sliver of light appeared as Hilva slid a huge barn door to one side. Gert ran to clear snow from its tracks and I stumbled to grab the door handle and help Hilva to heave it open enough for my horse to get through. I followed him in, brushing as much snow as I could from his back so he wouldn't take it inside, and marvelling at the fact that he was, as Hilva had already observed, massive.

Hilva and Gert came in behind us, holding up their lanterns. 'There's hay in racks all along that back wall, and the water troughs are at the far end,' Gert said.

I was horrified to see how unsteady my horse was on his legs as he made his way to the hay racks I could just about make out in the lanternlight. My knees buckled as everything he'd told me and everything I'd felt from him whilst he was tugging me, came flooding back and fitted together, all of a sudden making sense.

With his huge frame and feet – the complete opposite of the small, nimble-footed animals that thrived in the mountains – he was completely out of place here. He would have preferred to have waited down in the valley where the weather was less harsh and he had trees for shelter, as well as terrain upon which he could move comfortably. I'd felt him pick up pace after I rejected the offer of shelter from the elderly couple up on the ridge; he'd known, in the way that horses know, that without him, I wouldn't accept help. Ensuring that I did had nearly killed him, and yet, as I'd stood on Hilva and Gert's doorstep, he'd calmly accepted that as his possible fate. He'd been prepared to die in order to help me choose different words from those I'd wanted to say, those I'd felt compelled to say. Compelled by what? I wondered as my knees hit the ground and the weight of the pack on my back pulled me onto my bottom.

Your question is wise and one that will serve you well. Rest now. My horse's thought rang with approval, something I'd never experienced before. Worried for him as I was, I smiled an exhausted smile.

I can't do that yet. I need to keep an eye on you, and I don't have the answer to my question.

For now merely remember that you found your way to asking it. I require no observation. Rest.

I felt the straps of the sack on my back being pulled down my arms, but they were caught on those of the pack on my front. I frowned and shook my head. 'I can do it.' With heavy arms, I pulled the straps of both packs off of me.

'Goodness, this is heavy,' said Hilva, shouldering the smaller pack.

'And that's the smaller of the two. This one's even heavier,' Gert said. 'She's a strong lass, this one.' He offered me his hand. 'Come on, up you get, you need to be inside.'

I shook my head. 'I can't leave him. I need to make sure he finds the water, that he eats enough, that he's warm enough. He might need my cloaks over him once he lies down. I'll be fine in here, I'm used to sleeping outside.'

Hilva's face appeared in front of mine. 'That may well be the case, but you're soaked through. That's a fine cloak you have there, but it's almost frozen solid, as are your trousers. Your lips are blue and I don't like the colour of your face. If we leave you out here, you'll be dead within hours. You'll be no good to your horse then, will you?'

Anger churned in my stomach and tightened my jaw.

Your question, my horse reminded me wearily.

My question. I remembered. What was it that compelled to me to lash out at anyone who offered me help or advice? Until I had the answer, I needed to do as my horse had advised and shut up unless it was absolutely necessary to speak. I bit down hard on my lip, unable to feel the pain that should have resulted, even as I tasted the blood that leaked from the wound. Hilva was right. I should change into dry clothes and get warm. Then I would come out to check on my horse.

That will not be necessary. I will wake you should I have need. You know I can.

I nodded, suddenly feeling a little better. I took Gert's hand and allowed him to heave me to my feet.

'Can you walk back to the cottage unaided?' he asked.

I swallowed down the sharp response that up until an hour ago would have been unleashed with maximum effect, and managed a weak smile. 'Yes, thank you.'

He nodded. 'Come on then, let's get you into the warm.'

When I reached the barn door, I looked back into the dark where my horse was tucking into his hay. *Thank you,* I thought to him.

He registered my thought but didn't reply. I could feel him nestled in my mind like a warm bundle of reassurance in the middle of all the constant flittering around of my thoughts and emotions. I smiled. I could feel my bond with my horse. I was one of the Horse-Bonded.

Chapter Seven

I woke to bright light streaming through a gap between the curtains of the room in which I'd fallen asleep. I stretched and yawned, then remembered where I was and why. I sat bolt upright. *Are you alright?*

I felt my horse register my question, and his lack of need to answer it; I could sense sense for myself that he was warm, dry, fed and rested. I breathed a sigh of relief and looked around the room. Its grey stone walls were all that prevented me from vomiting at the violent shade of pink that had been favoured for the curtains, bedding, chair and rug. My eyes flicked back to the chair. I'd rested my back-sacks against it, but they were no longer there. Instead, there was a pile of what looked my clothes on its seat.

My heart hammered in my chest, and my mouth and throat went dry. Hilva and Gert had been through my packs. Was there anything that suggested I'd stolen everything in Kerk's pack? What about the pack itself? Did it have his name on it anywhere? I sat rooted in place as I racked my brain. Then my panic turned to anger. Gert and Hilva could think what they liked, I didn't care what anyone thought.

My horse increased his presence in my mind slightly; he wanted me to know he was observing my thoughts. My horse. I'd been tugged and I'd found my horse. I was loaded with stuff because I'd been on my quest to find him – Gert and Hilva would expect me to be carrying food and equipment bestowed upon me by my friends and family at my Quest Ceremony. They didn't need to know I hadn't had one, did they? And now I was a member of the Horse-Bonded, they would think to question me even less.

My heart calmed and moisture returned to my mouth. I got up and began to dress, grateful for the hot water bottle that had been placed between my trousers and shirt so that they were warm as I put them on, followed by several pullovers.

Once I was dressed, I made the bed and went downstairs. My stomach rumbled as the smell of hot milk wafted through a doorway at the end of the hall. That would have to wait.

My cloak was hanging on a hook by the front door; I remembered Hilva peeling it off me when we came in the night before. I flung it around my shoulders and hurried out of the door. As I followed a lone set of footprints through the thigh-deep snow that covered the front path, vague memories returned to me of what had happened after I'd arrived back at the cottage the previous evening.

I remembered being guided to a chair at a large kitchen table. What appeared to be a huge hunk of bread was placed in front of me, but on taking a bite, I found moist chunks of meat in its centre. A steaming mug of tea was placed in my hands and I cried in pain as warmth returned to them. After I finished my meal, I was gently manoeuvred upstairs by Hilva, who left me in a bathroom with a steaming bath that had a towel and nightshirt draped over one end of it. I barely spoke, which was a relief, as I could be confident that I hadn't said anything that ran contrary to my horse's advice.

Gert and Hilva's barn – the nearest of many solid-looking structures built from hundreds of small tree trunks that had been stripped of their bark, lashed together and painted with a dark stain – came into sight. Its roof was invisible beneath several feet of snow but the door, made of flat wooden planks lashed together, had been slid open halfway. A few goats stood in the doorway, peering out into the fenced paddock. They disappeared and were replaced by others who made the same observations and decision; they wouldn't be venturing outside.

I reached the door and peered into the gloom. *Where are you?*
That is something you need never ask.

He was right. I'd known he was standing, eating hay at the far end of the barn as soon as my thoughts had turned to the part of my mind that he now occupied.

'You can slide the door open further now it's stopped snowing, if you like, let a bit more light in,' called Gert.

I kicked the snow away from the metal runners that allowed the door to slide, then opened it almost as wide as it would go. I wanted to be able to see my horse; I didn't even know what colour he was.

I could just make out Gert high up in the loft that ran the length of the far wall, shaking hay loose from a bale and throwing it down into the hay racks.

My horse appeared out of the darkness. I grinned up at him in awe, for tall as I was, he was taller. He was powerfully built, his front legs spaced far apart to reveal firm chest muscles, matched by those of his neck, back and hind legs. He was completely black apart from brown eyes that looked deeply into me as if he knew everything about me – as if he'd been with me from the moment I was born until this very second, rather than just since yesterday.

I don't know what I'd expected, coming to meet him properly for the first time, but it wasn't this. All the hurt, anger and sadness I'd ever felt eased away as he held my eyes with his own. In their place was a warmth that stole through me, soothing me from the inside out and giving me strength – like when I used to sit in my tree.

'I suppose you're just getting to know him, seeing as you only found him yesterday?' Gert's voice sounded from right beside me, making me jump. I looked away from my horse, and everything I'd been feeling vanished. I scowled, but my horse reached out to Gert, sniffing his stubbled cheek. Gert smiled and lifted a hand. 'You're a beauty, aren't you, lad? Brave, too, coming up here to look for this lass of yours.' He turned to me. 'Hilva will have some porridge on the go, she'll keep it hot for when you're ready.'

I tried to turn my scowl into a smile and managed a grimace. 'Thank you. For everything. I'm sorry I haven't introduced myself, I'm Rowena.' I held out a hand.

Gert shook it firmly. 'I'm pleased to meet you. I don't know how this works, with the two of you only just having bonded, but if you're both up for it, I know there'll be some in the village who could use some of his counsel.' He nodded his head to where my horse stood looking between the two of us as if waiting for his turn to speak.

I didn't know how it worked either and I was irritated that I wasn't being given a chance to find out. The last thing I needed was to begin my time as one of the Horse-Bonded looking like an idiot. Before I could open my mouth to tell Gert so, I felt my horse holding my mind still, as he'd done when I was on my way to find him and he wanted me to pay attention. I looked at him.

His warm, brown eyes stared back at me. *Remember your question.*

The intensity of his thought combined with that of his gaze to push everything out of my mind except for the question at which I'd arrived the previous evening. I still didn't know why I had such a strong compulsion to lash out at everyone, but I remembered how much my horse had been prepared to sacrifice in order for me to ask myself the question, and that pulled me up short. But how to answer Gert without saying the words that I knew would get him to leave me alone, so I could figure it out?

'Right, well, I'll just leave you be, then. I'll see you at breakfast when you're ready.' Gert nodded politely, his watery blue eyes uncertain, and left.

'Huh,' I muttered to myself. 'I didn't say a word, and he left anyway.'

He read you as you do not allow yourself to read others.

I can read people. I always used to know when my brothers and sisters needed cheering up or...

I did not claim that you cannot interpret the behaviour of others. I observed that you do not give yourself the opportunity.

I don't? I mean, yes I do, but I don't usually need to. I know that when people start telling me what to do, it's because they think I'm stupid and incapable.

That is merely a belief to which you cling, my horse informed me.

I took a step back, looked into his eyes and felt again that he had been with me through it all, that I'd never actually been alone.

How are you doing that? I asked him. *You weren't there with me when I was growing up, but you know everything. You know how I feel, and not just because we're bonded, you feel it as if it happened to you, as if we were in it together, somehow.*

Cloud In The Storm you and I are one. You have a slight

appreciation of what that means now that we share a bond but when you achieve that which one day you will achieve then you will appreciate more.

How do you know what I'll achieve?

Because I have experienced that too.

My mouth dropped open but for once, no words, not even any thoughts or ideas for any, were forthcoming.

As we progress you will become more accustomed to the fact that very little is as you believe it to be, I was told.

I still couldn't speak, which shocked me almost as much as everything my horse was telling me. He didn't form words with his voice, the way I could. His thoughts were a part of him. If they weren't true, then he wasn't standing in front of me, because one couldn't happen without the other. I shook my head. How did I know that?

Our bond strengthens. Trust what you sense from it over everything you think you know. Over all of your experience of life thus far. It will help you to make decisions that will serve you instead of those that are merely familiar. It will help you to answer your question.

I nodded, feeling confused and panicky, as if the world were spinning faster and faster and I were being rapidly left behind. Yet I also felt a little excited. Everything my horse had told me was true, I knew that to my very core. So if very little was as I believed it to be, then maybe it was better?

Better and worse are merely opinions that can be assigned to anything and changed as if they never were. Everything is and is not. That is the truth.

I put my hand against his neck to steady myself. How could I have had such a good night's sleep, and yet feel so exhausted within less than an hour of being awake?

Your mind is unused to considering concepts outside its

experience. As you become more accustomed to opening to the truth you will find it less tiring.

I'll take your word for that.

You should nourish your body. It may not be in as desperate need as your mind but it should not be neglected.

Ouch, say it like it is, why don't you?

You respond with humour in place of anger.

I felt his approval and smiled. *Okay, I'll go and leave you in peace for a bit. Can you tell me your name before I go?*

It is customary for you to choose it for yourself.

I stroked his face, my hand almost disappearing in his thick, black fur. *Okay, so I try to think of something like you call me? Storm Cloud, wasn't it? I don't know whether to be proud or insulted.*

Cloud In The Storm.

I nodded, liking that better. *So I'll think of something along the lines of Cloud In The Storm, then.*

Do not think. Feel. He flooded me with himself. Where before he'd taken up a small part of my mind so I could be aware of him any time I wanted, now he was all of it, an unlimited reservoir of strength and love that was available to all, because he was all. No judgment existed within him, for there was nothing to judge. He welcomed everyone and everything equally into his world, for he was everyone and everything, yet his world was everything and nothing. He was safety and protection even though there was no danger, for it couldn't exist while he did – and he always would.

I opened my eyes to find that I'd thrown my arms around his neck and was hugging him as I'd hugged the branch of my beloved tree so many times; the tree from which I'd felt an echo of everything that I now felt from my horse. *Oak. Your name is Oak,* I told him.

Chapter Eight

Oak knew why I'd chosen his name. He'd probably known I was going to choose it, I decided as I walked away from the barn. I grinned as I felt his approval of my acceptance of the fact.

How is it that I felt from the tree what I can feel from you? I asked him.

You recognise that which is true. It calls to you even as it sits unrecognised within you.

Do you ever answer a question with a straight answer?

The human mind craves the security of knowing yet prefers the complexity of thinking over the simplicity of the feeling. I encourage the latter.

Okay, no more, Oak. I give in, I'm going to have some breakfast, and you'll be pleased to know that I don't intend to think. At all.

∾

I knocked the snow off my boots outside Gert and Hilva's cottage, and left them on the mat just inside the front door. I hung my cloak back on its hook, then followed the sound of voices to the kitchen. My hosts were sitting in chairs of wood so pale it was almost white, at a square table of the same wood, eating porridge with what looked like small, red berries in it.

Now that they were without their outdoor layers and I was fully awake, I could see that they were elderly. While Gert was tall and lean, Hilva was of average height and portly. Hilva's grey eyes sparkled but Gert's watery blue ones were more thoughtful.

Hilva jumped up out of her chair and rushed to the stove, where she began to spoon porridge into a bowl. Gert nodded to the chair opposite him. 'Have a seat.'

Hilva put the bowl of porridge in front of me, sprinkled some berries on top and said, 'Stir them in, they're even nicer when they're warm. How's your horse doing? Gert said he seemed happy enough.'

I grinned up at her. 'Thank you. Gert's right, he's more than happy, and also, as it happens, immensely self-satisfied.'

Hilva sat back down. 'Well it must be a relief for him that you both found your way here last night.'

I blew on a hot spoonful to give me time to push aside my first choice of retort to her implied suggestion that there was any doubt we would have, even though I knew there had been. Remembering Oak's counsel, I settled on merely nodding as I chewed my mouthful, then said, 'This is delicious.'

She smiled. 'I'm glad you like it. You may have noticed that I've been through your packs? Snow had got inside them and everything was frozen solid. I've dried and aired all of your clothes, and your food is in the pantry where it won't spoil before you repack it. Your family provided for you very well, didn't they? I suppose they had to, with you leaving just as the snows were imminent. What a time for your horse to tug you! Maybe he didn't know where you lived, that he was putting you in danger, pulling you away from the safety of your home just before the snow was due to hit?'

I frowned as I blew on another mouthful of porridge. I hadn't considered that. *Why did you...*

Because the time was right, Oak told me gently.

But we could have died.

And yet we live. An extreme circumstance can be useful in highlighting necessary change in the clearest possible way.

My frown deepened. *You're referring to my question that I still don't have the answer to.*

Oak didn't need to reply for me to know I was right.

'Are you alright? Did you burn your mouth?' Hilva said.

'No, I'm fine. I just asked Oak – that's my horse's name – why he risked us both by tugging me when he did, and I'm thinking about his answer.'

'It must be very confusing, suddenly having a horse telling you things,' Hilva said gently.

'You have no idea,' I muttered.

'Oh, I nearly forgot, this fell out of one of the pockets in your back-sack when I was hanging it over the airer to dry.' She pulled an envelope from a pocket in her trousers and placed it on the table in front of me. 'It's a good job the snow didn't get to it, or it would have been mush by now. It's addressed to you, but unopened, so I thought you must have forgotten about it.'

I stared at it for some time before recognition dawned. It was the envelope that had fallen out of my portfolio bag. I didn't recognise the spiky handwriting on the front. I tore it open and pulled out the two sheets of paper within. The first was a letter.

Dear Rowena,

Please find enclosed your Certificate Of Qualification as a fully-fledged and may I say, extremely talented, Tailor. I regret that I was unable to hand it to you in person, but you left in such a hurry, you quite took me by surprise. Your sisters have assured me that everything in your portfolio is your own work, a question which I fear offended you, yet which I was duty bound to ask as part of the qualification process.

As I'm sure you know, I'm long overdue to retire. Having examined in detail the extensive works in your portfolio, and been astonished to the point of speechlessness by their quality, I would be honoured if you would consider taking over the running of my shop. Please do come and see me at your earliest convenience.

Yours in hope,

Jewner

I dropped the letter and stared disbelievingly at the certificate still in my hand. It was an elaborate document. Its borders were embossed with images of needles, pins, scissors and reels of thread, in red and black. The writing within the borders was Jewner's and specified my name and everything of which I was now capable of contributing to my fellow humans of The New. At the bottom, Jewner's title and signature accompanied formal pronouncement of my qualification as a Tailor.

This couldn't be! Was this Heron and Kestrel's work? Had they produced it in the hope I would get work once I left Clearview? No, there was no way they could have produced a document like that, nor written a letter in such old-style handwriting. My mind raced, but I could come up with no answers.

'Rowena are you alright? Is everything okay?' Gert said, but all I could do was stare at the certificate in disbelief.

Oak nudged my mind. I felt his confidence in me, his knowledge that I would come to the truth. I trusted our bond. What had he said to me about that?

He repeated his earlier advice, but this time it was accompanied by a sense of increased importance. *Trust what you sense from our bond over everything you think you know, over all of your experience of life thus far.*

Where everything else in my life had always been so confusing, so hurtful, what he and I shared was different. His calm composure gave me hope that there was a way to make sense of it all. I took a deep breath and thought back to what had happened in Jewner's shop while keeping what I could sense from Oak at the forefront of my mind.

Jewner had examined my work and then politely asked me a question. I'd interpreted it through what I thought I knew of people, through my belief that no one would give me a chance, that everyone saw me how my mother saw me. I lashed out at him, then ran away before the hurt could get any worse.

A part of me paused to note that I'd answered the question which Oak deemed so important; I lashed out at people because I believed they saw me through my mother's eyes. I protected myself from them as I'd always felt the need to protect myself from her. I sensed Oak's approval and moved on with our observations.

My sisters had ensured I qualified, and must have hidden the envelope in my portfolio as a surprise for when I went to unpack it. My heart sank and my lower lip trembled. They would have noticed it was gone, they would know I had it, yet there was no letter from me in its place, thanking them for all they had done to help me.

Hilva put her hand on my arm. 'What is it? Is it bad news from home? You were pale before, but you've gone as white as the snow.'

I shook my head slowly. How had I got it so wrong?

Regret serves no purpose other than to highlight which adjustments are required.

What else did I get wrong, Oak?

I thought back to the couple who had invited me to stay with them in Tallwood, and saw them through my bond with my horse. Their faces were warm and kind. They were tired after their trek along the ridge from Highpasture, yet their concern was for me going on alone when they knew what might happen. What nearly had happened. They didn't know me, I looked strange in my black clothes and I was rude, yet still they had invited me to stay until it was safer to travel.

I thought back further, to the Pedlar who had woken me in the mountain pass. I'd made a silly mistake and he probably saved my life, yet I was ungrateful and rude to him. Still, he'd offered to help me, but I hadn't let him.

I hesitated. In my mind's eye, I stood in the mouth of the pass, looking towards Clearview. I couldn't bear to go over events there. What if I'd got all of that wrong too? No. My mother was vile towards me and always had been, there was no way I'd been wrong about that. Oak nudged me, pushing my mind back to my home village.

'We can't help you if you don't tell us what's wrong,' Hilva said gently. 'That looks like a qualification certificate. That's good news, isn't it? But why didn't your examiner present you with the certificate personally? What happened?'

I looked at her, miserably. 'I've made a dreadful mistake. And not just one of them, I think I've made lots of them. I can't do this here, I need to go to Oak.'

'Okay, I see that, but please, finish your porridge first?'

'I don't...' the rest of the words I'd been about to speak stuck in my throat before I could finish telling her that I didn't need her telling me how to look after myself. I didn't trust myself to say anything, to even think anything. I nodded and with a shaking hand, put a spoonful of porridge into my mouth. I concentrated on eating, on the porridge that stuck in my mouth and felt like glue as it went down my throat. Better to concentrate on that than on what awaited me.

I could feel Oak with me in my mind, patient and strong. His confidence in me never wavered, neither did his belief – no, it was more than that, his knowledge – that everything was alright. I tried to hold on to that feeling, even as a small part of me nagged away that he'd seen his own death that way too; he'd been prepared to die in order to give me the opportunity to make a different decision from that which came so automatically to me. He hadn't viewed his demise as an issue, but with the same lack of judgment he attached to everything else. If he'd been prepared to put himself through that, what was he prepared to put me through?

Trust our bond.

I do, Oak, but I'm scared.

I walk by your side. When he'd told me that as we began to pick our way through the snowstorm in the dark, I'd taken him literally, and taken comfort from his physical presence and strength. When he told it to me now, I understood his full meaning; whatever I faced, he would face it with me. I wasn't alone.

I stood up. 'I apologise for my behaviour,' I whispered. 'There's just something I have to do.'

Gert went ahead of me to the front door. He wrapped my cloak around my shoulders as Hilva appeared with my hat, placed it on my head and buckled the straps attached to the ear flaps under my chin, as I would have done for my youngest siblings.

'You take your time, dear. Gert will be off to help Simon with his sheep – he's getting on a bit and he's by himself – but I'll be here ready with a mug of hot tea when you get back. Whatever's troubling you, your horse will help you, you'll see.'

I swallowed down my irritation at her thinking I didn't already know that, and managed a weak smile. *I'm coming*, I thought to Oak.

No. You have arrived.

Chapter Nine

I fought my way through the snow to the barn on trembling legs. The sky was clear and a vivid blue, and the snow sparkled, as if each snowflake had caught a ray of sun for itself and was determined to use it to announce its individuality, its presence.

Oak was waiting for me at the fence of the paddock that surrounded the barn, the black of his coat making him seem even bigger in contrast with the white snow. When I was within a few strides of him, he turned and walked to the barn. I followed him to just inside the doorway, where he stopped alongside a bale of straw, the first in a line around the outside of the barn, presumably placed to keep out any ground-level drafts.

I sat on the bale and looked up into his eyes. The same knowledge of me that I'd seen in them before, the same acceptance, gazed back and combined with the constant sense I could feel from him that everything was okay. When he nudged me back to the vision in my mind that I'd halted, I went.

I was again looking in the direction of Clearview, my packs on the ground beside me. Behind me was the mountain pass I'd taken – the path that had allowed me to run away from everything that had hurt me… and towards even more reasons to feel hurt and lash out at people. In front of me were the answers, if I would continue to trust my bond with Oak, and go and look for them.

As soon as I made my decision, I found myself standing in the playground of Clearview's school. I looked down at myself and then all around me. It was a familiar scene. I was a twelve-year-old girl being teased about my clothes. My mother was a Tailor, yet my trousers were too short. Didn't she care about me?

I punched my tormentors to the ground just as an eight-year-old Heron ran over, shouting for me to stop. Her trousers were also too short. My heart almost stopped. How had I not noticed that at the time? I blinked furiously and looked up at Oak. He breathed in and out, slowly and deeply, his eyes warm and soft as he watched me. Everything was okay.

I was back in the playground.

'Mummy's just busy,' Heron said to the girls now sitting on the ground, rubbing their jaws and sobbing. 'Her cloth delivery was late and she's having to work like mad to catch up on all her orders. She said she'd make us new clothes as soon as she can, so you leave my sister alone.'

I was grabbed by the shoulders and marched indoors by a teacher to yet another detention. Later that day, I stole some scraps from my mother's workshop, ran to my tree and attached them to the bottom of my trousers, making them longer. Where were Heron's trousers? I wondered. Had I only altered my own?

Oak gently pulled me away from where I sat with my younger self in the tree. I was mortified at my selfishness. How had I seen the situation so differently from how it was? I would never have allowed behaviour like that from my brothers and sisters. How had I thought it was okay?

My mind flew back further. I was small, about six I judged. Heron was two and Finch was a baby. My mother was breast-feeding Finch while spoon-feeding Heron her breakfast. I was a big girl, I could feed myself. My mother smiled at Heron as she took her final spoonful, and wiped her mouth. Then she looked down at her suckling baby, smiling as she stroked his head, already thick with brown hair. She glanced over at me and her expression changed. The sparkle in her eyes disappeared and her smile faded.

'Sit up straight when you're eating, Rowena,' she said, not unkindly but not with the motherly love that shone from her when she looked at or spoke to Heron and Finch. My chest tightened and my stomach began to ache as if I'd been punched there. I didn't know what I was feeling, then, only that it hurt. A lot.

But I knew now. The pain of rejection was still as excruciating now as it had been then, and on every occasion in between.

Oak nudged my mind towards my mother, encouraging me to watch her more closely, his loving acceptance over-riding the pain that had arisen in me afresh. I trusted him.

I scrutinised my mother's face as she looked at me. Her eyes were full of an agony that far surpassed anything I'd ever felt. One glance at me had caused her to feel like that? I really looked that much like my father? How was I seeing it now when I never had whilst living with her?

More memories began to replay in my mind and I experienced afresh the ways my mother's discomfort around me had manifested; the stiffness when she reached for my hand; the dullness in her voice when she asked me to do something or reprimanded me; the pain in her eyes when she looked past me rather than at me, as she so often did.

Oak wound his way through my memories as I re-experienced my attempts to get my mother's attention when she wouldn't look at me, in increasingly unacceptable ways. If I asked her a question and she answered while looking slightly past me, I would throw what I was holding, sometimes at her. If I told her something that had happened at school and she either didn't answer straight away or answered in anything but the soft, kind tone she always adopted with my siblings, I would shout at her. When she hugged and kissed my brothers and sisters, I would demand that she do the same for me, but when I felt the stiffness of her embrace and saw the reluctance in her eyes when she went to kiss me, I would scream at her and push her away.

The more she hurt me with her dullness, her coldness towards me, the more I wanted to hurt her back. As time went on, disappointment and dislike added to the pain and sadness in her eyes when she looked past me. I responded by avoiding her as much as possible, and being as caustic as I could think how to be when I was around her – to which she began to respond in kind.

In blocking out everything I saw and felt from her, I left myself unable to recognise kindness from anyone else. Instead, I saw everything that everyone said and did through a filter constructed from my own beliefs – that I was unwanted, unlovable and unworthy. *But I was all of those things.*

You were none of them. Consider why your mother tried so hard to prevent you from being able to leave.

What? She made me work in her shop because…

Cloud In The Storm. Consider.

Oak's calm strength soothed me. I took a deep breath and looked back, through my bond with him, at the life my mother had established for me. I was stunned at how differently I interpreted her actions.

My sisters and brothers were the most important thing in my mother's life. She adored them – and yet she had always entrusted them to me. She saw how much I loved them, how happy I was with them, so she made sure that spending time with them, caring for them was a big part of my life, even though she couldn't help herself putting it across that it was one of the very few ways I could make myself useful.

My mother was a Tailor, and a very good one. She made out that she only taught me to sew so I could take some of the burden of making and repairing clothes for the family off of her shoulders, but in fact it was because she knew how much I enjoyed sewing. She devoted much time to teaching me, even when it meant she got behind with her work.

She was a perfectionist, yet when I began working in the shop, she trusted me with the large and difficult orders that challenged me and gave me enjoyment, as well as with the simpler tasks. True, she put me in the shop when I wouldn't have a chance to be in contact with her customers, but with good reason.

My heart thumped so hard, it felt as if it were rising up into my throat as I realised why taking me on as her Apprentice was never an option for my mother. It wasn't as she'd said and as I'd always believed, because she didn't think I was good enough to be a Tailor in my own right – but because she loved me as fiercely as she'd loved my father and she knew if I ever qualified, I would leave her just as he had.

Further, she knew I would struggle to live away from a family who tolerated my behaviour, who gave me a home regardless of how I behaved and how much trouble I caused. She kept me there in the only way of which she could think, because in her own damaged way, she thought she was doing the right thing for both of us.

I felt as if my whole life were disintegrating before me. While much of it was as I remembered, there was so much I'd missed even as it was happening, so much I'd misinterpreted, so much unnecessary hurt I'd caused my family. My mother had struggled with me, there were no two ways about it, but I'd made the situation so much worse. Where in time she might have got over my resemblance to my father and been able to show me the love I now knew she felt for me, I'd kicked the door shut on that chance and then hammered away on it so that it could never be opened. My mother was foul to me because I'd taken her pain and multiplied it a thousand-fold.

But she was my mother, I argued with myself. I was just a child, and she rejected me.

The illusion of rejection is in truth merely the unfulfillment of expectation.

WHAT? Are you seriously telling me that as a child, I had no right to expect being loved and wanted?

You were loved and wanted. You see that now. You were happy until you compared your relationship with your mother to that which she shared with your siblings. Had she been allowed the time to reconcile your similarity to your father then the issue of rejection in which you believe and to which you assign your troubles would never have arisen.

I couldn't believe it. *You're actually telling me it was all my fault?*

This does not concern fault or blame. Both are merely distractions from the truth. You have experienced much pain as a result of your expectations not being met and have caused much in return. As a child you were incapable of doing other than responding to your interpretation of the events in front of you. As an adult the events of your childhood give you a perspective from which you can learn.

Learn what? That rejection doesn't exist? That it was all in my head?

You have seen for yourself that no one is perfect. That the pain experienced by one can be passed to another and returned a hundredfold. Behind it all was a need for love. Yet that love existed. If you choose to see that it exists everywhere then you will be able to move forward. If you continue to choose to see rejection when those around you do not meet the criteria that you have set then the life in front of you will be no different from that which you left behind. His thought was as gentle as always, but its message couldn't have shaken me more.

I don't know how long I sat thinking, but when Oak lay down in the straw that formed a deep, insulating layer over the floor of the barn, I was shivering with mental exhaustion as well as with the cold. I slid down to the ground and curled up between my horse's front and back legs, needing both his body heat and to be in physical contact with the one who held my sanity. I didn't know who I was, or where to go from here. All I knew was that I was with him.

Chapter Ten

I was being shaken. As I came to, Hilva's voice was near my ear. 'Look, Gert, she's all curled up with Oak. Aren't they cute? Oh, Rowena, you're back with us. I'm sorry to disturb you, I can see that Oak's keeping you warm, and I can see you're still exhausted after your ordeal yesterday, but I just wondered whether you like goat's cheese? I'm planning to use a fair bit of it in our lunch, so I just thought I'd check?'

I sat up and rubbed my eyes. Did I like goat's cheese? I'd had it lots of times, I knew that much, but I couldn't remember how I felt about anything. Oak increased his presence in my mind very slowly and gently, which only confirmed my fear as to my fragility.

Do not fear. Merely show yourself the kindness and patience you showed your siblings when they were learning that which was new to them. Take your time. Do not answer until you have reconsidered that which you now know.

I put my head in my hands. My memories were crashing around in my mind; the ones to which I'd held on for so long colliding with those that made lies of them. I didn't trust myself to know what anyone meant when they said anything, anymore. I must look a proper idiot. A familiar feeling arose within me and I latched onto it; anger as a way of protecting myself was comforting in its familiarity. But there was something about it that no longer felt right. What had Oak told me to do?

I have to stop experiencing rejection because apparently, it doesn't exist, I told myself and Oak. *And I need to see the love that exists everywhere. I don't think I can.*

Oak waited patiently. I could feel his need to relieve himself and to eat, but he didn't move. *You chose to love and be loved by your sisters and brother when you could have chosen jealousy.*

'Rowena?' Hilva said. She crouched down in front of me, her eyes full of concern.

My sisters and brothers. When Heron looked at me like that, it wasn't because she thought I was useless, it was because she was worried about me – it was because she loved me. 'See the love that exists everywhere,' I murmured to myself.

'Um, okay, well that's a nice idea, but what about the goat's cheese? I really think you need to eat something, and soon,' Hilva said.

I stared at her. Her expression didn't change. She wasn't laughing at me, she wasn't taunting me, she was just concerned. I thought about my situation. I was sitting in the straw with my horse in the freezing cold, talking nonsense while goats urinated and pooped all around me. No wonder she was concerned. I began to grin, and then to chuckle. When I laughed out loud and couldn't stop, Gert's face appeared next to Hilva's as he crouched down next to her.

'Is she delirious?' he said.

I laughed even harder, until tears ran down my face.

'I don't know. What do we do?'

I shook my head. 'I'm not delirious, I just have no idea who I am anymore and I can't relate to anyone unless I pretend they're my sister. I'm twenty years old and my whole life has been a lie. Now I'm bonded to Oak, who knows who I am and what I need to do, but he can't live my life for me, can he? He can't tell me what everyone means when they talk to me, he can't answer out of my mouth with the right words, I have to do that, and I don't know how to. I'm one of the Horse-Bonded, now. People will expect me to be composed and wise, but I can't even understand the real meaning of anything anyone s...says.' My voice broke into a whisper as the first sob escaped me, followed in quick succession by a whole lot more.

Hilva put a hand on my shoulder. 'Come on love, you're cold, you're exhausted and you're overwrought. We need to get you back inside, to bed. When you've had another sleep and more to eat, you'll feel a whole lot better. Gert, help me get her up?'

I shook my head as they each took one of my hands and pulled me to my feet. 'I won't. I'm a mess and I don't know how not to be.'

There was a rustling and a grunt behind me and Oak got to his feet, his presence in my mind calm and steady as ever, as if nothing out of the ordinary were happening. He spread his hind legs and began to relieve himself as Gert and Hilva lead me away. Just as we got to the paddock gate, there was a thumping behind us in the snow.

Gert turned around. 'Where are you going, Oak? There's plenty of hay and water for you back there, don't worry, we'll look after her.'

Oak shuffled forward in the snow, gently nudging himself between Gert and me. *I walk by your side.*

I put a hand to his neck and rubbed it, leaning my forehead

against him. *Thank you, Oak, but you need to eat. I've kept you from your hay for long enough.*

He remained where he was without reply. I sighed. 'He wants to come with me.'

'Far be it for us to argue with him,' Hilva said. 'Come along then, let's get you in the warm.'

We trudged the short distance back to the cottage in silence. Hilva held on tightly to one of my arms as if afraid I would fall. My free hand remained on Oak's neck, his huge physical presence as calming and reassuring as the warmth that emanated from his body and mind. I would normally have run for my tree in a situation such as this. Now, the horse who was everything to me that my tree had been and so much more, was by my side.

When we reached the gate to the front path of the cottage, Oak stopped to allow Hilva and me through, then followed, leaving Gert to come last.

'Um, is he coming inside?' Gert said.

Oak moved to the side of the front door, rested a hind leg and sighed.

'I think we can take that as a no,' Hilva said.

Oak, please don't stand there in the cold, I'm fine. Please, go back to the barn and eat? I said.

He merely looked at me, his eyes all-knowing as ever; I was only just about holding myself together. I felt him expanding within the corner of my mind he normally occupied, until his mind surrounded my own. He held me firmly, reassuring me that I was who I'd always been, that I would be okay. But he knew I needed more than that. He wouldn't leave me.

Emotion choked me. I'd never felt so loved, so protected, so cared for. I was everything to this horse, I could feel it as he enclosed me within himself. He'd left those of his kind to come to me, to save me from the snowstorm – to save me from myself, and he would do whatever was necessary to help me.

I love you, Oak, I told him.

You merely see love where it already exists. With practice you will find it easier to see in others. Rest now. I will remain here.

I allowed Hilva to take me indoors, remove my cloak and guide me up the stairs to bed. I crawled under the covers and pulled them tightly around myself. Something else closed more tightly too. Oak squeezed my mind, very gently, almost like a physical hug. He was beneath my bedroom window. He was with me.

Rest, came his thought and with it a sense that he would rest with me. I closed my eyes and slept.

When I woke, it was getting dark. I sat up in bed, blinking, and tried to get my bearings. Oak! I rushed to the window, pulled it open and peered out. Oak stood dozing on his feet in exactly the same place I'd left him. There were people gathered around him, watching him. Judging by the flattened snow all around him and on the path, he'd had a lot of visitors while I slept away the afternoon.

He jerked awake and stretched his neck, holding it upright and rigid before relaxing it. Then he stretched each of his back legs out behind him.

'He's awake,' someone said.

'Where's his Bond-Partner? I've got loads of questions for him,' said another.

There was a knock on the door. 'Gert, Hilva, the horse is awake, can you get his Bond-Partner out here?' called another voice.

Irritation flared in me. They clearly knew that Oak had been standing there for some time, and the second he was awake, all they could think of was what they wanted from him? I tore down the stairs, lifted my cloak from its hook and onto my shoulders in one movement, and flew out of the front door to stand between Oak and all of the people gathered around him.

'I'm right here, there's no need to crash on the door, although judging by the mess you've made of Gert and Hilva's front garden, you don't know the meaning of respect. Now get gone, the lot of you. Oak will be available to give you advice when he's ready, and not before. Go on, go.' I scowled at them all and to a person, they took a few steps backward and then turned and almost ran to the front gate and the snow-covered street outside.

'Thank you, dear,' said Hilva, wrapping her own cloak around her as she stepped out into the compacted snow and slush created by so many feet. 'They just kept coming. I did ask them to leave him alone while he slept, but, well, you know, people are people. We rarely have Horse-Bonded and their horses coming up this way, so when we do, I'm afraid there's a tendency for everyone to rather forget themselves.'

'Don't mention it. I'm sorry for the mess they've made,' I said.

Gert appeared beside her. 'I'm sorry Oak was bothered.'

I turned to Oak and rubbed his forehead. 'I really don't think he was.'

'Well you sound much better, anyway,' Hilva said.

I frowned, uncertainly. 'I feel it. Strange.'

It is beyond your expectation. It is not strange, corrected Oak.

Okay, fine, but what's happened to me?

You allowed yourself to stand aside from your personality and see your life through the perspective afforded you by our bond. In so doing you opened your mind to the influence of your soul. It was imperative that you slept while your mind adjusted. Now it has.

You knew I'd sleep better if you were here with me physically as well as in my mind. I felt overwhelmed all over again by everything he was doing for me.

We share a bond. We are what we need to be for one another, he told me, simply.

I hugged his neck, hoping that I put everything I felt for him into my arms as I held him, and then realising that it didn't matter because he knew. *I suppose you're going to tell me off for having a go at those people,* I thought to him, still holding on tight. *I didn't see a lot of love there though, only an intention to fulfil their own needs whilst disrespecting yours, Gert's and Hilva's.*

I advised you to refrain from seeing rejection in everyone who addresses you. I did not advise you to forego your personality.

I let go of him, stood back and frowned. 'Huh.'

'When you suddenly go quiet, it's because Oak is advising you?' Hilva said.

I turned to see her and Gert standing on the doorstep, their cloaks draped over their heads and held tightly around their shoulders in an attempt to keep the bitingly cold air from snatching their body heat. 'That's one word for it. Confusing and shocking me are others.' I grinned. 'I only met him yesterday and I can barely remember my own name, but I do feel better now, thanks to him and thanks to you. You're freezing, you should go inside. I'll go to the barn with him and then be back, if it's okay for us to stay with you just a little longer?'

Hilva stepped towards me and took my hands in hers. 'It's an honour to have you both, and you're welcome to stay as long as you like. Hurry back though, dear, your stomach is rumbling so loudly, for a moment I thought there was a storm coming. And don't worry about the goat's cheese, we had it for lunch. I thought it best to avoid anything for dinner that might need an opinion, in case you were still a bit addled.' She winked, and I surprised myself by smiling at her. She wasn't suggesting I was an idiot, she was teasing, the way my sisters and I teased one another. I'd seen it in her eyes, and heard it in her voice. Maybe this wouldn't be so difficult after all.

'Is there anything I can do for the goats while I'm there?' I asked.

'I've already seen to them, thanks, just shut the door behind Oak and hurry yourself back. Here you go, you'll need a lantern,' said Gert.

I took it from him with thanks, again surprised that I felt no need to tell him that I knew it was getting dark and had foreseen the necessity for a lantern. As I walked down the path, Oak took his place by my side.

I'm doing it, aren't I? I'm reacting to people better? I asked him.

You need not ask that to which you know the answer.

I guess not. I'm doing it, I know I am. It all felt so hopeless earlier, but maybe I can do this?

It will not always be easy but if you could not then I would not be here. There was a slight edge of warning to his thought, but it was accompanied by such confidence in me – no not just in me, in us both, in our bond – that I dismissed it. He'd taken my life and ripped it apart until I couldn't see how to fit the shreds back together, yet in no time at all, I was beginning to feel positive, excited even, about the life that lay in front of us.

Do you have everything you need? I asked as Oak wandered into the barn.

You know I do. Relax in the company of your fellow humans. Do not think further on the events of today. Your mind requires the rest. Cloud In The Storm you have done well.

I couldn't mistake the pride that accompanied his thought. A lump formed in my throat. No one had ever been proud of me before.

Why do you call me Cloud In The Storm?

He didn't reply.

I ran to catch up with him. *Oak? Why do you call me that?*

You once more ask a question to which you know the answer, was all he would say as he began to pull hay from the racks.

I pulled the barn door closed behind him and began to walk back to the cottage. Cloud In The Storm. I knew from experience that storm clouds threw out rain, hail, snow, lightning and thunder, as if punishing anything and everything in sight. I sighed, and surprised myself by grinning. I couldn't argue with his view of me. And I kind of liked it. What had he said? To refrain from seeing rejection everywhere, but not to forego my personality. Cloud In The Storm was my personality. I loved the name he had chosen for me.

I enjoyed my evening with Hilva and Gert. Between them, they cooked up a delicious meal of goat pie topped with a thick layer of creamy mashed potato, and steaming, spiced vegetables.

I avoided mentioning my mother and Kerk, but told my hosts all about my sisters and brothers, making them laugh with the funny things Wren had begun to say. They told me all about their grownup daughters, all three of whom had moved away to other villages to marry, but came home regularly to visit. They told me of their love for their home, their village, their friends, their life, and I could see their love for one another. I felt a slight pang. I would never have that with anyone. But I had Oak, and he was more than I'd ever hoped for, and, I decided, more than I deserved.

'You have that serious, distant look again,' Gert said. 'Is it Oak? Is he okay?'

I smiled faintly. 'He's fine, thanks. I was just thinking how lucky I am that he chose me as his Bond-Partner.'

'I don't think luck comes into it, dear,' Hilva said. 'As far as I've always been told, the horses know everything. Oak will have chosen you for a very good reason.'

I nodded thoughtfully, then frowned, wondering why I was worth the effort.

For the same reason we are all worth the effort. We all have worth.

'You shouldn't frown so much, dear. You have beautiful eyes and a beautiful face, doesn't she, Gert? And you distort them each and every time.'

Gert grinned. 'Rowena isn't one of our girls, Hilva. You shouldn't talk to her as if she is.'

I smiled wearily at them both. 'Thank you, both of you, for everything. This is the best evening I've ever had.'

Gert and Hilva both looked at me, their eyebrows raised. 'That's lovely of you to say, Rowena, but you have such a lovely family, you must have enjoyed being at home?' said Hilva.

Unable to bear the warmth in their eyes, the thought that my life could have been so different had they been my parents, I looked down at the last few morsels on my plate. 'I didn't enjoy being at home at all. My mother and I didn't get along.' I looked back up at them and they both nodded solemnly.

Suddenly, Hilva's eyes lit up. 'Gert, I think this is an occasion that calls for your homebrew.'

Gert's eyes sparkled. 'It does! Don't move, Rowena, I'll be right back.'

'Homebrew?' I asked Hilva.

'Gert prides himself on his ale. I warn you though, it's strong,' she said with a wink.

A door slammed and Gert reappeared. 'Brrr, it's cold in the cellar. This'll make your toes curl.' He heaved a small barrel onto the table, tapped a spout into it with a hammer, and poured three large glasses of foaming ale. He passed one each to Hilva and me, then raised his own glass. 'To Rowena. To your future with Oak as one of the Horse-Bonded, and to you as a qualified Tailor. We couldn't be happier or prouder to have you staying with us.' He took a long swig and so did Hilva. Then they both looked at me as I sat staring from one of them to the other.

'Is there something wrong, dear? Is ale not to your taste?' Hilva said.

'I've never had it before, but I'm sure I'll like it. No, it's just that with everything that's happened, I forgot I'm a Tailor. I'm Horse-Bonded and I'm a Tailor!' I smiled and couldn't stop.

Hilva smiled too. 'Yes, you are. Whatever your troubles have been, I think they're well behind you, Rowena.'

I raised my glass. 'To my troubles being behind me,' I said and took a sip of ale. It was earthy and bitter, but I liked it almost as much as the warm feeling that quickly swept through my body. I grinned, and Gert chuckled in delight. Little did I know, as we drank the evening away in laughter and merriment, that my troubles had barely begun.

Chapter Eleven

$\mathcal{M}$y head was pounding and I felt nauseous. I sat up in bed, leant over to the bedside table for the glass of water Hilva had insisted I bring up with me, and drank the lot. The dull light of dawn peered through the gap between the bedroom curtains.

Oak, are you okay?

I felt him register my question and knew instantly that he was. He'd eaten, drunk and rested well and was currently munching, slowly and contentedly, on yet more hay.

I washed and dressed, then made my way downstairs to the kitchen. Hilva was stirring porridge while Gert sat at the table, his head in his hands. He looked up as I walked in.

'Morning,' he said with a grimace. 'How are you feeling?'

'A bit sick, actually. I had a headache but that's gone now.'

He raised his eyebrows. 'A bit sick? That's it? You had the same amount of ale as me and I feel like I've been hung upside down and swung around by my ankles.'

Hilva chuckled. 'I think our Rowena has a stronger

constitution than you, and a good deal more sense.' She looked at me. 'You drank the water I gave you?' I nodded. 'Thought so. See, Gert, water is what's needed, not more of what gave you the headache in the first place.' She smiled at me. 'Sit down, dear, if you can tolerate Gert's moaning. The porridge is ready.'

'I'm not sure that eating anything is a good idea,' I said.

'Trust me, it is. I've had plenty of opportunity to test hangover cures over the years as a result of Gert's homebrew, and water, followed by a breakfast of porridge and tea, comes out on top.'

I grinned as I sat down. 'What about you? Are you okay?'

She smiled. 'I'm fine. I drank about half the amount you and Gert put away. I know my limits, unlike some.'

'I think I've just learnt a bit about mine,' I said and closed my mouth firmly as my stomach lurched.

Hilva put a steaming bowl in front of me. 'Get this down you, and you'll feel a whole lot better. What are your plans for today?'

I hadn't thought about it. 'I don't know. I feel like I don't know anything. I was in such a regular routine at home, then when I was tugged, I focused on finding Oak, and I've been stumbling around ever since. I suppose I'll do whatever Oak tells me to do. Unless… is there anything I can do for you? Help with the goats, housework, or anything?'

Gert slurped a mouthful of porridge, his head now resting on one hand so that one side of his mouth was permanently open. 'I think you have far more important things to do than that.'

Hilva nodded. 'Remember all those people crowding around Oak yesterday? You and he are in high demand. I'd keep the fact that you're a Tailor under your hat, because you'll be sought out for that too, if anyone finds out. We have a Tailor here, but she's so overworked, she makes mistakes and her apprentice isn't up for working on the really heavy winter garments we all need in winter.'

I shook my head as I swallowed a mouthful of porridge. 'This is all very weird for me, having people thinking of me as being useful. I think I'll go and see Oak, and then see where the day goes from there.'

'That sounds like an excellent idea. Be sure to come back at lunchtime though, you've little enough covering on you as it is. I can't have you missing meals like you did yesterday.'

'Leave the girl alone, Hilva, like I said before, she isn't yours to boss around.'

'While she's staying with me, I'll see her properly fed and looked after,' Hilva said with a wink at me. 'Don't mind him, he's always grumpy after he's had a few. He'll be right as rain by lunchtime.'

I stepped out onto the front doorstep to find that a thin scattering of snow had fallen during the night. I drew in a breath of air that was so sharp, my airways dried instantly and my teeth hurt. I pulled my scarf up around my mouth and my hat down lower over my brow.

When I reached the gate, the few people in the vicinity, either leaving their own cottages further up the street, or passing by to the livestock barns, hastily diverted their gazes from me and hurried on their way. I kicked the snow. Not everything had changed, then.

On the contrary.

I began to walk to the barn, where I knew Oak waited for me. *People avoid me. They always have.*

The reason is different now. Remember my counsel.

Your counsel. Stop seeing rejection everywhere. Okay fine, but when people take one look at me and run, how am I meant to see it?

Through our bond. Calm confidence accompanied his thought and wove its way through me.

I thought back to those who had turned away from me. Then I remembered how many people I'd told in no uncertain terms the previous day, to get gone until Oak was ready to counsel them.

I sighed. *It's so easy to see it when you help me, but I can't do it on my own.*

Then it is fortunate that you are not on your own.

I smiled, feeling better. I could see him now, a large black shape against the white that made the surrounding scenery all but invisible. *What shall we do today?* I asked him.

It is usual for newly bonded partnerships to go to The Gathering. There is much for you to learn there from your fellow bonded. We will leave.

What? Now? Without giving anyone your counsel?

That would not be wise. You are not ready.

To act as your interpreter? I only have to tell them what you say, don't I? I'll be fine.

Oak tossed his head. When I was almost upon him, he peered down his nose at me. *There may be some benefit to your proposal. We will visit the village.*

I opened the paddock gate and then closed it behind my horse, even though the goats peering around the barn door showed little sign of wanting to venture out. Oak didn't wait for me, but walked purposefully towards the village. I jogged the few steps necessary to catch up, and walked at his shoulder.

Now that the snow had been sufficiently trampled that we didn't have to labour to get through it, I was able for the first time to take in the view of the large, sprawling village that was Mountainlee.

The snow on the rooves of its grey stone cottages glistened in the sunshine, even as smoke from the hundreds of chimneys added to as many small, dark grey clouds before drifting slowly away. Heavily clothed people hurried along its streets between cottages and shops, and in the direction of the barns Oak and I had just left behind us. Those we passed nodded but kept their faces down against the wind that blew down the mountainside.

We passed Gert and Hilva's cottage at the end of the village, and turned to walk up the main street of trampled snow. A few people began to walk hesitantly towards us. Oak came to a majestic halt and looked about himself. I stopped beside him.

'He's beautiful,' a woman called out, keeping her distance as her eyes flickered from me to him, uncertainly.

'I heard he was big, but he's massive, and such a handsome horse,' a man said, also from a distance.

'We're lucky to have you both here at this time of year, we all know that,' a woman said, hurrying down her front path to where Oak and I stood. 'We're sorry for messing up Gert and Hilva's garden yesterday, and for crowding your horse, we were just so excited to see him.'

I nodded. 'Well Oak is available to give counsel now, so anyone who wants it can approach in turn and we'll do our best to help.'

Immediately, voices spoke all together.

'What, right here?'

'In the street? I mean, it's not very private, is it?'

'That's not how it's normally done, normally we take turns visiting the horse in the paddock of the person hosting their Bond-Partner.'

The rapidly gathering people were all looking at each other in consternation, and then back at me. I flushed red and sweat prickled the back of my neck. I took my hat off as my heart began to race.

'Not done this before, love? You do look young for a Horse-Bonded,' the woman standing on her path said sympathetically.'

Our bond. Remember.

I pushed Oak's thought to one side. The villagers thought I was an idiot. And I was, to think I could do this, to think that I, the disappointment of the Harrol family, could ever be anything other than just that. 'YOU DON'T WANT OUR HELP? FINE, YOU CAN GO TO HELL THEN, THE LOT OF YOU,' I shouted.

Silence fell. Everyone looked at Oak and then back at me, their mouths open. He took a step closer to me. So, he was by my side. Big deal. He couldn't stop people looking at me the way they were, could he? He couldn't stop the stabbing pain in my stomach as the looks on everyone's faces confirmed what I already knew. I turned and marched away.

'Where are you going? What about giving us your horse's counsel?' someone called after me.

'What did we say?' someone else said.

There was a thumping sound behind me and Oak appeared by my side, his feet sliding everywhere at once as he fought to stay upright on the compacted snow. My rage didn't allow me to stop. I needed to get away from them and I needed to get away from him.

I began to run. I slipped and slid my way up to the barn and then past it. I ran past more barns of all shapes and sizes and in even greater number than the cottages of Mountainlee. When I was finally clear of them, all I could see was the bright white snow that dazzled me until my eyes hurt. Oak hurled himself through the now untrodden snow in order to stay with me as, sweating, I staggered onwards.

Finally, heaving, I came to a stop, sinking to my knees in the snow. I'd dropped my hat, and my scarf had unwound and fallen off somewhere. I still had my gloves, but my cloak had been swept over my shoulders as I ran. Oak stood patiently beside me.

Cloud In The Storm you must rise. You will not survive long as you are. There was an urgency to his thought, an importance that penetrated my anger.

'Why didn't you do that when they were all having a go at me? Why didn't you get through to me, why didn't you help me?' I railed at him. 'I got it wrong. It was my first time out with you and when they questioned me, I felt stupid, like I always have. I couldn't help being angry, and you didn't stop me, you didn't push your thoughts through to me like you just did, you stood there and told me to remember our bond, when you must have known I couldn't think straight. Why didn't you help me, Oak, why?'

You now appreciate the strength of the pattern to which you adhere. We will leave for The Gathering. You should collect your possessions. He turned around, took a few steps and then stopped and looked back at me.

'That's all you have to say?' I said weakly, knowing that it was. 'And that's it? We're leaving things like that?'

We are not in a position to help anyone. We will return here when that is no longer the case.

I began to shiver. My skin was icy cold; the sweat that soaked me from head to toe was beginning to freeze. A pang of fear shot through my chest. Oak was right, if I didn't get moving, I'd be dead within minutes. How could I have been so stupid? Why was I always so stupid? I wrapped my cloak around myself and began to trudge back through the deep snow with Oak, as ever, by my side.

His calm confidence seeped into me. Through our bond, I thought back over what had happened. My reaction to the villagers' questions had been immediate. I hadn't looked to Oak for help, and when he'd managed to get through to me, to remind me to see what was happening through our bond instead of through my own distorted filter of human behaviour, I'd shoved him aside in rage. It was one thing knowing what to do, I realised, but a different thing entirely actually doing it.

Worry not. We will address the pattern together.

We already did that, but then as soon as I had my first major challenge, I crumbled.

Your recent appreciation of the strength of your pattern will assist our efforts. Our time this morning was well spent.

You should find another Bond-Partner. I can't be one of the Horse-Bonded, Oak, I just can't.

He stopped and glanced at me, his brown eyes soft and knowing. *The pattern of behaviour to which you have clung for so long feels threatened. It attempts to push me away so that you can feel rejected in a new and even more painful way and its continued existence is ensured. We will continue to address it until you no longer feel its influence.*

I frowned. *You talk of it as a pattern of behaviour, but I can sense that you think of it as if it has a life of its own.*

It is an aspect of you that will fight hard for its survival. The more you step away from it the harder it will fight. Do not concern yourself. It is no match for our bond.

But how am I going to step away from it? If it's not one thing that tips me over the edge, it's another. And when we get to The Gathering, what then? If I feel stupid and worthless among the villagers here who need our help, how am I going to feel among those who know so much more than I do, and who can already ride and will probably laugh at me when I try? I can't go there, Oak, I can't. I can't do any of this.

Cloud In The Storm. Do you think you are the only one who has experienced difficulty following bonding to one of my kind?

I'm sure I am.

Then you are mistaken. It is a fallacy which your fellow bonded do nothing to dispel that the Horse-Bonded are chosen because they stand above their fellow humans. It is far more often the case that they are chosen because they will be well placed to help their fellow humans once they have been assisted in overcoming difficulties of their own.

It is?

At The Gathering you will be among friends. That is not to say that they will remain such if we do not first decrease the strength of your pattern. By the time we arrive we will have achieved much.

Oak walked on and I walked beside him, deep in thought. My shivering got steadily worse and I hurried my pace. If I didn't get to Gert and Hilva's soon, I wouldn't be going anywhere.

I found my hat and scarf as the first barns came into sight. I brushed the snow off them and put them back on without missing a stride. When I made out people moving about around the barns, however, I almost stopped in my tracks. I didn't want to talk to anyone; I knew how that would end.

Then do not converse with anyone. You are adept at appearing unapproachable.

I can't argue with that.

As we came within hailing distance of the nearest people, I chose my best scowl and kept my eyes in front of me. It was no surprise that we were left alone. When we reached Gert and Hilva's cottage, Oak waited outside the front door. I found my hosts sipping tea at the kitchen table.

Gert looked at me through narrowed eyes. Hilva stood up. 'There you are, dear, are you alright?'

I couldn't meet their eyes. 'Not really, no. I need to leave. I have problems, I think you already know that. I shouldn't have offered Oak's counsel, because I can't hold a normal conversation with anyone.'

Hilva ran to my side and clasped my arms. 'But you're lovely, I mean you've been lovely with us. You just need time to adjust to being bonded to Oak, that's all, we've seen how much it's taken out of you.'

I shook my head and tried to smile. 'You're very kind, but it's more than that, you know it is. Oak is adamant that he can help me, but he tells me we need to leave for The Gathering.'

'You can't leave now, there's more snow coming, the Weather-Singers announced it this morning,' Gert said. 'You and Oak will never get far enough south before it catches up with you, what with you being on foot and carrying so much gear.'

We will be moving at speed. Bring only that without which you cannot survive, Oak instructed me.

'Oak says we'll be moving at speed, and to pack lightly. These long legs of mine can eat up the ground when there's a need, I'll keep up with him. I have to do as he says. I want to do as he says,' I told them.

Hilva's eyes filled with tears, which she tried to blink away. 'Of course you do. I seem to remember one of the Horse-Bonded who visited before saying it took them a few weeks to get here from The Gathering, but that was in the summer. You pack your clothes and I'll look out enough food for four weeks.'

'Thanks, Hilva.'

She wiped her cheek, nodded and hurried to the pantry.

'Are you sure about this, Rowena?' Gert said. 'You really think you can outrun the snow?'

'Oak's been right about everything else,' I said, firmly. 'If he says we can do it, we can do it. I need to go and pack.'

I took the stairs two at a time. Hilva had stored my clothes in the wardrobe and chest of drawers of the room I was using, and hung my back-sacks on the back of the door. I took the smaller of the two sacks and threw it on the bed. It was too cold to change my clothes outdoors, so I would change into fresh ones now and take just one spare set with me in case of emergency, plus the extra clothes I would need when I had to stop and sleep.

The thought of sleeping brought with it a memory of snuggling up to Oak's warmth in the barn. His coat was thick and clearly kept him warm, but he too was vulnerable to the chill that would result if he sweated. How were we going to move at speed without either of us sweating? I wondered, suddenly.

I am well used to taking care of myself. You will wear suitable clothing.

I smiled at Oak's patient counsel, even though I sensed that he felt he stated the obvious. I quickly took off the clothes I was wearing, used them to rub the remaining sweat from my skin, then redressed. As I selected what I would take, I put my old cloak to one side. Then I thought of Hilva and how she had admired the new one I'd been wearing. I put my old one by my back-sack, ready to wear.

When I was ready, I folded everything I would be leaving behind and piled it neatly on the bed. Most of it was the new clothes I'd made for my portfolio. Hilva could either keep the items for herself or distribute them to her friends; maybe they would think slightly less badly of me.

I lifted my pack, only a third full, onto one shoulder, draped my old cloak over the other, and went back to the kitchen. Gert was just adding my hunting equipment to my cook pot, crockery and cutlery that were already laid on the table. Hilva appeared, her arms full of parcels.

'These are for breakfast, lunch and dinner, to make sure you eat three times a day. I've labelled them clearly,' she said, putting them down on the table. 'Wait there and I'll get the rest.' She disappeared again.

'I'll just take my mug, my cutlery, and my cookpot so I can heat water and warm my food when I have time,' I said to Gert. 'Can you use my hunting gear?'

He looked down at the table. 'I don't hunt much now,' he said. 'There'll be someone in the village who can use it though, or I can store it for you in case you come back?' There was a hopeful tone to his voice that warmed my heart.

'If you don't mind storing it, I'd love that,' I said.

He grinned. 'Hilva and I would love it too. You're having a difficult time, we both see that, but we also see the person trying to get out from underneath. You can do it, Rowena, and when you do, you'll be a credit to the Horse-Bonded. Hilva and I believe in you and Oak.'

I gulped and looked down at the shaggy brown rug that covered most of the grey slabs of the kitchen floor. When Gert's arms drew me into a hug, I hugged him back fiercely. When he finally let go, he lifted my chin so that I was forced to look into his old, watery blue eyes. 'Come back soon, do you hear me? It's a rare person who can drink me under the table, and I want you to prove it wasn't a fluke.'

I laughed as I quickly brushed away a tear that had defied my efforts to keep it from brimming over my lower eyelid. 'Deal. You just make sure you have more homebrew ready and waiting.'

He grinned and turned to Hilva as she came bustling back into the kitchen, her arms full. Right, this is all of them. I hope you have enough room in your... oh you do, you've indeed packed lightly. Are you sure you have enough clothes for the night? I know you're going south, but if the snows do catch you...'

'Hilva, don't worry, I have what I need. Everything else is on my bed, for you or anyone else who would like them. The cloak hanging by the door, I would like you to have.'

'Oh no, dear, I couldn't. I mean, it's beautiful, but it's yours and your need is far greater than mine.'

'It isn't, actually,' I said as I packed the food parcels into my back-sack. 'It'll be too hot for me to wear when I'm moving at any sort of speed, and too heavy to carry.'

'But what about when the temperature drops during the night? Even away from the mountains, it's still winter.'

'I have a cloak, and I have Oak. He's like a furnace. I'll snuggle up to him and I'll be fine.' I packed my cook pot and mug on top of the last parcel and looked at her. 'Hilva, please, have the cloak. You've been so kind to me, it's the least I can do.'

She rushed around the table and hugged me tightly, her grey head below my chin. Then she held me at arm's length. 'You look after yourself and that horse of yours. Do you hear me?' she said fiercely. 'And once you've done what you need to do at The Gathering, once you're ready to be out and about again, you make Mountainlee your first destination. Okay?'

I nodded and smiled. 'Okay. I was going to anyway, Gert's just promised he'll have more of his homebrew ready for me.'

She laughed and then was serious again as I donned my cloak and my back-sack, and made for the front door. Oak whickered as I stepped outside. Gert and Hilva held their hands up for him to nuzzle, and stroked his neck as they told him to look after me.

I hugged them both again. 'We'll be back as soon as we can. Thank you for everything.' I walked down the path, then turned and waved once Oak and I were through the gate. Gert hugged a sobbing Hilva to him as they both waved back.

We left the village and instead of taking our well-worn path north to the barns, turned south through deep, untrodden snow, towards some trees in the far distance. I hoped that before too long, as our altitude decreased, the snow would be thinner on the ground and our path easier.

To The Gathering, then, I thought to Oak. *Have you been there before?*

I have not. The Gathering exists for the bonded to learn from one another. I have not been bonded before.

Then how do you know where we're going?

Many other bonded horses are there. I need only follow my sense of them.

Huh. And we'll be moving at speed, even though there's snow on the ground and I'm on foot. I take it you have confidence in my fitness. I've never been much of a runner, but as soon as this flaming snow gets a bit shallower, I'll give it a go.

It is true that you are capable of moving swiftly for a human but that will not be sufficient for us to outrun the weather that is coming.

Then how will we outrun it?

We will not. I will.

But what about me?

You must learn to stay in place on my back.

Chapter Twelve

I stopped in my tracks. *Ride you? Now?*

It is necessary.

But isn't that one of the main reasons we need to go to The Gathering? So that the other Horse-Bonded can teach me to ride?

We cannot wait until we reach The Gathering for your learning to begin. If I do not carry you then we will not survive long enough to reach it.

Then why didn't we stay with Gert and Hilva in Mountainlee until the worst of the weather has passed?

Being alive is not about avoiding that which is difficult. It is about embracing the learning that accompanies a challenge.

Even if the challenge kills us?

The greater the stakes the greater the opportunity for learning.

It seems kind of reckless.

Humans have an intrinsic need for safety and comfort. You already know the consequences when those needs supersede everything else.

I nodded as I trudged along beside him. The people of The Old thought that if they rigidly controlled both their environment and one another, they would be safe and comfortable. They actually just became more and more paranoid until their insanity caused them to obliterate one another. *Does that mean we should do the opposite though, and just rush headlong into a situation we know to be dangerous?*

There is the illusion of risk in both accepting and avoiding this challenge. The risk to you of avoiding it is greater than accepting it.

Because you think I'll learn from it. But what about you? You don't seem to need to learn anything, so the risk to you is greater by accepting it than avoiding it.

I am not at risk either way. Neither are you in truth. Accepting the challenge ahead will take you closer to knowing it for yourself.

Thunder and lightning, Oak, let's just get on with it then, shall we? It can't be any more exhausting that trying to understand whatever it is you're trying to tell me.

There is a mound over there. We will head towards it and you will use it to climb onto my back.

When we reached the snow-covered mound, I prodded it with my foot and then kicked it. It was solid, a large rock, probably. Oak moved alongside it.

I remembered the heat that had emanated from him when I curled up against him in the barn. Would it be enough to keep me warm once I was no longer having to make my way through the snow? Or would it make me too hot? How much effort would it take to ride? Oak waited patiently and without comment as I considered how much clothing to wear. I settled for removing one thin layer. I packed it into my sack, replaced my cloak and then hoisted the sack onto my back, putting both arms through its straps so it was secure.

Okay, I'm ready.

Then mount.

How?

There was a pause. *I have no advice.*

But what if I get it wrong and I hurt you?

Then you will learn from the experience and try again.

I climbed onto the rock, grateful for its size and that it felt almost flat on top. I stood there for a few moments, looking at Oak's back, now level with my stomach. The rock was sizeable but my horse was huge. How was I going to get one of my legs over his back?

I decided to jump up and towards him in the hope I would land with my stomach across his back, and could then turn around and swing a leg across. I hesitated, then slapped both of my cheeks with my gloved hands. 'Come on Rowena, you can do this,' I told myself firmly. I counted to three and then leapt. I hadn't jumped far enough. However hard I tried to hold on to him, I couldn't stop myself sliding to the ground.

Oak didn't move. Irritation nipped at my stomach, but I took a deep breath and pushed it to one side. I clambered back onto the rock and tried again with the same result. I'd seen the Horse-Bonded mount their horses from the ground before without a saddle to help them, and they made it look easy. I had a rock to stand on, and I still couldn't do it.

'Oak, can you move a bit closer to the rock? I mean you can see I'm having trouble, help me out, can't you?'

Oak shuffled as close to the rock as he could, to the point that it made it more difficult for me to climb back on top of it. We were still in sight of Mountainlee. I hoped no one was watching. I was just giving them more proof that I was an idiot. They would be laughing at me.

Your opinion of yourself need not be affected by those of others.

Now you offer counsel? When I'm struggling with one thing, you offer help with another entirely – one that's no use to me whatsoever?

It is all part of the same challenge. Were it of no use I would not have offered it.

Well I'll have to take your word for that, won't I, seeing as, as usual, I have no idea what you're on about?

Oak didn't reply. He stood patiently by the rock, facing the way he wanted to go.

Right, well I'll just try again then, shall I?

I managed to clamber back onto the rock, then stood up, trying not to overbalance back off it. I put my hands on Oak's broad back and despite myself, felt a little comfort from the warmth beneath my fingers. I felt his calm, his patience, his steadiness, and took a deep breath. I flexed my legs, leapt up and forward, and landed across his back. Now I just needed to try to get my leg across him, so I could sit up.

I shuffled forward a bit and felt him brace beneath me. I twisted around a little and managed to get one of my legs over his back, kicking his rump on the way. *Sorry.*

Sit up.

What a good idea, why didn't I think of that? Do you think I'm not trying?

You are investing more energy into worrying that others might think you foolish. Focus on your task. Sit upright.

I braced my hands against his back, pushed myself upright and shuffled forward a little to a spot just behind the slope of his withers, where his back was narrowest. My cloak was tangled beneath me, which would be uncomfortable for both of us very soon. I leant forward, pulled it out and rearranged it over his back and rump, pleased to see that in bad weather, it would protect him as well as me.

Okay, now what?

I will move forward so that you can accustom yourself to my movement. With that, he started to walk. Forced as he was by the deep snow to take exaggerated strides, I lost my balance and tilted backwards. Instinctively, I tried to put a hand behind me to save myself, but missed his back, my hand landing on his side instead. The next thing I knew, I was on my back in the snow.

'WHAT THE HELL?' I shouted, spitting snow out of my mouth as I sat up. 'You lurch forward with no warning, and I'm meant to, what, just KNOW how to sit there?'

Your next attempt will be more successful now that you know what to expect, Oak informed me, already moving back into position by the rock.

'I'm not getting back up there until you tell me what to do.'

You have just learnt that which you must do. Cloud In The Storm you are squandering time that is necessary for our survival.

Casting a quick glance back towards Mountainlee, and satisfied that I couldn't see anyone watching, I brushed myself down. 'Fine, but if I fall off again, I'm walking.' I clambered back onto the rock and then, more confident this time, jumped towards him, landing on my stomach. I twisted and easily got my leg across him. I sat up, feeling pleased with myself. As soon as I was back in position with my cloak once more arranged over his rump, I looked around for a way to secure myself. 'Um, Oak, do you mind if I hold on to your mane? It's either that or I lean forward and wrap my arms around your neck, and I've never seen any of the Horse-Bonded ride like that, they're always upright.'

That will be acceptable.

Remembering his lack of warning before moving the last time, I quickly wrapped big handfuls of his thick, bushy mane around each hand. It wasn't enough. As he began to walk, his big, lurching strides through the snow threw me from side to side, as well as threatening to leave me behind. I squeezed my legs around him and held on tight. That was better.

Oak stopped very suddenly and I landed on his neck. 'What now?' I asked him.

Your lack of movement hinders mine.

I sighed. 'Well I'm sorry to be a hindrance, Oak, this was your idea, not mine, remember?'

You must move with me or we will not get far, was all the warning I had before he lurched forward again.

I clung on to his mane to keep myself upright, and again clamped hold of him with my legs. Oak stopped.

'Thunder and lightning, Oak, I can't stay on if I don't hold on with my legs, I'll fall off the side.'

No reply.

'Oak, what do I do?' I relaxed my legs while I waited for his reply, and he moved forward again. I was forced to close them tightly around him again… and again, he stopped.

'Oak, you said we have to move quickly so the snows don't catch us, well we're moving slower than we were when I was on foot. Oak. OAK, ANSWER ME.'

Oak just stood there, his ears flickering back to me as I shouted and then forward again when I stopped. He was waiting to move on again.

Why won't you answer me? Oak? 'OAK?' I shouted again.

He flicked an ear back to me and then pointed it forward.

I felt useless. It was bad enough when everyone else made things difficult for me, but Oak? My horse? My Bond-Partner? I leant forward, intending to try to swing my leg back over his back and dismount. I couldn't do this. Not here, not now.

Then you will not do it ever.

His thought shocked me into sitting back upright. *What?*

You are merely experiencing the version of your life that you expect to experience. Choose a different version and you will experience that. His thought was as calm and patient as ever, as if he were making an everyday observation.

I slumped where I sat. *I have to see what's happening, through our bond. Why do I find it so hard to remember to do that? I can't do it when I'm with people, we know that, but I can't even do it when I'm alone with you, without you telling me to.*

I did not instruct you to do it. You remembered. We must move on.

I felt his warmth both beneath me and through our bond, and calmed down. I looked back over the last few minutes. What had he told me? That I had to move with him. It was clearly important, but what did he mean? Irritation flickered in me again at my lack of ability to understand and his refusal to enlighten me.

Oak increased his presence in my mind slightly and I remembered. Irritation and anger would get us nowhere. I took a deep breath in, then out. Oak would rather die, literally, than give me further instructions, so this was obviously important. Move with him. The words hung in my mind and I suddenly felt their importance. It wasn't just about moving with him physically. I had to move with him with all of myself. I had to stay with him in our bond as well as with my body.

I felt a flutter of anticipation from Oak. I was on the right track. I kept my sense of him foremost in my mind. He was strong, confident and capable. So was I. I could do this. I wrapped his mane more tightly around my hands.

When I clamped my legs tightly around him, he stopped. When I relaxed them, he moved. He needed me to move with him... my legs must be stopping that, somehow. I was curious. That was new; normally, I would have been angry. Curiosity was better. How could I keep astride him without clamping on with my legs?

Oak moved forward suddenly – and yet it hadn't been suddenly. I'd known he would do it and now, through our bond, it felt as if it were happening in slow motion. My body was thrown a little to one side, so I pushed slightly with the leg on that side until I was central, then relaxed again. When I got a little left behind, I used his mane to rebalance myself and then shifted my upper body forward a little so that the weight of my back-sack didn't leave me vulnerable to that happening again.

As my horse lurched through the snow beneath me, I felt all of the aspects to his movement, and moved different parts of my body in response, so that my body stayed in balance with his. I felt his every stride, his every footfall, every single pull and relaxation of all his muscles... his every breath.

I felt his delight that I was immersed in our bond instead of remaining on its periphery in my own little world of misery. And I felt how easy it was to experience life his way; feeling my way through it, responding to all the different sensations because it was the obvious and natural thing to do. There was no confusion, no upset, just two bodies and minds working in such harmony that for the first time in my life, I was free of fear, anger and worry. It was exhilarating. I smiled and laughed until my lips cracked and my teeth ached with the cold.

I lost track of time, of my surroundings, of absolutely everything except for Oak's body and mine, and the constant conversation between them that gave my mind a break from all that weighed me down. When his movement began to slow, I felt the tiredness, the soreness in both of our muscles. I was already leaning forward, ready to swing my leg over his back, by the time he came to a halt. I slithered to the ground and was surprised to find that it was solid beneath my feet.

I took a step back from Oak and looked around. Where was the snow? We were standing in woodland, and not the conifers of the mountains, but the deciduous woodland that told me we had left the mountains behind and were at least as low in altitude as my home village of Clearview, probably lower. I peered up at the sky, easily visible between the leafless branches, and found the sun a little lower than its highest point; it was just past midday.

Our progress was rapid once you allowed yourself to feel your way.

I staggered towards him and flung my arms around his neck. *Oh, Oak, thank you, that was amazing! I can hardly stand and there's nowhere I don't hurt, but by the bitterest wind of winter, it was worth it. Everything seemed so obvious and easy when I was in my bond with you. Will I always be able to do it? Am I cured now?*

The difficulty will be in choosing that state of mind when your pattern would pull you in the opposite direction. You will find it easier to make that choice when you are on my back for our bodies will highlight any lack of harmony between us. You will still have to notice that lack of harmony and make the choice to correct it however.

I won't need asking twice to ride you again, but I'm worried about the effect it's had on you, you're tired and hungry, and you're sore too, I can feel it.

I will become better accustomed to carrying you the more we move together so.

Okay, well I'll walk on my own two feet until we find a good place to stop for the night. We can't stop here. There was nothing for Oak to eat and I could sense his slight unease; he wanted to be out of the trees and in the open, where he could run from predators if necessary. I would eat as we continued on our way, and hope that we would soon find somewhere he could graze.

I quickly shrugged out of the straps of my back-sack and took a long swig of shudderingly cold water from my flask. I offered to cup some in my hands for Oak, but he declined. I replaced the flask in my pack, took out a food parcel and hoisted my gear back onto one shoulder, grimacing at my complaining back muscles. I'd only been sitting on Oak while he did all the work, how could I be so tired and ache so much? Then I remembered absorbing each and every movement of Oak's muscles, using one or more of mine. I may not have appeared to have been moving, but my body had been working nearly as hard as Oak's. Nearly. Pushing through all of that snow while carrying me had taken a lot out of him, yet he was still ready and able to push on. He was big and incredibly strong, just like the tree after which I'd named him.

I rubbed his neck as we walked onward through the trees. *Did we do it? Did we get far enough ahead of the snow that's coming?* I asked him.

It will be less severe now that we have reached more amenable surroundings but we will not escape it. We will endeavour to cover as much ground as possible before it overtakes us.

Then what?

Then is then. Now is all that concerns us.

I nodded. *Let's get you out of these woods.*

Chapter Thirteen

We walked all afternoon. The widely-spaced trees allowed us plenty of light and a relatively easy path, the undergrowth having shrunk back from the bitter cold of winter. The sky remained clear and the trees sheltered us from the breeze that moved the branches above.

I should have been feeling buoyant after everything we had achieved that morning, but I could feel Oak's thirst and hunger, and they worried me. I didn't know where we were, or when we would come across water and grazing for him.

We will come across them when they lie in our path, Oak told me.

What if they don't, though? Will you at least take some of my water?

I will not. Your human skin will be adversely affected by its temperature.

You won't let me pour some into my hands for you because you're worried I'll get cold hands?

We are a partnership. We have strengths and weaknesses. A strength does not exploit a weakness.

I frowned. *I'm a weakness?*

Only if you choose to see yourself as such. My thirst is merely less of a hindrance than your lack of digits would be were the cold to take them. He was matter-of-fact as ever.

Frostbite won't kill me. Thirst could kill you, though, as could your stubbornness.

Then it is fortunate I scent water ahead.

Oh, thank goodness. And look, it's a bit lighter in front of us, I think we're reaching the edge of the forest at last.

Half an hour later, we were indeed out of the trees. We stood for a moment, staring over an expanse of coarse grass at a huge lake in the distance that glistened in the last rays the sun had to offer for the day. The breeze had dropped and we were engulfed in silence. Our outward breaths hung in front of us as if reluctant to disperse into the frigid air.

We will rest here, Oak announced.

No, we'll move closer to the water. This grass is dry and tough, it'll make you thirsty, and I'll need to break the ice at the water's edge for you. And we'll be further away from the trees; I know you don't like being in the forest.

I do not. Yet we will not be in the forest. We will be near enough to the trees that you can feed a fire and benefit from their shelter. I will eat and drink as necessary.

But...

I need no assistance. He wandered off without a backward glance.

Well! I was only looking out for him, but if he thought he knew better, then... Oak stopped and looked back at me, pulling me up short in my thoughts. Then he continued onward a little further before dropping his head to graze.

I felt his contentment. His thick coat protected him even as heat from digesting the grass he was munching would warm him from the inside. I, however, could feel the cold biting at me through my boots, gloves and clothing and I'd only been standing still for a few minutes. I would need a fire if I were to remain stationary for any length of time without Oak's body to warm me, and it was less cold next to the trees than out in the open. Oak had been right. I scowled, but as I watched him graze, his placid calm wove its way into me and I remembered. Being wrong didn't make me worthless and stupid.

I sprang into action, casting around in the fading light for tinder and sticks with which to light a fire. When I'd found what I needed, I struck my steel grinder with my flint until sparks flew into the tinder. My heart leapt with relief as the first tiny flames flared into life. I added some dry twigs, which caught fire immediately.

My stomach rumbled in anticipation of the stew I began to picture in my mind as I opened one of Hilva's food parcels. She'd included some relatively fresh vegetables, one of my meat portions and a tiny packet of what smelt like herbs. I could use all of the water in my flask now that I knew I could easily refill it, so it would be a moist, hearty meal.

The light of my fire reached a decent distance into the forest, so I spent a good amount of time collecting more sticks while my stew was cooking. When I finally sat down to eat, I had a huge pile of very dry wood which would keep my fire going for hours if I could build it up enough for it to keep going by itself.

I smiled to myself as I ate. I was tired and sitting in the middle of nowhere in the dark in winter – but I was eating a hot meal that smelt and tasted delicious, while my horse grazed contentedly nearby. I could just about make him out in the moonlight, about halfway between me and the lake. His thoughts and feelings were far clearer. He had everything he needed, and that included me. I didn't think I could be any happier.

I built the fire up more and more, until I'd used most of the wood I'd gathered. I donned all of my extra clothing and then put my cloak back on. It wasn't as warm as the one I'd left for Hilva, but it would do.

I will wake you if necessary. Rest. Oak told me.

Thanks, I'll just sleep while you're eating. When you need to sleep, wake me and I'll build the fire back up so I don't need you to watch over me.

Oak didn't reply, which I took to be agreement. I lay down, rested my head on my back-sack, and listened to the fire crackling as I allowed my horse's contentment to fill me.

Light was penetrating my eyelids. That couldn't be right, I must be dreaming. But no, my eyes opened to see blades of frosty grass in front of my face. Where was Oak? Was he alright? Had something happened? Why hadn't he woken me?

I sat up, wincing at my aching muscles, and found him curled protectively around me, his belly providing my back with warmth. He rested his nose on one of his forelegs, so that his velvety muzzle was scrunched up and his warm breath came out of his nostrils sideways. His eyes were closed, his long, black lashes covering his lower eyelids, and he had frost on his whiskers, forelock and mane. His breaths were deep and even and he looked to be asleep, but I could feel the part of him that was alert for any unexpected sounds, any movement nearby, any sense that someone approached. And I felt the tendril he had extended to my body so that he would be alerted to any change that would mean I needed to be woken.

As I sat in the frosty grass, the air still and silent except for his breathing, I felt so much love for my horse that it almost hurt. How was I this lucky? He'd taken me away from the misery of my childhood and given me love, companionship, protection and a way to make something of my life. He seemed to want nothing in return other than for me to learn from him, and that wasn't even for his own sake, but for mine.

I leant my weight against him very slowly so as not to disturb him, and put my arms around his body, hugging him with all my love and gratitude. He was so peaceful, yet I could feel the warmth, strength and vitality that thrummed through him.

I remained huddled up to him until my stomach began to rumble. I groaned as I got to my feet and stretched; there was nowhere that didn't hurt as a result of my ride the previous day.

I cast about for more sticks; if Oak was going to rest longer, I would break my fast with something hot. I heard a grunt and spun around to find that Oak now lay flat out. Having spent the whole night watching over me, he had finally allowed himself to fall sound asleep.

I relit my fire and quickly built it up. When it was hot enough, I made myself some porridge and tea, which I enjoyed immensely while Oak slept on.

Once I'd finished, I got up to go to the lake to refill my flask, and wash my cookpot and mug. I grinned down at Oak as his ear flickered and his hooves twitched in his sleep. He would be okay here for a few minutes.

The frosty grass crunched beneath my feet as the cold air bit the back of my throat before descending, only slightly less sharp, into my lungs. The lake ahead of me was still and dark below the mist that hung above it as if waiting to pounce on anything that dared to raise a head out of its waters. It was an eerie yet beautiful sight.

When I reached the lake, I glanced back to see that Oak hadn't moved. I turned back to the bank of the lake and could see where he'd gone down to the water to drink, breaking the ice with a front foot, judging by the position, shape and size of the newly-formed ice. I didn't hesitate to follow his path and bash the ice in exactly the same place with my cookpot.

I trusted his judgement, I realised, suddenly. It felt strange. I was so used to relying on myself and making all my own decisions, my instant reaction to just do as he had done left me feeling as if I didn't know myself. Or maybe I no longer knew who I'd been? I frowned as I scrubbed out my cookpot with some grass, and then rinsed it in the lake. The sun's rays began to lift the mist away from the lake, and I caught sight of my reflection. I remembered Hilva telling me that I frowned too much. I probably did.

When I eventually turned to go back to Oak, he was standing. *You didn't sleep for long.*

I slept for as long as I was protected.

Protected? I kept an eye on you, but there's nothing and nobody around here, Oak.

You were not sufficiently alert to our surroundings to be able to arrive at that conclusion. Oak wasn't troubled, as such, but he wasn't as rested as he had wanted to be, either.

I began to hurry my steps. *You don't think I was looking out for you? I mean, I know I went to the lake, but you did that yesterday, you were nowhere near me when I went to sleep. I trusted you, why don't you trust me?*

Was your attention with me? Would you have known if anything approached me while I slept? His thoughts were fainter than usual. As I hurried closer, I could see that his head was lower to the ground than normal and he was resting a hind leg. He was dozing while keeping watch for himself.

My attention? I knew you were sleeping peacefully, and I was as quick as I could be, washing my stuff. I didn't leave you for long, nowhere near as long as you were away from me.

I need not be near you physically to sense how your body functions. To hear through your ears while you sleep. My body was not near yours but I was with you constantly and would have woken you the moment anything was amiss.

My heart sank. I felt awful. Then I felt angry. *I didn't know I had to do that for you, I didn't know that was what you needed in order to be able to sleep, why didn't you just tell me?*

I inform you now. The emotion that provides you with sanctuary from what you perceive to be your shortcomings is unnecessary. It will save much time and energy if you merely open yourself to learning without the complication of attaching emotion.

I've slept all night with you watching over me. You've slept for what, an hour or so, because I'm selfish and I'm useless. You should have just told me what you needed me to do and I would have done it. How did you know my mind was elsewhere, anyway? You were asleep.

It is the nature of my kind to know when we are safe to sleep and when a part of ourselves must be alert. I will eat now and then we will move onward. He very obviously turned his attention away from me as he stretched his neck and back legs, walked a little way and then dropped his head to graze.

I threw some sticks onto the fire with far more force than necessary, causing sparks to fly into the air and the fire to crackle loudly. Neither relieved the ache in my stomach that came with the realisation I'd let Oak down. I took off my extra night layers and repacked my clothes and cooking gear into my back-sack. Then I stood by the fire, stewing, while I waited for Oak to finish eating.

When finally, I could feel Oak beginning to think about moving on, I spread out the burning sticks as best I could with a long stick I'd saved for the purpose, then used it to scrape together handfuls of the frozen forest floor. I threw them on top of the flames until they were completely extinguished. When smoke stopped billowing from the remains of my fire, I spread its ashes around further. They would cool in no time at all. I hurled the stick away from me, still feeling horrible; ashamed, guilty, stupid and horrible.

I looked around for Oak, to see him standing by a large tree stump at the edge of the trees. He wanted me to get on him again.

I'm not in the mood, Oak. I'll only do something else wrong.

Then you will have more mistakes from which to learn.

I threw my pack down on the ground. *That's what this is all about, isn't it, you and me? You waiting for me to screw up so you can tell me where I went wrong, and I can feel useless.*

Your pattern is fighting hard. That is good. It senses it is under threat.

My pattern? A feeling of cold plummeted inside me, like the first – and last – time I swallowed an ice cube. My pattern. My well-practised pattern of behaviour that had caused me no end of pain and sorrow, had taken me over yet again.

Instantly, I reached for Oak, for our bond. Through it, I saw myself walking lightly on my feet to the lake, almost high with happiness. I felt Oak, even asleep as he was, sense the moment my attention left him. He woke and stood up to doze until I came back. He'd planned to go back to sleep, but my demand to know what had happened and then to rail at his explanation, to use the situation as another excuse for my insecurities to announce themselves, had woken him fully. Yet still, he attached no judgement to the situation. He'd been asleep and then he was awake. He'd rested and eaten, and now he was ready to continue onward to The Gathering, where I could continue to learn. Me. He was doing all of this for me.

Not solely for you. There will come a time when you will be in a position to help many horses and humans.

Me? Seriously? Are you sure, I mean, you know me?

Oak just stood watching me, his breaths deep and even, a calm constant in the middle of all my emotion.

I sighed. *I apologise for not watching over you properly this morning, and for the behaviour that followed. I'm sorry I didn't see that it was my pattern rearing its horrible, ugly head again, and get through this quicker. And I'm sorry we're both standing here in the cold while I sort myself out.*

Oak continued to stand and stare at me, his demeanour unchanged. He didn't need my apologies, I could feel it; he didn't see that I'd done anything wrong. I'd just made a mistake and then made it into a drama instead of learning from it and moving on. Moving on. That's what he was waiting for.

I heaved my back-sack into place and walked over to him. He whickered, a deep, throaty sound that melted my heart.

I swallowed and nodded. *Okay, let's do this.* I climbed onto the stump, which was a little lower than the rock from which I'd mounted the previous day. Never mind, I would make it. I persuaded my aching legs to jump the extra height I needed to land across Oak's back, then shuffled forward a little, swung my leg over and sat up, feeling pleased with myself.

We will practise moving our bodies together at greater speed, Oak informed me.

It makes sense, now that there's no snow.

I immersed myself in my sense of Oak and his body as I wrapped his mane around my hands and arranged my legs into the position that had allowed me to use them to stay in place the previous day.

Oak took a few strides of walk and then moved up to a trot. Just like when I rode him the last time, nothing he did was a surprise. I felt his every movement almost before he made it, and adjusted my body continually to remain in place. Unlike the day before, however, my body was stiff and didn't absorb his movement quite so easily. In addition, where the four-time gait of walk meant that Oak was always in contact with the ground, his two-time trot launched his body into the air, where it was suspended before landing on the opposite diagonal pair of legs before being launched back into the air again. The bouncier movement, combined with the extra speed it generated, gave my body far more work to do in order to stay in place. I managed not to fall off, but I bounced around quite a bit. Still, I did it... until I didn't.

In heading due south around the lake, we came to a narrow stretch of grass where the forest, which curved around the west bank of the lake, extended almost to the water. A rabbit shot out of the trees in front of us, startling Oak, who leapt to one side. I bounced horribly and just about managed to land on his back, but I was well off to one side with no chance of recovering my balance. I landed on the frozen ground, on my shoulder and hip, the breath forced out of my lungs so hard that I couldn't get it back. I lay there, gasping.

Hooves appeared in front of me and a soft, warm, black nose nuzzled my face. *You are unharmed. We will continue when you have regained your wind.*

I couldn't find the wherewithal to answer him. I managed to roll onto my front, still gasping, and crouched on my knees and elbows until I finally managed to draw enough air in to slow my breathing. I could feel warm air on the back of my neck.

I hurt all over, Oak. I can't get back on.

You can. You must. His thoughts were gentle but firm.

I sat back on my heels, rubbing my shoulder and then my hip. It was a wonder that nothing was broken.

Cloud In The Storm. We must continue.

I got to my feet, feeling disorientated. Oak walked towards a huge tree that had fallen on its side. I limped after him, rubbing my hip. When I reached the tree trunk, I was relieved to see that it was even bigger than I'd first thought. Where it was thickest, by the roots that stuck out both vertically and horizontally, it was a little higher than Oak's back. He was already moving to that exact spot, but I would have to climb onto the trunk further along, where it was thinner. I headed for a spot onto which I thought I could manage to climb.

Once I was upon it, I discovered that climbing onto the tree trunk had been the least of my problems. There were branches to negotiate as I limped painfully along its length, and the closer I got to the root where Oak stood waiting, the more rotten was the wood. While its condition explained why such a massive tree had fallen in the first place, it did nothing to help my situation. I screamed when my foot went through in one place, causing me to fall on my injured hip. It was only due to branches sticking up on either side of me that I managed to pull myself back upright and continue carefully, painfully, to where Oak stood watching.

Through it all, I never left our bond, I never distanced myself from Oak's calm confidence. I had a high pain threshold. I could cope with colder conditions than many, without discomfort or complaint. I knew how to look after myself and I was strong physically and mentally as long as I viewed my situation as he viewed it. We were capable of so much when we came from the place of love and strength that was so natural for him and so difficult for me. It was all I focused on as I fought my way to him.

I fell through the rotten wood again, this time with both feet but thankfully not very far. I clambered back out of the hole and crawled, now, to Oak's side. I put my hands on his withers, lifted a leg painfully over his back and sat there for a moment, panting. Then I wrapped his mane around my hands again, and shuffled into place. I felt Oak's approval, and smiled faintly.

He turned, took a few steps of walk and then moved back up to a trot, slower than before. It was painful, but just about manageable. And it was necessary. The snows wouldn't wait for us to clear the area before falling and making everything more difficult and uncomfortable.

I followed his movement, even managing not to bounce. But when, all of a sudden, Oak landed on slightly lower ground, I couldn't help it. I bounced into the air and landed on his back with a wince as pain shot through my hip. Yet my pain was nothing compared to his. I felt it as if it were my own – a sharp, lancing pain in my back – even as I felt him buck beneath me.

I was catapulted into the air, where I seemed to hang forever before the air rushed past me and, finally, I landed on the knee below my already painful hip, then on the hip itself again. Thankfully, my pack moved around to cushion my shoulder so that it, at least, had a softer landing. Pain gripped my hip and knee, taking my breath away every bit as much as the fall itself had done. Then a pain took hold of me that was far, far worse than anything my body could feel.

I'd followed Oak's counsel. I'd been with him in our bond. I'd given everything of myself to it, holding nothing back, even when he threw me the first time. He told me to get on his back, and then threw me straight back off. He didn't want me there. He said he did but clearly, he didn't. He hurt me. Not once, but twice.

I felt as if I were being stabbed repeatedly through the heart. No one wanted me. I couldn't trust anyone. I'd trusted Oak and I'd begun to believe that maybe, just maybe, I could trust myself; that I could know how to feel and what to do. And this was where it had got me. I'd loved, trusted and been rejected, just like always.

Tears leaked out of my eyes and dripped onto the frozen ground. I would stay here. Moving was too painful. Being was too painful. I began to sob and then, ignoring my body's protests, to heave. With each lurch of my body, I drew up from beneath my pain something that felt as if it might protect me. I recognised it. It was that which had always protected me.

I began to tremble with it as it numbed my pain. I rolled onto my front, got to my feet and unfurled myself until I stood tall. I leant towards Oak and pointed a finger at him. His eyes widened until the whites showed as he sensed what I was about to unleash.

'You're the worst of all of them,' I snarled. 'At least they never pretended to want me. You drew me to you, you protected me while I slept, you made me think there was nothing more important in your world than me. You dragged me out into the winter weather, you made me ride you, you made me feel that I was on top of the world, that I could be somebody. And you did it all so that when I fell, not just once, but the two times it took for you to try to break me, I would fall so hard that I would never get back up. Well you know what? You're not the only one who's strong. I am too.' I was panting, and not just because I'd barely taken a breath. Something raw and primal was in control of me, something that wanted the blood and pain of another in exchange for all the pain it had suffered. I blinked as the small part of me that had observed what was happening, retreated from the far larger part that sneered so threateningly at Oak.

He stood his ground. *The tree for which you named me gains its strength not by defying the wind but by allowing its branches to be moved by that which would otherwise tear it apart. Branches that are damaged or have grown too rigid are willingly released while the core of the tree remains grounded. The strength of oak arises not from its ability to resist that which threatens it but from its willingness to be vulnerable.*

The small, observer part of me thought it understood, but couldn't make itself heard over the greater part of me that was consumed with protecting itself.

'I know how strong I am and I know you feel it too. Look at you, quivering before me, you're only just about making yourself stay here. Any moment now, you'll turn and bolt like you want to, but you know what? I DON'T CARE. Leave me here in the middle of nowhere, I don't need you. You're pathetic. You're all pathetic. I don't need you, any of you.' I glared at him as I picked up a large stick.

Oak's ears flickered back and forth. I could actually hear his heart thumping as he shifted about on his feet, the instincts of his species urging him to flee the danger he could see and feel before him.

My eyes narrowed and I grinned. 'You're frightened of me. You thought you could break me, you thought you could push me aside, you thought I was weak, but look at us both. Who's the weak one now?' I raised the branch and took a sudden step towards him, my rage delighting in the fact that he took several hurried steps backward, even as the observer in me was horrified. What was happening to me? Why was I threatening to hit my horse?

Oak snorted, lowered his head and stared directly into my eyes with his own. *I see you beneath that which you think protects you. It believes itself to be strong but since it comes from fear it is weak. Choose that which is love. Focus on what we share. Use my strength and make it your own for it is your own.*

I tried. The part of me that knew who he was, that knew who I was, tried to expand, to become more than merely the observer, to open my hand, drop the stick and run to him. But the pattern within me was like a cornered animal fighting for survival. It shoved me to one side and advanced towards Oak.

'You think you can worm your way back in?' I shrieked. 'I'll show you what happens to those who try to hurt me.'

Oak tossed his head as he fought to control himself and stay with me. He stepped backwards, remaining just out of my reach, never taking his eyes off me. *Cloud In The Storm. I see you.*

'DON'T CALL ME THAT. DON'T YOU EVER CALL ME THAT,' I screamed. The observer within me stirred again. Cloud In The Storm. My Bond-Partner's name for me. He saw me. I was a cloud formed due to pressure on all sides, then thrown around in the wind, hurling rain, thunder and lightning before returning to the gentleness, the softness of who I really was. This rage, this aggression wasn't me.

No. But the part of you that believes itself capable of being rejected now fights desperately for its existence. You named me for your tree not because it protected you with aggression but because it strengthened you with love. You can continue to allow your pattern to convince you that aggression will keep you from pain or you can choose to be vulnerable and discover your real strength.

'THERE IS NO CHOICE. I HAVE TO DESTROY YOU JUST LIKE YOU TRIED TO DESTROY ME. NO MORE. NO MORE WILL I ALLOW ANYONE TO KNOCK ME DOWN.' It was as if it was someone else shouting and spitting at Oak, and not me at all.

It is someone else. It is the part of you that is no longer necessary. The part of you on whom you have come to rely but who serves no purpose. You have our bond and all that it contains.

'I DON'T NEED OUR BOND, I DON'T NEED ANYONE, I'M BETTER OFF ON MY OWN,' I screeched, and rushed at him.

It was as if everything slowed down. As I leapt towards him, my hold on the stick loosened. When I landed, it slipped within my grasp. I took hold of the stick with my other hand; I could hit him harder if I brought the stick down double-handed. I took another leap but as I landed, the fingers of both hands relaxed and the stick slipped through them. I closed my fingers again, catching hold of the stick halfway down. I grinned. I could stab him with it instead, that would hurt more. I went to take the next stride and pulled up short. Oak had stopped backing away from me. He stood watching me, his ears pricked, his eyes soft.

I grinned. I had him. I would make him hurt every bit as much as he had hurt me. But the stick slipped out of my hold completely. I stopped and looked down, confused. Why couldn't I hold onto it?

Because it's not me, I affirmed to myself, as much as to Oak. *It's not me. I'm Cloud In The Storm.* I staggered, feeling faint.

Oak stepped forward and rested his muzzle on my uninjured shoulder. *You feel as if you are less than you were but you have cleared the way to be so much more.*

I reached a hand up wearily to stroke his face. *We don't have time to think about that now though, do we? You want me to ride you again, straight away. But why did you throw me? The first time, I get; the rabbit and fox made you jump. But the second time?*

You have no need to ask, he told me. There was no reprimand, just a gentle statement of fact.

Immediately, I reached for our bond and thought back. I'd bounced, landing hard on his back. I winced as I felt again the pain it had caused him. He was already sore there; it was the same spot on which I'd landed before falling off him shortly before. My seat bones were sharp and he'd reacted instinctively to the pain.

My heart sank. I wasn't a good enough rider to keep my balance bareback at speed. I couldn't ride him again until we got to The Gathering; I wouldn't risk hurting him again. But the snow was coming. It would be less severe than if it had caught us in the mountains, but it could still cause us problems.

You are skilled in your choice of work.

Yes, I am, but I don't see how that can help your back... oh, cancel that, I do see. We don't have time for me to make a cushion, though.

We do not have the time for you not to. You must make haste. I will build my reserves and then we will continue at even greater speed. Oak dropped his head immediately and began to snatch at the grass at his feet.

I limped over to the tree from which I'd mounted him, and sat on it, between some small branches. I hung my back-sack on one of them and rummaged in one of its side pockets for my sewing kit, an idea forming in my mind of what I needed to do. I took out two pullovers, holding them up against where Oak grazed a few feet away. I nodded to myself. They would do, it was a good job I had long arms. I got to work.

Half an hour later, I was ready. I limped over to where Oak still grazed.

It's not very strong, but hopefully it'll stay in place, I told myself as much as him.

I threw one of the pullovers onto his back, its neck and waist already sewn shut, its body stuffed with my carefully folded spare clothes. I placed the makeshift cushion where I would be sitting, then reached underneath Oak's belly for the second pullover, stitched to the first at the end of their sleeves. I folded it around itself to make a thick roll, then pulled it until the loose sleeve met the one hanging down from the pullover on his back. I took a needle from where I'd stuck it through my sleeve, already threaded with the thickest of my threads, and began to sew the two loose arms together.

Oak grazed on without concern.

When I'd finished, I took a step back. *It's not great, but hopefully, if I don't put it under too much strain, it will hold.*

Oak moved to stand by the huge tree root again. I groaned, but as the wind got up, I made myself limp over to him. The snow was coming.

Chapter Fourteen

That day was one of the worst of my life, and one of the best. My makeshift saddle proved strong enough to stay in place on Oak's back, but wouldn't have held under any strain exerted by my weight, so I had to be with Oak, in our bond, every step of the way in order to sit lightly atop it. I was in agony from my knee, my hip and my shoulder, none of which could be spared from having to work to keep me not only on Oak's back, but as balanced as possible so that I didn't hurt or unbalance him as he trotted for mile after mile over the grassy plains that stretched before us.

Yet my mind felt light and unburdened in a way that made me want to sing. The part of me that had threatened Oak seemed far away from me now, fallen by the wayside, no longer worthy of thought or attention. There was just me, Oak and our bond.

When he stopped to eat and drink, I slid painfully to the ground, my frozen feet announcing a brand new agony as I landed on them. The rest of me was hot, so I walked around until the warm blood from my body forced its way back into my toes. I was sore, exhausted and just wanted to lie down and sleep. A gust of icy wind from the north reminded me that I didn't have time.

I took a food packet from my back-sack, silently thanking Hilva for her thoughtfulness in organising my food so that a full meal was quickly to hand. I pulled it open, replaced my gloves and then ate while I walked in circles around Oak so that the cold couldn't take hold of me. I took tiny sips of water, warming the fluid in my mouth before swallowing it in order to preserve every bit of body heat I had.

When I'd finished, Oak chose a slight mound that had a large, coarse tussock of grass growing on it, as my best chance of getting on his back. I looked from the tussock to him in disbelief, but he continued to watch me in anticipation; it was the best we had, so we would make the most of it. I felt like crying, but I couldn't spare the time or the energy. The plains were dotted with the odd tree here and there, but otherwise offered no shelter. We needed to get across them, and we needed to do it quickly.

I put a foot onto the tussock of grass, hoping it was denser than it appeared. It wasn't. My foot disappeared into its midst. *This is no good, Oak, I can't jump on you from down here.* I looked all around, trying to see if there was anything I could pile up and stand on. There was nothing. It was hopeless, but Oak didn't think so, I could feel it. He had complete confidence in me. He offered no counsel because I didn't need it.

I was strong and capable. I could do this, I told myself. I looked around again. At least the ground was flat. *I'm going to have to take a run up and see if I can jump better that way,* I informed Oak.

He continued to wait patiently.

I shrugged out of the straps of my back-sack and laid it across his neck, apologetically. *Sorry, but I'll have a better chance of getting up there without it, and I won't be able to reach it once I'm up there. Once I'm up there,* I repeated, firmly. I would get up there.

I limped away from Oak, then turned to him and sighed. This was going to hurt. Oak increased his presence in my mind until all I was aware of was his confidence in me. The hurts of my body were only that. They could be ignored when necessary, and tended to if they found a more urgent message to tell.

I rocked back on my heels, then ran as fast as I could. As I neared Oak, I slowed. This wasn't going to work. He was too tall, and if I grabbed hold of my cushion in my haste to mount, I would rip it off. There had to be an easier way. I racked my brains, trying to remember how the Horse-Bonded who had visited Clearview had mounted their horses bareback. I couldn't.

Oak, I can't do it, I told him simply. *Can you help me?*

I was almost knocked off my feet by the rush of emotion I felt from him. His confidence in me had never wavered but now it was joined by approval, pride and… love. I was loved, completely and utterly. Everything he'd held away from me in order to give me the space to put my pattern to one side without giving it anything else to cling to that might mask it and leave it simmering until next it felt threatened, he now allowed me to feel.

For the first time in my life, I'd admitted that I couldn't do something – that I needed help. I'd risked feeling stupid, unlovable and unworthy. I'd allowed myself to be vulnerable.

I grinned, feeling silly, but in a totally different way from how I had used to feel. There was no need to use aggression to hide my lack of knowledge or ability before they could be used as weapons against me – when I was with Oak, I didn't care. Nothing that wasn't of my bond with him needed to be hidden or defended, because it was nothing. I knew that now.

Oak folded his knees and lowered his front end to the ground, followed by his rear end. He landed with a thump and then whickered to me. I hobbled to him, threw a leg over the other side of my pad of clothes, and sat on it. I took big handfuls of his mane, and held on tightly with my legs as he heaved himself back to his feet. I rubbed his neck. 'Thank you, my big, strong lad. Thank you.'

Oak walked forward a few steps while I adjusted my position, then leapt into a trot. I was with him all the way. When he decided to canter, I almost braced myself for the unknown, but then relaxed. As long as I was with him in our bond, I could stay with him.

I found the rocking movement of Oak's canter far easier to absorb and move with than his trot. I smiled through my tiredness, making sure to keep my mouth closed and the cold air out. I breathed through my nose, and was snorting almost as hard as Oak by the time he eased us back to trot, then walk.

He walked until he'd gathered his breath, then took off at a trot again. I marvelled at his strength and stamina. He was a powerful horse, there were no two ways about it, but he wasn't used to carrying me, let alone for this long. I smiled and smiled, then when Oak sped back up to a canter, smiled and snorted until he slowed to trot and then walk again.

Oak's rotating periods of walk, trot and canter seemed to give us the best combination of speed and endurance. His legs ate up the plains and spewed them out behind us. By the time the light began to fail, I could see trees in the distance.

I glanced back over my shoulder at the darkening sky. As yet, it was clear of clouds, but the north wind was gradually gathering in strength. The snow clouds could appear at any time. We needed to get into the forest and try to find shelter, but I worried about Oak. He wasn't comfortable in woodland, and there would be nothing for him to eat.

I will eat before we enter the trees.

Okay, that makes sense. I guess we should be able to see our way at least for a bit, with the moon being out and the trees not having any leaves.

I know for where we must head.

You know a good place to shelter? You've been here before?

I have not. There are two who pass through here often. They have shelter and await our arrival.

Oh, thank goodness. How do they know we're coming? Wait a minute, they're horses?

One is of my kind. The other is of yours.

A horse and a human? Bond-Partners? I'm going to meet one of the Horse-Bonded?

I felt Oak's agreement as he picked his pace back up to canter. I began to feel nervous, but then my cushion slipped beneath me. Immediately, my attention was back with Oak. Whatever happened, happened. As long as I was with my horse, everything would be fine.

Oak grazed well into the night. I didn't blame him; it might be some time before he ate well again if the snow fell thick and fast, and he knew I was warm by my fire with a belly full of hot stew and tea. But as the moon disappeared behind clouds, I began to worry. I didn't know how far into the woods were those who awaited our arrival, and whether the snow might fall so fast as to stop us reaching them.

When Oak finally finished eating, I worried even more at how thirsty I could feel he was. There was no obvious source of water, and he wouldn't even consider taking any of mine, even though I explained that he could drink it from my cook pot rather than me freezing my hands trying to cup it for him.

Your tendency to fret is borne of having cared for those less experienced than yourself. I am not such, I was informed as a gentle statement of fact. I couldn't argue because I could feel that it was true. His strength was more than just physical, it was total. Total knowledge, total confidence, total wisdom, expressed through a fit, muscular physicality. He was such a gentle soul, but so, so strong.

I found myself nodding as I gathered my stuff together and repacked my back-sack. *Okay, well let's get going then, shall we?*

By way of reply, Oak placed himself by a fallen tree and then stood patiently waiting for me to mount in the fading moonlight.

I can't ride you again now, Oak, it's a miracle you've managed to carry me all day with barely a break. I'll walk next to you. I promise I won't lose contact with you.

I felt his amusement. *You could not do that if you tried. My vision in the absence of light surpasses yours. We will move with greater speed if I carry you. It is necessary.*

I looked behind me to where stars had been visible almost as far as the eye could see, but were now rapidly disappearing from sight. I heaved my back-sack onto my shoulders with a grimace, rubbed my hip and knee and then hobbled over to him. It seemed as though this day that had been so amazing, so incredible in terms of my bond with Oak, yet so excruciatingly painful for my body and mind, was never going to end.

I managed to jump onto Oak's back, thankful that my body's memory of how to do it compensated for my mind, which was so consumed with trying not to scream with the pain that I couldn't think at all. Oak stood, stoic as ever while I shifted myself into position on my cushion. Some of the clothes within it had shifted away from my weight, leaving a slight bulge in front and behind me. I felt cradled and a little more comfortable, but worried that it might feel lumpy for Oak.

Are you comfortable? I asked him.

You are as aware of my body as I.

Our bond. I plunged myself into the part of my mind I shared with him, and felt for his awareness of himself. The shock of how his body was faring made me gasp. The saddle pad was fine but underneath it, he was sore from where my seat bone had stabbed him twice in quick succession, and all of his muscles were tired and aching, particularly those of his back, neck, shoulders and front legs.

I am unused to carrying your weight. That situation will change.

As always, he told the truth, yet I could sense that there was something that concerned him, something he was holding back from me. *What aren't you telling me? Am I causing serious harm, riding you when I don't know what I'm doing?*

On the contrary. You have rapidly become adept at being as easy a passenger as any human is capable.

So what's the problem then? If you don't tell me what to do to make it better, I'm getting off.

There is no problem. Merely the beginning of a path that we will travel together. Worry not. With that, he strode purposefully into the forest. I couldn't pull my mind away from his discomfort. If he were going to be sore as a result of carrying me, I would at least feel it with him.

Your resolve to focus on my body's aches and fatigue only highlights them for me when I would place my attention on taking us to shelter. Focus instead on that which is positive and we will have a fulfilling experience even though circumstances are difficult.

'Huh,' I said to myself. Then my head cleared as I understood; that was how we had made it through such a difficult day. My body was battered and bruised and yet I'd ridden Oak for hour after hour because I'd been flying high as a result of everything I could feel through our bond. Love, strength, companionship, togetherness and harmony were all so foreign to me, and so welcome, that I'd put all of my attention there and, I now sensed, my elation had carried Oak with me. I'd taken energy and strength from our bond, and delivered it in return.

Immediately, I placed my attention back to where it had been all day. I was with Oak every step of the way. When the snow began to fall, I barely noticed. Oak was forced to shift from side to side, often at very short notice, to avoid trees – both standing and fallen – and odd bits of undergrowth in his path. I often had to quickly duck or lean back as I felt branches in front of me or brushing my hat, but I made sure to keep my attention on the fact that we were together, in harmony, moving ever forward towards shelter.

When the snow was deep enough that the night time sounds of the forest stilled, my mind wanted to worry. I pulled it back to the steadfast confidence of our bond. We were fed, warm, fit and strong. Shelter awaited us and we would reach it.

The snow fell faster. I couldn't see it, but I could feel it on my face and it became a weight on my head, arms and legs. I left it in place. It was too cold to melt and soak through the cloak that covered me and lay over Oak's back.

I couldn't see anything. How Oak did was beyond me, but he never faltered. He just kept going, one footstep after another through the snow and the trees.

Eventually, I saw a light in the distance. I blinked the snow out of my eyes, and it was gone. Oak sidestepped a tree and it flickered into view again.

Oak whinnied, a deep, husky sound that caused his whole body to shake. He was answered by a much shriller whinny.

Another light joined the first, moving very definitely from side to side. Someone was trying to make sure we didn't miss them. I grinned to myself. As if. Oak knew exactly where they were. He made straight for the lights, no more trees in his path.

The moving light came from a burning stick that someone was waving around. Behind it was what looked like a wall with a gap in it, from which the main source of light emanated.

Over the deathly silence of the snow, a man's voice rang out. 'Welcome, both of you, you really are so very welcome.' There was a softness, a kindness, about his voice.

Oak stopped just in front of him and whickered. I dismounted, landing in several feet of snow which prevented me from taking the steps back necessary to keep my balance, and sat down suddenly.

The man offered me a hand. 'You must be completely exhausted. Come on, up you get, we'll soon have the snow brushed off you both, then you must come inside, in the warm.'

'Inside?' I said, shivering now that I didn't have Oak's body heat to warm me. 'Do you live here?'

The man chuckled. 'Goodness, no. My horse and I don't live anywhere, really. We just travel around and over the years, we've found all manner of places we can count on for shelter when the weather would defeat us. Can you shake yourself free of the white stuff while I do the same for your horse?'

I nodded. 'Of course, but I can take care of Oak. You go on in and we'll follow.'

'Would you truly prefer to see to him by yourself, or would you consider directing me as to how I can help?'

'Um, okay, well maybe you could brush the snow of his far side and I'll do this side? Don't try to take off the contraption he's wearing though, it's attached to him. I'll deal with it inside.'

The man nodded and I thought he smiled through the snow that continued to fall. 'That sounds like a story I look forward to hearing, but never mind that now, it's no good me standing here gossiping while you and... Oak, you said, didn't you? While you and Oak get colder by the second.' His footsteps scrunched away through the snow. The light from his stick appeared on Oak's other side, and snow began to fly into the air.

I began at Oak's head, flicking the snow off him with my gloved hands as fast as I could as I made my way along his body to his tail. It was quickly covering the cushion and Oak's back that had previously been covered, and it was frozen to ice where he had flicked it underneath himself, soaking the rolled pullover that acted as a girth.

As soon as I'd finished, Oak strode towards the gap in the wall, which, now that I was close to it, I could see was actually a crack in sheer rock, just wide enough for him to fit through.

'That's it, Oak, you go on in, we're right behind you,' said the man and beckoned for me to go ahead of him.

The moment I stepped out of the snow, I heard the crackling of a fire. I followed Oak down a short, narrow corridor of rock that curved slightly before opening into a huge cave.

At its centre was a large fire, above which hung two steaming cookpots on a tripod. A large stack of wood against the wall to my left promised a fire that could last for days, weeks, even. Hay bales stacked next to it told of preparation for horses, although where hay could have come from in the middle of woodland was beyond me.

Against the wall to my right was a stack of what appeared to be mattresses woven from vines and filled with moss that poked out of the gaps.

Water flowed down the far wall. Some of it froze on the ice over which the rest dribbled before coming to rest in a large pool, also covered with ice except at the edge where it been smashed to allow access to the water beneath.

Between the water and the fire lay a horse. His body was mostly white with patches of light brown, he had a dark brown face with a white stripe down the front of his nose, and a thick, black forelock with a pronounced white streak. His eyes were bright as he watched our entrance, and his ears pricked towards us, but he didn't attempt to get up.

Oak made straight for the water, whickering to the prone stallion on his way past as if they were old friends. I smiled delightedly at the two of them as I tried to stamp the warmth back into my feet.

The man stood by my side and stretched a gnarled hand out towards the horse. 'I would like to introduce you to my Bond-Partner, Peace.' He held out his hand to me. 'I'm Adam. I'm so pleased to meet you.'

Chapter Fifteen

I shook Adam's hand. He was shorter and stockier than I, with thick, white, shoulder-length hair. His handshake was firm, yet as gentle as the green eyes that looked up at me. I liked him immediately.

'I'm pleased to meet you too. I'm Rowena. Is Peace okay?'

Adam nodded. 'He's fine. He would get up, but he's not long lain down, and both activities are an effort for him nowadays.'

'He's beautiful. I can see he's tired, I'm sorry we've disturbed you both.'

'Not at all, not at all, it takes far more than the arrival of new friends to disturb Peace and me.' He released my hand, then beckoned for me to follow him as he hurried over to the fire, where he began to stir the contents of the larger of the two cook pots. 'This soup is nearly ready, and I have some bread warming. I do love it when it's warm, don't you? Come and stand closer to the fire and get some heat back into you. Then, when Oak has finished drinking, you can relieve him of that incredible-looking saddle you've made for him. I suppose it's to cushion him from your seat bones?' I nodded. 'What a marvellous idea. Well then, when you've helped him out of it, we'll get him some hay, then you can take a seat with some soup and bread, and tell me all about yourselves.'

I nodded, frowning and smiling at the same time. While it felt as though the massive, oppressive cloud that had hung over me had drifted away since Oak helped me to step aside from my assumption that everyone saw me as my mother did, I still found it strange that I was comfortable with Adam telling me what to do, especially when I'd already decided to do the things he'd mentioned.

Adam continued to stir the soup in between fetching plates, bowls and spoons from a large back-sack that rested against the wall by the mattresses, and dragging two mattresses to rest, side by side, by the fire.

I removed my back-sack, hat and gloves, and laid them beside the rocks that surrounded the flames. Then I stood rubbing my hands together, trying not to wince as the heat warmed my boots, causing my feet to return to life.

Peace watched me and Adam in equal measures. When he looked at his Bond-Partner, his large, brown eyes softened to the point of almost appearing fluid in the firelight. When he looked at me, his eyes focused and brightened, as if recognising me.

I blinked as I felt Oak monitoring my thoughts whilst drawing in large mouthfuls of icy cold water. *Does he recognise me, Oak? I don't remember him, but maybe he saw me as a child? Did he and Adam visit Clearview?*

He knows you in the same way he knows me.

So you've met him before?

He and I have never met yet we have never been apart.

I groaned. *Oh no, this is one of those conversations I'm not going to understand, isn't it?*

If you so choose.

Then I can choose to understand and I will?

You can decide to accept. Acceptance opens a pathway between your mind and your soul down which understanding will travel in its own time.

A sudden lack of movement caused me to look at Adam, who was standing, holding a bowl and a ladle, and smiling at me. 'Don't let me interrupt,' he said.

'Huh? What? Sorry?'

He shook his head. 'I'm so sorry. I see that in trying not to interrupt your conversation with Oak, I've managed to do exactly that. I just wanted to ask whether you like your soup hot enough to blister, as I do, or whether I should spoon yours out now, so it can cool while you're seeing to Oak, who has finally, by the look of it, slaked his thirst?'

I glanced at Oak to see that he had indeed finished drinking and was standing looking about himself. I fumbled to get my sewing kit from my pack. 'Blisteringly hot works for me, thank you,' I said as I pulled out my small unpicking scissors. 'I'll just be a moment.' I rushed to relieve Oak of my cushion of clothes, which was now dripping.

I unpicked the stitches that held the arms of the pullovers together at his side, twice stabbing myself with the point of the scissors as my fingers, wet and increasingly cold from the wool of the pullovers, refused to obey me. When the cushion finally came loose, I ran my hands through his coat where it had been in contact with him. I was relieved to find that it hadn't rubbed him anywhere, and thanked the light that he had a thick winter coat to protect him. He was warm beneath my fingers and the heat slowly returned to them.

Thank you, Oak. Thank you for everything you've done for me today. I had no idea that being bonded could be like this. It's hard, but it's... it's... I was too tired to think what it was.

It is productive. Rest now. We are with friends. Oak wandered off in Peace's direction. When Peace's tail twitched, Oak halted and rested a hindleg.

I turned at a scraping sound. Adam was holding a mattress in each hand and dragging them to where Oak stood. He nodded towards Oak and Peace in turn. 'They seem to have come to an accord over how close they're comfortable being to one another for now, so we'll just put these two down by Oak in case he fancies a lie down. We can't have him lying on the hard, cold ground, can we?'

I rushed to take a mattress from him, and placed it next to the one he lowered to the ground beside my horse. I glanced across to where Peace now lay out flat, and saw the vines and moss of similar mattresses poking out from beneath him. 'Thank you, that's really thoughtful. You seem very well prepared in here.' I nodded to the firewood, hay and mattresses stacked against the walls. 'Is this a kind of hangout for the Horse-Bonded and their horses?'

Adam chuckled 'I suppose one might call it that. Peace and I pass by here from time to time, and in the past, we've often had others along with us. That was at warmer times of the year, mind; there aren't many as willing or able to travel in weather as cold as Peace and I are. Mind you, I think this will be the last time we'll be any distance from The Gathering when the snow hits. The cold this winter has taken its toll on Peace in ways it never used to touch him. But you don't want to hear about all that, let's get some hay shaken up for Oak, and you fed, then we'll see about some herbs to ease your and Oak's soreness, shall we?'

'You're a Herbalist? Oh, thank goodness,' I said as I followed him over to the hay bales, where he handed me a couple of sheaves.

'I am. Your village Herbalist didn't give you any supplies during your Quest Ceremony then? Or have you used them all? How long have you been travelling?'

I turned away so that he couldn't see me flush, and took the hay he'd given me, to Oak. When I rejoined him at the fire, he was ladling soup into a bowl. I hoped he'd forgotten his first two questions, and answered the third. 'Um, it's all a bit of a jumble, but let me see, Oak and I found each other three days ago, so nearly a week, I think? It feels like longer.'

Adam grinned as he passed me the bowl of soup, followed by a plate with some thick slices of bread, and indicated for me to sit down on one of the mattresses. 'It's not easy, the first few weeks and months being bonded, but don't worry, any confusion you're feeling at the moment is completely normal.'

Relief washed over me. 'It is? Did Peace teach you that everything you ever thought you knew was wrong too?'

He stopped ladling soup into his own bowl for a moment and glanced across at where his horse slept. He smiled a sad smile. 'He tried. He's still trying.' He blinked and looked back at me. 'I'm sure you're being too hard on yourself if you truly believe that everything you knew was wrong, but if you're open to thinking that way this early on, your bond with Oak must already be strong.' He looked over to where Oak dozed, then back at me before continuing to fill his bowl with soup.

I gulped, swallowing my mouthful too quickly and burning my throat. 'He's all I have,' I said, and then immediately regretted it. Why did I say that to a complete stranger?

Adam lowered himself slowly to the mattress beside me. 'Is that really true?' His voice was soft, and there was no challenge in his eyes. He emanated warmth and a sense of safety, as if nothing could hurt me while he was near. He reminded me of both my horse and my tree.

I looked down at my soup. 'This is delicious, thank you.'

'No thanks are necessary. It's lovely to have your company, yours and Oak's.' His voice resonated with truth and again, I felt safe, as if anything I said or did would be okay.'

'No, it's not really true,' I blurted out. 'I have sisters and brothers, but they're so far away.'

'And not just in terms of distance, I think,' Adam said, softly. He tore a piece of bread from one of the slices on his plate, and wiped it around the top of his bowl, cleaning the dregs of soup that clung to the smooth wood. There was no tremble to his hands, just a calm, measured focus, as if it were a task of utmost importance.

'How... how can you know that?' I said.

He looked up at me and smiled a warm smile. 'I hear the voice of my soul, as Peace calls it. Before I met him, I knew it as intuition.'

'Do you understand everything he tells you?'

'I tend to now, but it took a long time to get to this point. So much of what Oak will tell you, he won't expect you to understand straight away, but one day, it will make sense.'

I nodded. 'That was what Oak was telling me when you interrupted us. Not that you really did, I mean I think the conversation was over.'

He chuckled. 'I see you've also learnt when to stop asking questions because no answers will be forthcoming. It's the equivalent of them dropping a stone into an ants' nest and running away, isn't it? It can take some getting used to.'

I grinned back. 'You've no idea how relieved I am to know this is all normal.'

Adam swallowed a mouthful of soup. 'You're bonded now,

Rowena. I can't assure you that you'll ever feel normal again. I think you'll find as time goes on, though, that being continually challenged by Oak is both an honour and a privilege you will come to hold almost as dear as Oak himself.' There was sadness in his eyes as he glanced at Peace.

'How old is he?' I asked.

'Forty-something. If I'm completely honest my dear, and I do try to be, I avoid keeping count, now.'

'You've been bonded a long time?'

He nodded. 'I'm approaching seventy. I was twenty-nine when Peace rescued me from myself.' His eyes glazed over.

I cleared my throat. 'He rescued you?'

'He did. In so many ways.' He blinked and looked squarely at me. 'But we don't need to go into that. Not when you and Oak are waiting so patiently for me to attend to your aches and pains.' He scooped up the last of his soup with the last of his bread, put his bowl on the ground and waved his hand towards the cook pot, now hanging higher up the tripod so that its contents didn't burn. 'Help yourself to more soup, there's plenty there, I rather got carried away when Peace told me we would be having company. I'll get some herbal preparations together for you and Oak, then you can both get a good night's sleep.' He got to his feet far more easily than I would have expected for a man of his age, hurried over to his back-sack and began rummaging in it.

I helped myself to a little more soup and another slice of bread, which was indeed all the more delicious for still being warm, placed as it was atop one of the stones that surrounded the fire. A scraping noise made me look over to where Adam knelt on the cold ground, grinding herbs together in a small stone bowl with a piece of rock, open packets of herbs all around him. He was intent on his task, all of his concentration going into each and every stroke of the rock against the bowl. Eventually, he poured the bowl's contents into a mug, selected more herbs from some of his packets, and began grinding again.

I finished my soup and bread, then took my and Adam's crockery over to where a bucket stood by the pool of water. I used the bucket to rebreak the ice at the water's edge, and lowered it in until it was half full. When I'd washed the bowls and plates, I looked about for somewhere to empty the dirty water. There was nowhere. I sighed. I would have to brave going back outside.

As soon as I was in the curved passageway of rock, I appreciated fully how much warmth and shelter Adam's cave and fire afforded. The bitterly cold wind that buffeted the trees outside had blown snow in to the entrance, creating a drift almost as high as I was tall, against one wall. I slipped and slid past it before stepping out into snow that was almost knee deep. In the light that made it around the curved rock behind me, I could just make out a few snowflakes drifting to rest on those that covered the ground. I threw the dirty water out into the night and hurried back into the cave.

'Just in time, just in time,' Adam said, smiling as he got to his feet. 'This is for you.' He held out a wooden mug of steaming tea. It was a disgustingly bright green, but unlike other herbal preparations I'd had reason to take from time to time, it smelt delicious; herbal yet sweet at the same time. 'Drink this, and you'll soon feel a whole lot better. I have Oak's ready too.'

I held out the bucket. 'Here.'

Adam shook his head. 'I don't think he'll need that, I rather suspect he knows what I have for him. I'll just offer him the herbs in one of the bowls you've so helpfully washed up, shall I, and see what he thinks?'

'Er, yes, fine.'

Adam took his grinding bowl over to where I'd left our soup bowls, and tipped the herbs into one of them.

Oak watched Adam's approach. I could feel his anticipation and knew he would take the herbs, even before Adam held the bowl out to him. As he scooped them up with his lips, I blew on my herbal tea and took a sip. It was as delicious as it smelt, and strangely, not just because of the taste; I felt different almost as soon as it touched my lips. A sense of calm and wellbeing wove its way through me, as if everything was alright. I recognised it. I'd felt it from my tree, I felt it whenever I allowed my bond with Oak to be prominent in my mind, and I felt it when Adam spoke to me.

He appeared in front of me. 'Well, that went splendidly, Oak polished off his preparation. Is yours going down okay, Rowena, or would you like me to sweeten it a little more?' When I didn't answer, he said, 'Are you alright? Are you cold again? It doesn't take much exposure does it, when the weather's as unpleasant as it is? Come and sit by the fire.' He stood to one side of me and opened his arms out, creating a corridor down which I felt compelled to walk.

I sat down as instructed. Everything was okay. It really was. My soreness was fast disappearing, even the shooting pain in my hip – but it was more than that. I felt relaxed.

Adam poured boiling water from the smaller of the two cook pots into a mug, to which he added some herbs. 'This'll ease the aches and pains of an old man,' he said with a smile. 'Peace had his earlier, a right pair of old codgers, we are. Feeling warmer?'

'Yes, thanks.' I took a deep breath. Everything was okay. 'You're going to think I'm crazy, but this tea makes me feel like my bond with Oak does, and how my tree used to. Maybe if I'd made tea from its leaves, it would have had the same effect?'

Adam sat up a little straighter. 'Your tree? At home?'

I nodded. 'I'm from Clearview. Sometimes, when I needed to get away from… things, I would run to a tree in the woods. It wasn't just a normal tree though, it was a huge oak tree and when I was near it, I always felt better. I felt good about myself, as if I wasn't the idiot everyone said I was.' I sighed, remembering everything I'd seen when I looked back at my life, with Oak. 'Not everyone,' I admitted. 'Someone. Someone who was important to me.'

Adam was silent for a while. Then he smiled. 'A huge oak tree, so big that nothing grows anywhere near it?' he asked.

My eyes flicked to his. 'Yes. How do you…'

'With bark covered in notches and bumps?'

'Yes, how you do know that? How can you possibly know about my tree? No one does, except for me.'

Adam glanced across at Peace and then back at me. 'It's been a long time since we visited Clearview, twenty years or more I think, but I remember that tree. Peace and I, that is to say, I, wasn't welcome in Clearview when we first arrived in the blistering heat of summer, so we camped in its shade for several days. I think it's fair to say that we left a little of ourselves behind when we left it.'

'You weren't welcome in Clearview? Why not? Everyone's welcome there, except for me.'

'In your case, my dear, I find that very hard to believe. In mine, I'm afraid it was very much warranted. But that's all in the past, now.'

'What do you mean, you left a bit of yourselves behind?' I felt Oak increase his presence in my mind, and thought for a moment he would offer insight, but he was quiet.

Adam looked from me to Oak, then back to me again as he blew across the top of his tea. 'You named your Bond-Partner after the tree?'

'Yes. Well, kind of, not after the tree as such, but what I felt from the tree. Oak, he… showed himself to me, who he is inside, I mean.'

Adam nodded.

'You don't look surprised.'

He winked. 'I'm not. Please, do continue.'

'Well, when Oak filled my mind with who he is, I felt as if he was this unlimited supply of wisdom, peace, and calm. As if while I was with him, I would always be safe, protected, just like I used to feel when I was in my tree.'

'And if you had to assign just one word to everything you know Oak to be, everything you felt from your tree, what would it be?' Adam asked in such a way that I felt I had all the time in the world to answer.

I didn't need more than a second. 'Love.'

Adam nodded, his smile wide. 'Love. And that, my dear, is a good place to leave this conversation.'

It was as if a part of me understood what he was trying to tell me while the rest of me was left floundering – yet I couldn't find it in me to question him further. I frowned in confusion. 'Are all of the Horse-Bonded like you?'

Adam grinned, ruefully. 'Thankfully, no.' He leant forward and gently took my empty mug from me. 'Lie down now, and rest. Peace will wake me if the fire goes down, we won't let you get cold.'

'Thank you.' My eyes closed as I lay down on the mattress of moss and vine, but I fought the sleep that tried to take me as I checked in with Oak. He was dozing but a small part of him was alert, just as when he had watched over us both before.

You can sleep, Oak. Peace has the first watch, apparently. Wake me when it's my turn? I don't think Adam will.

Rest easy Cloud In The Storm.

I smiled as I drifted off to sleep.

Chapter Sixteen

I snorted. Something was rubbing my face and blowing hot air up my nose. I opened my eyes to see a pink nostril attached to the equally pink lip that was wiggling from side to side on my cheek.

'Woah!' I hurled myself away from it and sat up with a start.

Peace merely peered along his nose at me. White hair dotted the dark brown of his cheeks and formed thick, white eyebrows above bright eyes which held a look of mischief that belied his age.

Adam laughed from across the fire, whose flames were lashing around both cookpots as they released steam and the scent of porridge into the frigid air of the cave. 'Don't mind Peace, he likes to share his affection with as many people as possible, and not always at convenient times, I'm afraid.'

Peace stretched his neck out to me and turned his head to one side, wiggling his upper lip. I grinned and reached out a hand to him. He wiggled his lip on the back of it, then wiggled up my arm, shoulder and neck to the top of my head. I stroked his cheek, chuckling. 'You had a good sleep then, huh, Peace? Wide awake and full of life this morning, are we? Are you going to let me get up so I can see to Oak?'

Immediately, Peace stepped back. I got to my feet, amazed that where I'd had pain, I now just ached, and rubbed Peace's neck. His fur was much thicker than Oak's but as I looked more closely at him, I could see his ribs protruding underneath it.

The thud of hooves on rock announced Oak's approach. Peace glanced at him, his ears angled backward. Oak stopped where he was. A flash of anger shot through me. It wasn't for anyone, horse or human, to tell my horse where he could go, especially if it prevented him coming near me.

We merely cooperate according to the instincts of our kind, Oak told me.

I put my hands on my hips. *But why are you deferring to him? Look at you and look at him, you're bigger and stronger. Surely, he should be moving out of your way?*

Strength is not relevant here and also not what you continue to believe it to be despite us having visited this subject before.

I sighed and walked over to my horse. *It's too early for this,* I told him as I rubbed his nose.

His ears were pricked towards Peace, who stood watching us. *There will always be an excuse to delay learning that which is difficult.*

I moved along his neck and body, stroking him and checking for any signs of soreness I may have missed the night before. *Okay, fine, strength isn't what I think it is, and you've told me that before, well you're going to have to remind me, what with me having just woken up and all.*

Strength has little to do with physical prowess and nothing to do with aggression. It is the willingness to be vulnerable. To risk being defeated in the knowledge that defeat does not exist.

I stopped what I was doing and stood back from Oak so I could see his face as he turned to look at me. *That makes no sense.*

He blinked and then held my gaze, leaving me in no doubt that what he was about to tell me was important. *Strength is resilience and there is only one source from which resilience can arise.*

Our bond?

That which forms our bond. That which you felt from your tree and which allowed you to endure your childhood. That which you feel from those who offer us shelter.

'Love?' I said out loud. 'Strength comes from love?'

I felt Oak's satisfaction as memories of my experiences in my tree collided with Adam's admission the previous evening, and all of my experiences with Oak… and made sense.

He turned away from me and wandered over to where Adam was shaking hay loose from several sheaves. Peace ambled after him and took his place at Oak's side. There was no sign of flickering ears or swishing tails as they both began to munch contentedly.

My mouth dropped open.

Adam raised his eyebrows on his way past me, back to the fire. 'Everything alright?'

'So Peace won't allow Oak too close to him, but he'll stand right next to him when he decides to?'

Adam chuckled. 'The horses do what they do for many reasons, some purely their own, others to do with us. Judging by the look on your face, whatever just transpired was at least partly the latter. Have some porridge? I find it usually helps.'

'Porridge will stop me feeling as if the world has tilted and I'm about to fall off?'

'In my experience, yes, usually,' Adam said, cheerfully. 'We'll break our fasts, and then you and Oak will each need another dose of herbs…'

'Oh, yes please.'

'… then we'll clear out the horse dung, pack up and be on our way, shall we?' Adam began to ladle some porridge into a bowl.

I sighed. 'I guess. Where are you and Peace going?'

'Same place as you, I should imagine; we always go to The Gathering for the worst of the winter. There are some villages on the way whose inhabitants will be pleased to offer us warmth and shelter. I think we can count them as your first assignment as a member of the Horse-Bonded.' He winked as he handed me my breakfast.

Instantly, I remembered my last attempt at acting as a translator for Oak's wisdom. I shook my head. 'I can't. Not yet. And no one will want to ask me for help, anyway, not with you and Peace there, I mean you're experienced and clearly known to them, why would they want anything from Oak and me?'

'Why wouldn't they? They'll be delighted to meet you both, and Peace and I need more rest than we used to. You and Oak will be helping us enormously by sharing the load.'

Oak?

Much will be learnt by all.

But I really messed up last time.

You have learnt much since then.

I nodded slowly. Maybe it would be okay. At least Adam and Peace would be there. Or, we could let them go their own way via the villages while Oak and I made our way to The Gathering alone, bypassing any signs of human habitation?

I looked across at Adam contentedly eating his porridge, and then across to where the horses stood side by side, eating. Oak's rounded, muscular hindquarters were a stark contrast to Peace's angular rump and legs that, although thick with bone, lacked muscle and trembled very slightly, causing him to shift regularly from one to the other. I couldn't leave them to go on alone. The first snow was here and would probably be followed by more before long. What if they got into trouble? They might need Oak and me.

'Is that a yes?' Adam looked across the fire at me, his eyebrows raised.

I sighed and then smiled at him. 'It is.'

Adam slapped his knee. 'Wonderful! More porridge?'

Adam bustled about the cave, tying up the hay bale from which he'd fed Peace and Oak, cleaning his cook pots and storing them in a cavity near the log pile, dousing the fire, clearing out the fire pit and laying tinder and sticks ready for whoever stopped by next. I heaved all of our mattresses back onto the stack, then gathered the uneaten hay and horse dung into an old sack Adam gave me, and dumped it outside.

When the cave was straight, I re-stitched Oak into my cushion of clothes, then turned to where Adam and Peace waited by the cave's exit.

'I take it you don't ride Peace anymore?' I said.

Adam rubbed Peace's shoulder and shook his head with a sad smile. 'It's been four, maybe five years since I last sat on his back, but I enjoy walking with him.' Peace turned to him and Adam put his forehead to his horse's. 'We hold each other up, don't we, old friend?'

A lump formed in my throat. Adam's love for his horse was in his every move, his every gesture. When he looked at me, it was with the same peaceful expression that his horse wore, as if his bond with his horse joined the two of them so completely that they were two halves of the same whole. I hoped that one day, Oak would be as much a part of me as Peace and Adam were of one another.

That is already the case. You have merely to recognise it, Oak informed me. His thought was accompanied by a feeling of warmth, of satisfaction that made me think I'd achieved something, even though I didn't know what it was. I had to accept that which I didn't understand, and in time, I would get it, that was what Oak had told me. This time, it was easier.

I smiled at Adam. 'I enjoy walking with Oak too, and with the snow as deep as it is, he'll find it much easier if he doesn't have me to carry, so I'll stay on foot as well. Oak and I will go first, so that we can clear the way for you both, shall we?'

Adam smiled warmly and nodded. 'That would be very much appreciated, thank you.' Without taking his hand from Peace's shoulder, he stepped to the side. Peace moved with him, creating space for Oak and me to pass them both. 'Lead on, Oak will pick up the way from Peace,' Adam said cheerfully.

I felt Oak's intention change from following to leading, and he stepped forward. Peace flicked an ear towards my horse, following his movement but otherwise not reacting as Oak passed by him whilst staying close to the wall of the cave so as to give Peace as much space as possible.

Peace needed it, I saw that now. Any bumping from Oak's large, powerful frame would give his old, tired body much to do to keep itself upright. He'd let Oak know on several occasions how much space he needed and Oak was taking heed. My shoulders slumped as I followed Oak. Why had I not seen that at the time? Why had I taken affront on Oak's behalf?

You have recognised and discarded the pattern that ailed you. Now you must address the habits and beliefs that accompanied it and yet linger. Worry not. Each time we revisit them you will gain greater understanding.

I sighed. *Good to know.*

Oak stepped out into the snow. No more had fallen since I'd thrown out the wash water the night before, so it remained just below my knee in depth – still plenty deep enough to be a nuisance.

My breath caught in my throat as I stepped out behind my horse and an icy gust of wind blasted us both. I put my head down, pulled my cloak tighter about myself and followed the southward path that Oak began to carve through the crispy, sticky snow.

When I glanced over my shoulder to check that Adam and Peace were following okay, I saw that Peace was walking the path that Oak was creating for us all, but Adam was treading his own path at his horse's side, his hand still on Peace's shoulder as if he were, as he had said, holding his horse up.

I opened my mouth to tell him to save his strength and follow Peace, or at least walk in front of his Bond-Partner and clear more snow out of his path if he was adamant that his horse needed additional help. Something about the way Adam strode through the snow, determined to stay at his horse's shoulder, gave me pause, however. I moved out to the side of the path Oak was creating so that I walked in front of Adam, kicking my way through the snow so he could walk with a little less effort.

I'm worried about Peace, I told Oak.

He does not appear strong but recall what you have learnt about strength.

I thought back to what seemed like days ago, but was only a matter of hours. 'Strength is resilience,' I muttered to myself. That was all very well, but surely resilience had a limit?

Consider once more that which you saw in me when you gave me a name.

Immediately, I was flooded with everything that was my

horse. I remembered the word for it that Adam had encouraged me to use, the word that I found so difficult to say but so desperately needed to feel. Love. Adam and Peace's had strengthened me when it oozed out of the tree in which they had left it. Oak's had given me the strength to push my pattern aside and ride for hours whilst exhausted and in pain. It strengthened me now as I fought my way through the wind and the snow, giving me energy I would never have known I could access. I felt my way around it but could find no edge to it. It stretched on and on in more directions than my brain could understand. It was limitless.

Love is limitless. So that means resilience is limitless – and strength is limitless. Adam is giving Peace strength by giving him love?

It is love that sustains them both.

I stopped in my tracks and turned around to stare with fresh eyes at the elderly pair who followed in our wake. I could almost see their bond as a physical entity. It joined them, surrounded them, was them. They moved as one and breathed as one, supporting each other with their physical companionship as well as through their bond. I wanted to help, to give them more strength.

Do not interfere. We have our path to tread and they have theirs. Our presence is enough of a distraction to them.

Adam looked up. 'Are you alright?' The north wind whipped his words to me. 'Shall Peace and I take a turn in front?'

'Absolutely not. Let me know if either of you need to stop for a break, okay?' I shouted back to him.

Adam shook his head. 'We're better off keeping moving. We'll keep going until we reach Mettletown.'

'How far is it?'

'At our current pace, I should think we'll be there by midafternoon. Are you alright to eat as you walk? The sooner we get there, the sooner the horses will have food and shelter.'

I raised my hand by way of reply, pulled my hat down further over my ears as the wind threatened to blow it on ahead of me, and strode onward beside my horse.

Chapter Seventeen

*T*he wind was relentless throughout the rest of the morning and into the afternoon, but thankfully, didn't bring snow with it. Grateful that it blew from behind me, I managed to eat as I walked, as did Adam, while Oak and Peace trudged onward without complaint.

When we eventually broke out of the trees, a white expanse of snow lay before us, on the far side of which rose smoke in numerous spires.

'Mettletown,' Adam announced as he and Peace came to a halt beside Oak and me.

The opportunity presents itself for you to address further the habits and beliefs which accompanied your pattern, Oak informed me. *You will need to view that which will transpire through our bond. You should accept assistance to mount so that our bodies may highlight any lack of harmony between us.*

We don't know how deep the snow is out here in the open, though. I'll get on you closer to the village.

You will require time to reacquaint yourself with all of the aspects of moving your body with mine if you are to use our bond to full effect.

But…

Cloud In The Storm. I will continue once you are in position.

I stamped my foot. *For the love of summer, you're stubborn, Oak.*

Adam chuckled quietly and then laughed openly when I glared at him.

'What's funny?'

Adam carried on laughing. He looked at Oak standing at my side, then at me. His eyes were kind and warm, as if he were laughing at a joke we were sharing. 'Oh Rowena, I'm so sorry,' he said. 'I was just thinking back to how abominably I behaved in the early days of being bonded with Peace. When you went so quiet and still, I imagined Oak was telling you something you weren't altogether thrilled about, and your very dainty stamp of your foot was so in contrast with my shockingly inappropriate responses to Peace's counsel, I couldn't help but see the funny side of it.'

'What did you do?'

'Please believe me when I tell you that my temper is best left in the past.'

'Your temper? You?'

He smiled. 'Shall we carry on before we all freeze solid where we stand?'

'Oak wants me to ask you for help getting on his back.'

Adam glanced at Oak. 'And are you?'

'What?'

'Asking?'

I took in a deep breath of icy air through my nose, and blew it out of my mouth. 'Yes, I suppose so.'

'Never have I been asked for a leg up with so much enthusiasm,' Adam said with a grin. 'Come on then.' He moved to

Oak's side and bent over, cupping his hands. 'Put your knee here, then jump on three and I'll lift you. Got it?'

I did as he instructed and was amazed to find myself heaved high into the air far higher than Oak's back, so that I almost fell off the other side.

'Well you have a good jump on you, I must say,' Adam said. 'All good? Great. Do you want to go first, or shall we?'

My bond with Oak became more of me from the moment I sat on his back, so I knew his answer without needing to think about it. 'We'll go first, but you won't have my trail to walk in now, Adam. Will you be alright? Couldn't you walk in front of, or behind, Peace just for this last little bit?'

'Don't you worry about me my dear, I'm both stronger and fitter than I look, I shall be just fine. Onward to Mettletown!'

Oak gave me no opportunity to wonder whether I was up to the task ahead of me; he strode forward into the snow, which thankfully proved shallower – only a few feet deep – than I'd feared. I immersed myself in feeling how and where he would move just before it happened, and within a few minutes, was able to relax back into moving with him, staying balanced upon his back even when the depth of the snow altered, causing him to lurch.

I felt his weariness after the previous day's exertions – thankfully, most of his soreness was a mere echo of what it had been, thanks to Adam's skill with herbs – and the morning's efforts, but as he'd instructed me when he searched for Adam's cave, I focused instead on our strength and harmony so that we carried each other through the snow.

The wind blew us across the open, snow-covered expanse, in places whipping up loose flakes of snow and slamming them into our backs as if hurrying us on to Mettletown. When I turned to see if Adam and Peace were okay, Adam called out cheerfully, 'That wind's vicious, isn't it?' All I could do was nod while squinting to keep the stinging flakes out of my eyes.

The grey stone cottages of Mettletown stretched away from us in two opposing rows. I could just about make out the snow-laden fencing of paddocks behind each cottage, and the outbuildings they contained, and my heart lurched with an unexpected longing. Mettletown was smaller than my home village, but its cottages and layout were so similar.

A small portion of my mind strayed from Oak's as I wondered how Heron and Kestrel were doing, and whether they had forgiven me for taking off the way I did; whether Finch had shown aptitude for any of the Skills at testing; whether Wren understood that the little bird I'd left for her was from me. I swallowed hard. This was not the time.

As we drew closer, I made out several figures watching our approach. They were swathed from neck to toe in thick winter cloaks that they held tightly around themselves against the wind, and like Adam and me, their hats were pulled down over their brows and their faces were covered as they stood, jigging up and down on the spot.

A memory of the villagers of Mountainlee waiting for Oak and me with similar anticipation shot through my mind – and then engulfed it. I stiffened, and Oak halted beneath me. A cold sweat broke out on my forehead. No. I couldn't sweat, I would freeze. But wasn't that better than having to go through the same humiliation I'd experienced in Mountainlee? I wasn't good enough then. How much had changed? I tried to remember everything I'd been through with Oak over the past few days, everything I'd thought and felt, everything I'd learnt, but the more I tried to remember, to order my mind and figure out what to do, the more my mind just swam with thoughts to which I couldn't grasp hold, and the more I panicked.

I wasn't good enough. I never would be.

'Rowena? Is everything okay?' Adam called out from behind me. I panicked even more. Adam needed a rest, but now he would have to see all of the people who were amassing as word spread that two horses were arriving with their Bond-Partners; I couldn't see any of them, I was useless. I should never have agreed to come here. Maybe if Oak and I had decided to travel on alone, Adam and Peace would have sheltered in the cave until the weather was more amenable.

Oak lurched forward beneath me, almost leaving me behind.

Oak, we have to turn around, I can't do this, I'm not ready, I told him, holding firmly to his mane while I tried to regain my balance.

You will not falter so long as you choose our bond over everything that would distract you. Until now you have processed events this way utilising hindsight. Now is the time to interpret what is before you. Allow your body to remind your mind of the path it must take.

I felt his confidence in me, and relaxed. Immediately, my body was stable and moving easily with his, my mind almost entirely immersed in our bond – almost. There was a small part of me that felt strange. Exposed. Without the defences upon which I was used to relying to keep myself from being berated and put down, I felt incredibly vulnerable... and yet totally okay about it. How was that possible?

Strength is the willingness to be vulnerable, Oak reminded me, his thought so faint that I almost missed it. Or was it my thought? Absorbed as I was in my bond with my horse, I couldn't tell.

More than a dozen people were now gathered, waiting for us. I smiled at them as Oak's hooves touched the snowy cobbles of Mettletown. From their eyes, I could see that they smiled back before looking to where Peace stood waiting while Adam stamped the loose snow from his feet.

The villagers all rushed past me. A flash of hurt and anger shot through me – but that was all it was. It didn't build on itself, it didn't take root and give me cause to shout and rail, or storm from the scene.

'Adam,' said a woman, reaching to hug him, 'it's so good to see you and Peace, thank goodness you made it, you've normally passed through here by now.'

'Peace, my old friend,' said a man, his voice muffled underneath his face covering as he rubbed Peace's neck. Peace took hold of the peak of the man's hat and pulled it off, then swung it around in circles before releasing it. Everyone laughed delightedly. 'You have your fun and games, old lad, don't you worry about the top of my head freezing off,' chuckled the man, making no move to retrieve his hat.

The minutes passed, one by one, as more and more people appeared out of their cottages, wrapping themselves against the cold as they hurried to welcome Adam and Peace as the old friends they clearly were. They all smiled and nodded to me as they passed where I sat astride Oak, who had stepped away from Adam and Peace in order to give them more room.

It was an effort to keep myself from reacting to what a small part of me wanted to see as the dismissal of someone clearly not wanted or needed by anyone, but I smiled back at them with Oak's calm acceptance of the situation.

It seemed the whole village was intent on greeting Adam and Peace before they would be allowed to move. While Peace appeared to be thoroughly enjoying all of the attention lavished on him as he nuzzled and nudged people, stole their hats and wiggled his lips in their hair, every now and then, I saw Adam lean a little more against his Bond-Partner. When he staggered as a particularly vicious gust of wind caught him, irritation flared in me. Couldn't these people see he needed to get in the warm, to rest? I caught myself, expecting to need to refocus on my bond with Oak... yet I was still there with him.

You need only relinquish the aspects of your personality that do not serve you. Again, I couldn't tell whether Oak was counselling me, or whether the thought had sprung from where Oak's previous counsel had lodged itself within my own mind. I didn't stop to wonder at it.

Oak felt my intention and responded immediately. 'Excuse me,' I called out as he nudged his way amongst the crowd. Everyone was focused on Adam and Peace. I pulled my scarf down below my mouth. 'EXCUSE ME,' I shouted. The nearest people turned around in surprise. 'YES, I'M TALKING TO YOU, AND TO THE REST OF YOU WHO CAN'T SEE PAST YOUR OWN SELFISHNESS.'

There was a lot of nudging and some people took hold of the shoulders of people nearer to Adam and Peace and shook them until they turned to face me. Adam rubbed Peace's neck and grinned at me.

'It's customary to offer hospitality to visiting Horse-Bonded and their horses, isn't it?' I called out. 'Is this your idea of hospitality? Keeping a tired old man out in the cold until he's barely able to stand? I can see you all love him and Peace, so show it, will you, and get them out of the weather? Oak and I are here if anyone needs counsel so urgently that it can't wait, just show us to wherever you have whatever level of privacy you need, and we'll get to it, shall we?'

There was a stunned silence.

'NOW,' I yelled.

Everyone leapt into action. The man nearest to Adam took his cloak off and wrapped it around Adam's shoulders, and a woman put her arm around Adam's waist and pointed up the street. I could see her mouth opening and closing, but the wind took her words away from all but those closest to her. She gestured, angrily until the crowd parted in front of her. Then she guided Adam, his hand on Peace's shoulder, to where I hoped they would soon both be safe from the relentless, bitter cold.

Adam winked at me as they passed us. He'd pulled his scarf back up over his face, but I could see a bluish tinge to his skin that I didn't like.

'Adam will need a hot bath before he does anything else,' I said to the woman, 'but there's no point him going to yours unless you have an outbuilding big enough for Peace. Do you have that, and hay?' She nodded and picked up her pace, hurrying Adam and Peace along with her.

The rest of the crowd looked warily at me as they gathered around Oak, whispering to one another. Again, I felt vulnerable, as if I sat naked, completely exposed to the biting wind and the words and opinions of those in front of me, all of which could rip me to shreds. Oak's steady confidence thrummed through me. They could only rip me to shreds if it were possible. I smiled around at everyone and almost as one, their shoulders relaxed and their eyes smiled back at me above their face coverings.

'Adam has asked me to take your questions for Oak to answer, so that he and Peace can rest before we continue on to The Gathering. I'm sure you understand. I'm Rowena, by the way.'

'Why don't you have a proper saddle?' a girl piped up. 'Aren't you a proper Horse-Bonded?'

Pain slashed through me somewhere deep inside. Immediately, Oak shifted beneath me. My mind leapt to his reminder and rooted itself firmly within his. A dull ache replaced the pain and faded to nothing.

I looked down at the girl, who I guessed was the same age as my eight-year-old sister, Swift. Her eyes were wide with curiosity. I grinned. She reminded me of Finch at that age, when he'd been in his incessant pursuit of information phase. 'What's your name?' I asked her.

'Her name is Shirlee, and she didn't mean to be rude, did you Shirl?' said a woman standing with her hands on Shirlee's shoulders.

Shirlee shook her head emphatically.

'Well, Shirlee, why don't you ask Oak a question and see?' I said.

Shirlee shook off her mother's hands and walked boldly up to Oak until she stood beneath his muzzle. She tilted her head back until it rested on the base of her neck. 'Oak, how old are you?' she said.

Immediately, Oak showed me a rapid set of memories of the seasons, one following the other. I counted them and said, 'Oak is five, so a bit younger than you.'

'Why did you have to wait for him to tell you? Didn't you know?' Shirlee said.

Another flash of pain. Oak shifted beneath me again and I blinked as the pain faded away. I felt weary and yet, strangely, as if I could go on taking more and more of the questions that hurt... and yet didn't.

Strength is resilience and there is only one source from which resilience can arise, Oak reminded me gently. I smiled as I understood; so long as I had the love of my horse and our bond through which to feel it, I could take whatever was thrown at me.

I dismounted and crouched down so that Shirlee didn't have to crane her neck to talk to me. 'No, I didn't know. Oak and I only bonded a few days ago, and I haven't had a chance to ask him.'

'You're newly bonded?' Shirlee's mother asked. She looked at Oak and then back at me. 'So, you're on your way to The

Gathering for the first time? You haven't had any training or anything?'

I stood up straight and put a hand to Oak's neck, where it sank into his fur. The woman's hazel eyes were tired and there was pain there. The dark half-moons beneath them confirmed a persistent distress. She needed help, but didn't trust me and Oak to be able to help her in the way that she knew Adam and Peace could.

I barely noticed the punch to my stomach that hadn't happened. Its pain drifted away while I stood in place, undefeated. 'Yes, I'm on the way to The Gathering for the first time, and it's true, I haven't had the chance to have training from the other Horse-Bonded. But I've had a little help from Adam and Peace, and a lot of help from Oak.' I rubbed his neck. 'If you need help from a Herbalist, then of course you'll need to see Adam, but please, only visit him for that reason. If you need the counsel of a horse, then Oak is more than happy to provide it, and he assures me I'm more than capable of passing on his advice.'

Shirlee's mother looked from one of my eyes to the other, then held out her hand. 'It's good to meet you, Rowena, and you, Oak.' She nodded to him as I shook her hand. 'Please, come and stay with Shirlee and me, as our guests? I have a big lean-to in the paddock for the sheep, but I've got fewer than normal because of... well anyway, what I mean is, there's plenty of room for Oak. There's straw on the ground for him to lay on and plenty of hay, and everyone can visit you and Oak there for counsel once you've both warmed up and had a rest.'

I smiled gratefully. 'Thank you, we'd love to stay with you both. Hear that, everyone?' I called out. 'We'll be at...' I turned to the woman in front of me, my eyebrows raised.

'Her name is Rudi,' Shirlee said.

'We'll be at Rudi's,' I continued. 'Give us an hour or so and then come knocking.'

Rudi took Shirlee's hand. 'Come along then, the sooner we all get out of this wind, the better.'

I was taken very literally at my word. I'd barely had time to see Oak to the lean-to, shake extra hay up for him away from the sheep who huddled away in one corner, cut him out of my makeshift saddle, and then have a sandwich and a hot cup of tea in front of the fire in Rudi's kitchen, before the first knock sounded on her front door.

'I'm assuming by the look on your face that when you said to give you an hour or so, you thought they'd give you longer than that?' Rudi said, her grin lighting up her face and making her look younger than the forty-odd years I'd supposed she was.

I grinned back. 'What should I have said?'

'That there are no problems in this village that can't wait until tomorrow, when you and Oak will have had a chance to get your bearings and settle in,' Rudi said, and then muttered what sounded like, 'even mine.'

'Shall I ask whoever it is to wait? I can see there's something troubling you. Maybe Oak and I can help?'

Rudi ran a hand through the bright orange, curly hair that tumbled down her back to her plump waist. She looked as if she were going to accept my offer, but then shook her head. 'No. Thank you, but it can wait, in fact it's not really... anyway, no, you go and see who that is. Do you want another mug of tea to take outside with you?'

I nodded. 'That would be great, thanks.' I took the mug from her and made my way along the narrow, grey stone hallway to the front door, where I'd left my back-sack.

I donned an extra pullover, my hat, gloves and cloak, then

opened the door to find six people queueing down the front path. On the doorstep stood a man with dark brown eyes, the only one of his features I could see. He stamped his feet against the cold and flapped his arms about himself. Behind him was another man, judging by the size of him, swathed in a grey cloak with matching hat, gloves and scarf. He caught my eye, flicked a glance at the man in front of him and rolled his eyes. I grinned.

'Send anyone who needs to wait, in here,' called out Rudi from the kitchen. 'You can fetch them out to Oak one by one.'

'You, come with me,' I said, pointing to the man directly in front of me. 'Everyone else, well you heard Rudi.' I stepped outside and waited for them to file past me. The last four were all women as far as I could tell as the wind slammed into me, eating into my clothes as if they weren't there.

Can't I pass on their questions to you, and then your counsel back to them, from inside? I don't have to be near you to hear you, I thought to Oak.

They will not trust you. Not yet.

Out in the freezing cold it is, then. I shut the front door. 'Follow me,' I said to the man, and walked quickly down the path, along the fence of the front garden and down the side of the cottage, to the paddock. He hurried along behind me, stamping his feet with every step as if he were the only one affected by the cold. When we stepped out of the wind and into the shelter of the lean-to, Oak looked up from his pile of hay.

Good luck with this one, Oak.

He watched us both calmly. *Luck does not exist. Patterns of thought and behaviour are all that concern us.*

There was no hint of disapproval in his reply, but I felt chastened. *Okay, fine, yes, sorry.*

I pulled my scarf down to my chin and turned to the man. 'I'm Rowena, and as you've probably gathered, this is Oak. You are?'

The man also pulled his scarf down past his face. His lips were blue and his teeth chattered. 'P...pleased to m...meet you, I'm Saul.' He held out his hand, which I shook. He moved slowly and carefully to Oak's side, as if worried he would scare him away. 'Hello, Oak.'

Oak watched him, his ears pricked, his eyes soft. When Saul was close enough, my horse reached out and sniffed his face.

I pulled my cloak off and threw it around Saul's shoulders. He flinched and turned to me. 'W...what are you d...doing?'

'Looking after you. You clearly aren't wearing enough clothes, surely you know how to deal with the cold, living somewhere as exposed as this?'

'I'm wearing twice as many clothes as most here need, but I still can't stay warm at this time of year,' Saul said. 'It's the reason I'm here.'

'You're out here, freezing to death because you can't deal with the cold?'

'No. Because my wife is as hardy as everyone else who lives here, but my daughter is like me. My wife was born here, you see. She's a Farmer, like most of her family. I'm a Bone-Singer. We met when I came here to apprentice to the Master Bone-Singer who worked here. I could work anywhere once I qualified but she wanted to stay here and work the land her family know so well, so I settled here with her. I hate it, but I love her.

'My daughter suffers in the winter like I do. She's just qualified as a Tree-Singer, down in Summerfield. You should see her at work, she can sing a sapling to a fully grown tree in just a month, she's so strong. She could have apprenticed here, but she chose to go south to have a break from the bitter winters we have here. Only trouble is, she met a lad down there and is now engaged to him, and neither of them want to live here. I don't blame them, but my wife won't accept it. Farmers tend to stay where they were born, you see. My daughter will be the first Wilson for generations to settle somewhere else. We're falling out over it, and I'm being accused of having encouraged Sara to leave her mother.' The words tumbled out of him, not even giving his teeth time to chatter.

'Okay, so your question for Oak is?'

'It's not enough that I suffer so much every winter, my wife would have my daughter do the same. How do I get her to see reason?'

The views held by another are not his responsibility.

What? But his wife's clearly a selfish cow. How do we help him to grow a pair and stand up for himself and his daughter?

It would be more appropriate to ask how we can assist him and those around him to operate from a different perspective so that what you suggest is not necessary. Cloud In The Storm. We are of less help to those who require it if we must discuss my counsel before you deem it worthy of being delivered. You are the voice that can be heard when mine cannot. I request that you be that voice. Oak watched me intently, but his eyes remained soft and there was no hint of displeasure in his thoughts.

I sighed. *Wind my neck in. Okay, fine, but I don't think he'll like hearing what you've told me to say.*

His opinion of my counsel does not diminish its worth.

I turned to Saul, who was stamping his feet again. 'Oak says that the views held by another are not your responsibility.'

Saul frowned, opened his mouth to say something and then shut it again. He watched Oak, who watched him in return while munching mouthfuls of hay.

'So I don't even try to get my wife to stop ranting? I don't try to talk her out of marching down south and bringing Sara back home whether she likes it or not? What sort of father does that make me?'

If he gives energy and attention to the thoughts and patterns of another then he must be prepared to watch them grow stronger. If instead he holds firmly to what he feels to be true then he provides the opportunity for others to join him in that truth.

My words gradually slowed as I passed on Oak's advice. This was how my horse behaved, always. I'd only known him a matter of days, yet he'd moved me further from the old version of myself than I would have believed possible by being exactly as he was advising Saul to be. His counsel was sound. I wouldn't question him again.

I sensed Oak's amusement. *That is unlikely. You should not attempt to relinquish your personality for it is the mechanism through which you live your life here. It is sufficient merely to identify and clear those habits that have arisen from mistakes and misunderstandings.*

But you told me not to question your advice.

I merely requested that you adjust your timing.

Well I didn't start this particular discussion, and Saul is still here.

It serves him that you are not watching him for his response. He requires that our attention is elsewhere so that he can contemplate my counsel.

I glanced over at Saul, who had moved to lean against some straw bales. He still stamped his feet and had begun clapping his arms around himself again, but his eyes were cast downward and he frowned slightly.

I'll check the water trough, and the sheep look like they could do with some more hay, I told Oak, who turned away from Saul slightly and lowered his head to his own pile of hay.

By the time I'd managed to break through the ice in the water trough with the handle of a shovel, and shaken hay into several piles for the sheep who began snatching mouthfuls in between casting anxious glances at Oak's great bulk, Saul was at Oak's side. He stroked Oak's neck as my horse stood, munching rhythmically.

'Is everything okay?' I said.

Saul's brown eyes had a slight crease between them and weren't quite focused on me as he answered. 'I'm not sure. I think so, maybe. I feel like I have more questions but when I try to think what they are, I just keep going back to Oak's advice. It wasn't what I expected.'

I chuckled. 'Welcome to my life. If it's any help, I think you just have to let the advice settle, and then after a while, you'll get it.'

Saul nodded. 'Are you going to be here for a while? In case I need to come back?'

'A day or two, probably, until Adam and Peace are ready to go on. I want to get them to The Gathering before the weather gets any worse.'

He nodded. 'Understood. Thanks, Rowena, and thank you Oak.' He nodded his head to Oak, pulled his scarf back up over his face, and hurried away.

Oak's approval wove its way through me. *Cloud In The Storm. You did well.*

I grinned and rubbed his forehead. *And so, if I may say, did you. Ready for the next one?*

Chapter Eighteen

*I*t turned into a very long afternoon. Each time I went in shivering to Rudi's kitchen to fetch the next person in line to see Oak, she presented me with more layers of clothing to put on and a fresh mug of tea, insisting I drink it before I went back outside. By the time I went to put my boots back on for the last time, I couldn't squeeze my feet into them for all the layers of socks, and I couldn't fit another pullover over those I was already wearing.

'Wait there,' Rudi said, laying her hand briefly on my head as I sat on the bottom stair, straining to get my left boot on. She rushed up the stairs and came down carrying a pair of men's boots and a thick, black woollen pullover, both of which she handed to me. 'Put these on, they were my husband's. I know the boots will be too big, but they'll do to get you to the paddock and back.'

'Won't he mind?'

Tears filled her eyes as she shook her head. 'He has no use for them, now, but you do. You and Oak are doing a fantastic job, Mildred's already popped back with a casserole for us all for dinner and some carrots for Oak, as a thank you.' She blinked away her tears and swallowed. 'Anyway, the sooner you finish with Janna, the sooner you can get inside for the night.' She bustled away to the kitchen. 'Come on, now, Jan, rouse those old bones of yours so Rowena can get you the help you need and then get herself back in by the fire.' She practically shooed us both outside.

When I finally came back indoors, having first escorted an extremely grateful Janna back home and then checked that Adam and Peace were okay at the residence she pointed out to me on the way, I was exhausted.

Rudi called out greetings from the kitchen and advised that she was just dishing up the casserole. I lowered myself to sit on the bottom stair as dainty footsteps sounded behind me. Shirlee's hands were light on my shoulders as she leap-frogged over me to land with a giggle by the front door. She turned and dropped to her knees, grinning up at me as her small hands began to undo my laces while I tried in vain to persuade my fingers to untie my cloak.

'It's good to see you, Shirlee, now that I can see you without your hat and scarf on,' I told her. Her tightly-curled, orange hair matched her mother's exactly, except it was cut off at shoulder length. She was heavily freckled, even above her brow, which creased above brown eyes as she said, softly, 'These look like Daddy's boots.' Then, in a tone that was an exact imitation of her mother's when she'd been organising me and her other guests that afternoon, Shirlee said, 'Lift up your foot and I'll pull this one off.'

'Will your daddy be home soon? What does he do?' I said.

Shirlee bit her lip and stopped heaving at the boot for a moment. Then she pulled again, harder. 'Daddy doesn't come home anymore, but we don't talk about that, because it makes Mummy sad.'

I nodded slowly. 'Does it make you sad?'

Shirlee's eyes filled with tears but, exactly as her mother had done earlier, she blinked them away. 'Yes, but Mummy says we have to be strong.'

There it was, right in front of me – the exact same mistake I had made. My heart went out to the little girl at my feet; she was so young and so determined to find strength in the wrong place. 'Do you feel strong, Shirlee?'

My boot finally came off, and she sat back onto her bottom with a bump. She looked down the hall to the kitchen, and then back at me. 'N…no, b…but I have to be. For Mummy.'

I smiled. 'Well you're very good at pulling boots off. Let's have a go at this one, and then I have it on very good authority that there's a casserole waiting for us.'

Shirlee grabbed hold of my boot and pulled. 'Auntie Mildred brings one for us most days. Daddy used to do the cooking and Mummy hasn't got the hang of it yet.' Her little brow furrowed beneath the orange, curly fringe that matched her mother's, determined that the boot wasn't going to defeat her.

'Mildred is a nice person, I like her. She brought carrots too, apparently. For Oak.'

Shirlee's eyes lit up even as they remained fixed on the boot that was only just beginning to budge. 'Ooooooh, can I give them to him?'

'Of course, but in the morning, okay? I think Oak will be very pleased to see you then.' I managed to flex my ankle a fraction and the boot finally gave way.

Shirlee giggled as she landed on her bottom again. I stood and offered her my hands.

'Will Oak help my mum?' she asked as I pulled her to her feet.

'If she asks him to.'

She kept hold of my hands and looked up at me. 'She won't do that. She won't ask anyone. But it's okay, she has me.' She brightened. 'I'll give Oak his carrots in the morning, then.'

'In the morning,' I agreed.

Mildred's casserole was as excellent as Rudi's roast potatoes were not, but I enjoyed all of the meal anyway. It was hot, and the fire that roared in the grate warmed the room almost as much as the atmosphere generated by Rudi and Shirlee's affection for one another. They were like two flowers from the same plant, one just beginning to open while the other was in full bloom – yet a bloom that had closed slightly, as some do when the sun goes in.

They told me about themselves – Rudi was a Potter and Shirlee attended school for reasons that she carefully explained as if I couldn't possibly have known – and then asked about my family.

I described each of my brothers and sisters in detail and was delighted to feel a little closer to them all as a result. Crow and Swift in particular interested Shirlee, and when I explained that they too were at school, for the same reasons she was, she listened intently, nodding at all the places an adult would in a serious conversation. Rudi caught my eye and winked.

'You have a lovely way with her,' she said once Shirlee had gone up to bed.

'I've always found children easier than adults.'

Rudi put a steaming mug of what smelt like greenmint tea in front of me. 'You don't like talking about your parents,' she said softly, sitting down with her own mug.

'No. And you don't like talking about your husband.'

Her eyes flicked up to mine. I held her stare. Eventually, she looked down at her tea. 'No.'

I didn't know what to say next. I wanted to tell her about my life, the huge, glaring error I'd made that had made a difficult situation a hundred times worse, I wanted to help her, to stop her making the same mistake, but I didn't know where to start.

I thought back to my afternoon with Oak. His counsel for each of the six people who had asked for his help had been consistent. Not one of their situations or problems had been alike but in each case, he'd shown no inclination to address them at the level at which their questions were asked. The details of conversations, misunderstandings and arguments between people held no interest for him whatsoever, indeed as the afternoon wore on, I began to get the impression he found them tedious, if to be expected of us humans.

He always seemed to be trying to get the people concerned to look at their own part in what was bothering them, as if by sorting out their own thoughts and feelings, the problems concerned would look after themselves.

Giving energy and attention to the thoughts and patterns of another merely results in those thoughts and patterns growing stronger. Holding firmly to truth gives the opportunity for others to join that truth. I repeated his counsel over and over in my mind until I knew what I could do. But it would hurt. A lot.

Shirlee's little face flashed into my mind, her manner and expressions so like Swift's. I made my decision. 'My father left my mother while she was pregnant with me,' I said.

Rudi's eyes flicked up to meet mine. She opened her mouth as if to say something, but then her eyes hardened and she set her mouth in a firm line. Eventually, she said, 'That must have been very hard for her.'

'It was. Apparently, I look exactly like him, a constant

reminder of who she lost. She couldn't be the loving mother to me that she was to my brothers and sisters.' I took a deep breath, in and out. *Strength is the willingness to be vulnerable, to risk defeat while knowing I can't really be defeated,* I affirmed to myself.

I walk by your side. Oak's thought was so faint, I barely caught it, but his love was all I needed.

'I saw my mother's difficulty with me and took it to mean she didn't love me,' I said. 'I thought I was unlovable, worthless. If I'm honest, deep down, I still do.' I was mortified to feel a tear trickling down my face. Vulnerable wasn't a strong enough word for how I felt – I'd exposed the part of me that bled, for Rudi to do with as she wished. Yet strangely, there was the tiniest part of me that felt relieved, as if the worst had happened and yet here I was, still in one piece, at least for now.

I watched Rudi. If she confirmed that I was right, that there was something about me that was abhorrent, I had no idea how I would come back from it... and yet that tiny part of me stood firm, reassuring me that I would.

I walk by your side, repeated Oak. I grabbed hold of his thought, his love, and held on to it for all I was worth.

'You poor, dear thing,' Rudi whispered. She held on so tightly to her mug that the knuckles of both hands went white. 'My husband, Marcus, died six months ago. I'm terrified I'll never get over losing him, and that I'm not enough for Shirlee on my own. Marcus was a Baker, and an amazing one. He did all the cooking – I've always been terrible at it, and with him always being so good, I never bothered to improve – but now I have a little girl to feed and I can't do it properly. I lied to you earlier, Mildred didn't bring the casserole for you as a thank you, she brings them most days because she knows, like everyone else here knows, that I can't look after my own child. I'm a failure. I couldn't keep my husband here with me and I can't keep my child healthy, so she'll probably leave me too. I try to be strong, to not let her see that I barely make it through each day, and I'm trying to teach her to be strong, but I'm failing at that too. She cries herself to sleep every night and nothing I do or say makes it better for her...'

My heart went out to her as she stepped out of her own, private world of misery and into the one of excruciating honesty that I'd created with my own admission.

Cloud In The Storm. Focus. Your effort is not yet concluded.

I tried to concentrate on the words that continued to spill out of her as she admitted all of the ways her fear of failure manifested itself.

'...and I have no idea why I'm telling you this. I can't tell anyone, I can't ask for help because if I do, I'll lose the miniscule shred of self-respect I have left.' Rudi looked up at me, her eyes now red-rimmed and her cheeks wet with tears.

I'd done it now. I'd opened the way for her to drop her defences, to stop trying to be strong in the wrong way. Now I had to try to help her to be strong in the right way – me of all people. I had no idea where to start.'

You have already begun.

I did what I did for Shirlee... ahhhhh. Strength comes from love.

I reached a hand out across the table, and Rudi took it, hesitantly. 'I would have given anything to have my mother look at me the way you look at Shirlee,' I told her. 'So, you can't cook. Big deal. You can love, Rudi, and for a child, a mother's love is the most important thing. Shirlee told me that you both have to be strong. You love each other. Focus on that, and you'll have all the strength you need. You can cry, you can grieve, you can admit that you don't cook vegetables for long enough, and you'll be fine, because you'll be focusing on what's important and not on what really, really isn't. And by the way, another two minutes and the potatoes would have been perfect. Calm down, take your time, taste things, poke things with a fork, let things that are cooked wait for things that aren't, and before you know it, you'll be eating meals that go down just fine.'

Rudi sighed. 'You make it sound so simple.'

'The cooking bit is. The rest isn't, I know that, and I can tell you now, it's going to carry on hurting for a while, but remember where to put your focus and you'll find real strength. I'm only just beginning to learn to do it for myself, but I know I'll do it because I have Oak to teach me. Shirlee will do it because she has you to teach her.'

Rudi stood up, suddenly. 'I need to go to her.'

I nodded. 'Yes, you do. I'll clear away here and then if you don't mind – cancel that, even if you do – I'm going to have a rummage through your cupboards, which, judging by your skill as a Potter,' I held up my mug as evidence, 'will be full of the food you've traded for your work. Your cooking lessons will start bright and early in the morning and by lunchtime, you'll have Mildred's dinner prepared and ready for Shirlee to deliver to her. Got it?'

Rudi paused by my chair and put a hand on my shoulder. 'I don't know what to say.'

I stood up. 'Give me a hug, then.' She flung her arms around me and held on tight. Her sobs started off small and quiet, but soon racked her body. When she'd cried herself out, I gently disentangled myself. 'Go to Shirlee,' I said, softly.

She scrubbed at her face with the sleeves of her pullover. 'I can't go like this. I need to wash my face.'

'You don't. Shirlee copies you. She thinks that being strong means holding everything in. Show her that it doesn't.'

Rudi nodded and just about managed a smile. 'In case I'm a while, your room is the second on the left upstairs, and the bathroom is opposite it. Do you have everything you need, you and Oak?'

'Yes.' I smiled at the realisation. 'We really do.'

As soon as the first birdcalls announced that the day was ready to begin, I leapt out of bed. I washed quickly, dressed and shot downstairs. I wrapped myself in my outdoor clothes and jogged outside to break the ice on the water trough, shake up more hay for Oak and the sheep, and remove Oak's enormous piles of dung, depositing them on the nearby dung heap.

He was well-rested and content, so as dark, angry snow clouds began to release their charges, I shot back inside, brushing the snowflakes from my hat and cloak before returning them to their pegs. Shirlee was sitting at the table, looking expectant.

'Mummy says we're having cooking lessons,' she told me. 'She thinks I'll be a better cook than her, what with Daddy being as good as he was, so she wants us to learn together and she says you're going to teach us.'

I grinned. 'I am. What do you fancy for breakfast?'

'Jumbled eggs on toast. Daddy used to make it for me.'

Rudi came bustling in with an armful of washing, which she deposited in a basket. She looked tired, but smiled at me. 'Morning, Rowena, I hope you slept well?'

I nodded. 'I did, thanks. Shirlee tells me we're making jumbled eggs?'

Rudi took a sharp breath, glanced at Shirlee, and breathed out, nodding slowly. 'Jumbled eggs were her father's version of scrambled eggs. I think he put onions in, and tomatoes and butter, but I don't really... I don't really know.'

'Right, well Shirlee ate them often enough, so come on over

here, Shirlee, and we'll all three of us have a try together, shall we?'

We stayed in Mettletown for four days, during which time Rudi and Shirlee cooked a lot, laughed a lot and cried a lot. It was heart-warming to see them enjoying the fruits of their labours and growing ever closer as together, they worked their way through their loss.

'We should all stay here for the winter,' I told Adam on our fourth morning there. 'I know your hosts love having you here, and Rudi has already asked me to stay at least until the snow is gone. It will mean I can make sure she and Shirlee are well on track before leaving them.'

Adam looked up at me from the comfy chair in which he sat by the fire in his host's living room, and smiled warmly. 'It's almost as if we find ourselves teaching what we need to learn, isn't it?'

'It is. So then, you understand why Oak and I need to stay here?'

'Helping someone through their worst fear is an admirable thing to do.' Adam continued to smile up at me, his green eyes twinkling.

'Why am I sensing a but?'

'If you're sensing one of those, then I think your very wonderful Bond-Partner is better placed to help you with it than I.'

'You think I want to stay on here because I'm nervous about going to The Gathering,' I accused him.

'Ah, so that's it.'

I sat down in the chair opposite him. 'Well, I suppose I was nervous about the thought of it, but now, after what I've learnt from being here, well, now I think I'll be okay.'

Adam smiled. 'I think you will be too. Peace and I will be leaving within the hour. You and Oak will leave with us?'

'Within the hour? Today?' I rolled my eyes and sighed. 'You know very well I won't let the two of you go on alone. Okay, fine, we'll come with you. You said we'd be stopping off at more villages along the way. How far to the next one?'

'We'll be there by nightfall.'

'You know we've had another few inches of snow since we've been here? Are you sure you and Peace will be alright?'

Adam smiled. 'We will appreciate following in your and Oak's footsteps again, but yes thank you, we'll be fine. Now, I have something prepared for Rudi and Shirlee.' He got to his feet and beckoned for me to follow him to the kitchen, where he presented me with a glass jar of what looked like the same bright green tea he had given me. 'Please warm this up for them. If, having smelt it, they feel disposed to have some, it will ease the news of your departure.'

'What's in it? It looks disgusting, but I know it smells and tastes amazing.'

'Just a few herbs I like to cobble together as a pick-me-up for when someone is tired in body and mind. You've done a fine job helping your hosts along on their way, this will give them the energy to stay on it when you're gone.'

I narrowed my eyes at Adam as I took the jar from him. 'Who are you, Adam? I mean really? I had no intention of leaving today, but you've talked me into going by saying hardly anything at all. You're Horse-Bonded and you're an amazing Herbalist, but you're more than that, aren't you?'

He shook his head sadly. 'No, I'm not. But I'm trying very

hard to be.' He stood up a little straighter. 'I must pack. Peace and I will be ready when you are.'

I looked at the jar in my gloved hand as I walked back to Rudi's. It felt as if I carried with me a bit of the calm, peaceful energy that Adam exuded, and I found myself wondering again at how he had, several times now, drawn me out of myself without seeming to try.

I walked into Rudi's kitchen to find her and Shirlee covered in flour from head to toe, and shrieking with laughter. 'What on earth are you two up to?' I said with a grin.

'Mummy found Daddy's notes from when he was an apprentice Baker,' said Shirlee. 'We're making bread like he used to, but he says in his notes that when you knead the dough, you have to be very free with the flour, so I threw some at Mummy.'

'And I threw some back,' laughed Rudi.

'You're making bread, wow, good on you both,' I said, putting Adam's jar down by the stove. 'I'm just going to put this on to warm. If you fancy some, help yourself.'

'Oooooh, what is it?' said Shirlee.

'It's herbal tea that Adam made. I can guarantee you're going to want some, it's delicious.' I poured the contents of the jar into a pan and set it to warm on a low heat. 'I'll be back down in a bit.' Before they could reply, I turned and made for the stairs.

I quickly packed my gear, glad that I'd done my washing the previous day, then went back downstairs, dropped my back-sack by the front door and went into the kitchen. Flour hung in clouds as Rudi and Shirlee kneaded their respective lumps of dough with vigour.

'Well I'm glad you're both taking the recipe so seriously,' I said with a smile. 'It smells like that tea is ready.'

Rudi wiped her brow on her sleeve and turned to me as Shirlee wiped her own forehead on her sleeve in imitation. 'Lovely.

Would you mind pouring it for us? Over to the sink with you, Shirlee, and wash your hands and face. Then we can drink our tea while the dough rises, and have a think about where we're going to start with cleaning up all the mess we've made.' She touched a floury finger to Shirlee's nose, leaving a white mark at the tip.

Shirlee giggled. 'Daddy used to do that,' she said and stopped laughing.

'And what did he call you, Shirlee? When you had a white nose?' Rudi said.

A smile spread across Shirlee's face. 'Snose. For snow nose.' She turned to me. 'Get it?'

I chuckled. 'I do. Well, Snose, your dough looks like it's beginning to rise already. Your mum will make a Baker out of you yet.'

Shirlee's smile widened further. 'Like Daddy? I could be a Baker like Daddy? I'd love that.'

Rudi took her by the shoulders and guided her to the sink. 'You can be whatever you want to be, little one. We'll just carry on working through Daddy's notes and see how you feel when you're of an age to make your final choice, shall we?'

'Hurraaaaaaaaay!' Shirlee put an arm around her mother and hugged her.

I poured Adam's tea into two mugs, and set them on the table. Shirlee sat down and sniffed her mug. Her eyes lit up. 'It smells nice.' She took a sip as Rudi sat down next to her.

'It does indeed smell delicious, thank you,' said Rudi. 'Just as well really, or I'd never have persuaded myself to drink it. It's a vivid shade of green, isn't it?' She took a sip and raised her eyebrows. 'Wow. Aren't you having any, Rowena?'

I shook my head. 'I'm actually going to be leaving, shortly.'

'Noooooooooooo,' wailed Shirlee. 'You can't go.'

Rudi bit her lip. 'Do you really have to? You can't stay

longer?' Her voice shook a little. 'You've... you've helped us so much, and we'll miss you. Won't we Shirl?' She put an arm around her daughter's shoulders and hugged her close.

'And I'll miss you both, I've loved staying here. You've helped me too, you know, more than you can imagine.'

'I just pulled your boots off. You made Mummy happy again,' Shirlee said, her eyes full of tears.

'It wasn't me who did that, little Snose, it was you.'

Rudi smiled down at her daughter, her voice stronger. 'Let's drink up and get our coats, shall we? Then we can see Rowena and Oak off on their way.'

By the time I'd donned my outdoor clothing, stitched Oak into my makeshift saddle, and made my way around to the street with Oak just behind me, Rudi and Shirlee were waiting for us along with Adam, Peace and, it seemed, the rest of Mettletown. Many of the villagers had already lost their hats to Peace, who was currently swirling a bright red, woollen hat around in his mouth while a young, blond-haired girl shrieked with laughter as she jumped up and down, trying to catch hold of it.

Shirlee ran up to me and flung her arms around my waist. 'Will you come back and see us? I'll be able to bake you a cake by then,' she said, her voice muffled by my cloak.

'Of course I'll come back. I can't promise when, but you just keep baking new things, and then when I come, you can make me your favourite, okay?'

'Okay.' Shirlee released me and reached a hand up to Oak. He lowered his head and she kissed him between his nostrils. 'I want you to look after Rowena, okay?' she said, staring up at him so earnestly that a lump rose in my throat.

I hugged Rudi, who held on tightly and whispered, 'Thank you.'

'Thank you. For having Oak and me, for everything,' I said. 'Right, Adam, let's be having you and Peace, we have snow to trudge through and extremities to freeze off.'

'Right you are, right you are, we're coming. Peace, do let that poor girl have her hat back.'

Peace responded by flinging the now very soggy red hat into the air. It landed some distance away in a patch of untrodden snow, and quickly sank out of sight.

There was laughter and hilarity as all the children ran to find it, while Adam accepted the last few hugs and handshakes from his friends.

I'll walk so you don't have to work so hard, and I can clear a path for Adam, I told Oak. He didn't respond and I smiled as it dawned on me that had he wanted me to ride, I would already have received my instructions.

'Thanks Rowena, thanks Oak,' people began to call after us. I turned and raised a hand in farewell, happy that we'd been able to help. Happy.

Chapter Nineteen

We spent ten days travelling from one village to the next. The weather was atrocious, with snowstorms, biting winds, and several hailstorms thrown in for good measure. Despite moving at a slower pace than Oak and I would have done alone – I continued to walk next to him, clearing a path through the snow for Adam while my horse did the same for Peace – we always managed to cover enough ground to reach the various villages for which Adam headed, by the time darkness fell. I was increasingly grateful for his knowledge of the area.

Adam and I spoke little during the day, intent as we all were on enduring the conditions until we could rest and get warm again.

Each time we reached a village, Adam and Peace were greeted as if they were old and dear friends of every single villager, rather than occasional visitors there to dispense counsel, before being whisked off to the residence of whoever won the argument over hosting them. Oak and I were then fought over as the next best thing, before being similarly hurried off to shelter, warmth and food.

We stayed for two nights in each village. Adam continued to ask Oak and me to see anyone wanting counsel, so that he and Peace could rest. I strongly suspected that it was more so I would gain experience acting in my capacity as one of the Horse-Bonded, and was happy to oblige.

I found that I loved relaying Oak's advice. It always made sense to those asking for it – eventually if not immediately – and increasingly, it made sense to me. I felt as if with every response Oak gave to the questions asked of him, I left my old life another step further behind me and embraced this new one in which I found myself, with more confidence – and people responded differently to me as a result.

The smiles that greeted us all when we arrived somewhere new now quickly turned to hands being offered for me to shake, and excited chatter at old Bond-Partners being accompanied by new. People asked their questions of Oak more readily, openly and honestly. When I passed his counsel back to them, my awareness of how powerful the simplest words were when combined according to his direction, my trust and my confidence in him, all allowed me to dispense his advice with greater conviction. People nodded before they had received his message in its entirety, eager to understand, sure that it was right, that it would help.

By the time the stone buildings of The Gathering loomed in the distance, the anxiety I'd felt over whether I could cope with being around a lot of people, whether I would fit in there, had been replaced by excitement and more than a little relief that finally, we had arrived. The worst of the winter was still to come, and judging by the sky behind us, it was fast approaching.

'Outstanding,' Adam's voice carried easily through the morning air, which for once was still. 'Our record goes unbroken.'

I turned to see him grinning from ear to ear as he ploughed through the snow. It had a frozen crust on the top, so I'd been unable to kick through it for him, but Adam was stepping through it almost as quickly and easily as if it weren't there. 'Your record?'

He nodded, still grinning. 'Every year since Peace and I bonded, we've returned to The Gathering during winter. And every year, we manage to get back here before the very worst of it. We've cut it fine this year, there are no two ways about it, but we remain undefeated, don't we, old friend?' He rubbed Peace's shoulder with the hand that, as always, rested there. 'If you turn left to go alongside the river just down there, we'll soon be alongside some paddocks. When you reach a path that bisects them, turn up it. The going should be easier from thereon.' His voice quietened as he spoke to Peace. 'We'll soon have you in a nice, warm shelter with plenty of hay, and then you can rest your old bones. Maybe for a bit longer than normal, eh? Until spring, even?'

'You're not planning on leaving again, surely? Can't you retire? I'm here now, can't Oak and I take your place visiting the villages, so you and Peace can just enjoy the time... that is, I mean...'

'The time he has left?' Adam said, the sadness that laced his voice every now and then, returning. 'If only it were that simple; there are some villages that he and I still need to visit.' His voice brightened. 'But you can absolutely take our place dispensing counsel to as many others as you can, in fact, I think you should. Your no-nonsense approach lends itself very admirably to helping villagers of a more, shall we say, thick-skinned nature?'

I laughed. 'Are you very politely calling me bossy?'

He chuckled. 'I wouldn't dream of it. I just find your candidness refreshing, and would bring your attention to the fact that you do it well.'

'Well, thank you. Hello, are those the paddocks you meant?'

'They are. Judging by the absence of horses in them, my bones are correct in their assessment that a storm is coming. If you'd like to head on down to the paddocks nearest the buildings, there are some that are always left empty for newly bonded horses. Oak and Peace can make themselves at home in one of those, and then you'll know Oak is close by to where you'll be staying. We'll give them a good, deep bed of straw in their field shelter, and plenty of hay, so they'll be warm and cosy when the storm hits.'

I nodded gratefully, and rubbed Oak's neck as he carved his way through the crusty snow, strong and confident as always. I'd been apart from him for much of the time we'd spent staying with people of the different villages, but he'd been just outside the back door of every residence in which I'd had a bed. I was glad I wouldn't be too far away from him now.

You are never far from me. It is not possible, Oak informed me.

I know you're always with me in my mind, but there are times when I need to be with you in person, so that the world stops spinning. We've been bonded barely three weeks and I hardly recognise myself – you're the only thing in my life that's solid, that doesn't change.

Oak marched on without response. He understood. He'd known without me explaining myself. I smiled to myself. I was Horse-Bonded and I had the most amazing, beautiful Bond-Partner. I would carry on learning from him and from the other Horse-Bonded, who were hopefully all as nice as Adam. And, I suddenly remembered, I had my qualification certificate with me – I was a Tailor! I could contribute to The Gathering by doing something I loved.

'We're here,' called Adam. 'If you could manage to heave open that gate to your left through all the snow, Oak and Peace can take the closest paddock to the buildings. Well done, perfect. On you go, Peace.' Oak and Peace filed past me as I held the gate open, unable to wipe the smile from my face. 'Happy to be here, I see?' Adam winked as he passed me.

'Very.'

'Good. Come along then, we'll get some hay and straw shaken up in the shelter – there should be some bales stacked in there, ready – and then I think we're going to need to take some buckets of water in there, and shut the horses in. No,' he added hastily after a glance at my horrified face, 'that was clumsy of me to put it like that. We won't be shutting them in so much as the weather out. Do you feel that wind picking up? It's coming from the opposite direction from normal, so any snow it brings will blow directly into the field shelters. The other bonded are clearly of the same opinion, which is why you didn't see any horses or livestock in any of the paddocks we passed. Of course, if any of the horses want out, they have only to let their Bond-Partners know and their doors will be opened forthwith. Does that set your mind at rest?'

I nodded. 'I'll fetch the water then, shall I?'

Adam nodded. 'That would be appreciated. You'll find buckets stacked next to the water barrels, just inside the gate.'

By the time Adam had shaken up straw into a deep bed for Oak and Peace, I'd fetched as many buckets of water as I could find. We opened several bales of hay and shook it into four huge piles for Oak and Peace to munch on through the afternoon, then left the field shelter just as snow was beginning to drift on the wind. Adam and I pulled on first the bottom half of the door to the field shelter, then the top door, until they finally creaked shut; the hinges were rusty and clearly hadn't been used for some time.

'I think,' Adam said, flicking the catch on the top door to hold it shut, 'that we've earned ourselves a hot bath and some lunch. Don't you?'

'Sounds good to me. Where do I go?'

Adam grinned. 'If you'll just follow me to my rooms – as a Healer, I have a consulting room joined on to my bedroom – I'll dump my gear and then we'll go to the accommodation block and find you a room.'

I shook my head. 'You can just point the accommodation block out to me and tell me where to go for lunch, and I'll sort myself out. I'm not standing in the way of you and your bath.' I held a hand up as he opened his mouth to argue. 'You don't get to have your way in everything, Adam. I'm a big girl, and I'm perfectly capable of following directions.'

He smiled. 'Of course you are. Let's get out of this awful weather then, shall we?' The wind was beginning to bellow, and the snowflakes that rode it were getting larger.

'Lead on,' I said, pulling my scarf up over my face. *Oak, are you sure you're okay in there?*

I am content.

Okay, well if you feel uncomfortable and need to get out, just let me know and I'll be back here straight away. I'll be down to see you before dark, anyway.

Oak didn't reply, and since Adam was already through the paddock gate and trying to pull it shut against the wind, I hurried to help him. When it slammed, we pulled our cloaks tightly around ourselves and hastened along the path, passing between massive buildings of grey stone, each of which I judged to be five storeys tall. We entered a large, cobbled square around which were more of the enormous grey stone buildings. At its centre stood a huge statue of a person standing alongside a horse. I smiled and immediately put a gloved hand in front of my mouth as the wind penetrated the fibres of my scarf and hurt my teeth. People were slipping and sliding as they hurried, bent over to protect themselves against the snow and wind, between the buildings.

Adam pointed to a building on the far side of the square. 'That's the accommodation block,' he shouted over the wind. 'Any unoccupied rooms will have their doors wedged ajar. Start on the bottom floor and work your way up until you find an empty room, dump your stuff and then work your way to the middle of the corridor, where you'll find the bathrooms. There'll be fresh towels in cupboards outside each one. If you need me, my rooms are on the ground floor of that building, there.' He pointed to the building that ran down the righthand side of the square. 'When the bell rings, it means it's lunchtime. Make your way to the dining hall there,' he pointed to our left, 'and I'll see you inside. Are you sure you don't want me to show you?'

I shook my head. 'I'll be fine. How long do I have before lunch?'

Adam shrugged. 'I'm afraid I've rather lost track of time, but I shouldn't think it will be long.'

I nodded and hurried towards the accommodation block. I pushed the door open and had to lean against it to shut it behind me. Once I was out of the wind, it seemed deathly quiet. I allowed my cloak to fall open and pulled my scarf away from my face. I was standing at the end of a long, stone corridor. I hurried along it, looking for any doors that were ajar. I passed a man coming the other way, already wrapped in a long cloak and with his hat pulled down low. He nodded without comment as he pulled his scarf up over his face in preparation for stepping outside. All of the doors were shut, so I climbed the wide, stone staircase to the second floor.

Immediately, I spotted an open door. I stopped beside it and peered into the room beyond, which judging by the belongings scattered about, was occupied.

'Can I help you?' a voice called out from behind me.

I turned around as a short woman stepped into the corridor from the stairwell. She was wrapped from head to toe in brown, from her hat, scarf, gloves and cloak to her boots, but her eyes looked friendly and cheerful.

'Thanks, I'm fine, I'm just new here and looking for an empty room.'

'You'll be needing the next floor up then, I'm afraid. Welcome, I'm Quinta.' She held out a gloved hand, then looked at it and shook her head. She pulled her glove off and offered it again.

I pulled my own glove off and shook it. 'I'm Rowena, and really pleased to meet you.'

Quinta raised her eyebrows and quickly looked me up and down. 'Um, well, welcome Rowena, I'm sure you'll be, well I hope you'll be, very happy here. And I look forward to meeting your Bond-Partner. Would you like me to come up to the next floor and help you find a room?' She spoke rapidly, as if uncomfortable. No, I corrected myself, that was just the old me coming to the surface again. What had Oak said? I'd let go of the pattern, now I had to practise letting go of the habits that had gone with it. If I expected to experience rejection wherever I looked, then I would. Quinta was probably just in a hurry and offering to help when she didn't really have time.

'No thanks, I'll be fine. I'll see you around,' I said.

She hesitated and looked down at the ground and her eyes became slightly unfocused. Then she blinked and nodded, slowly. 'How rude of me, sorry, Noble had something to say to me – he's my Bond-Partner, obviously – yep, sure, see you around Rowena.' She smiled and seemed more comfortable. That was it then, she was just busy and needed to get on. I returned her smile and made for the stairwell.

I pulled off my hat and gloves as I climbed the stairs to the third floor. When I reached the top, I almost collided with a man of equal height to me but with considerably more bulk.

'Sorry,' he said. He looked me up and down as Quinta had, and frowned. 'Do I know you? I don't think I do, but I recognise… aaaah.'

'You recognise what?'

He looked past me for a second, then seemed to remember I was there. 'Nothing, sorry, I'm in a bit of a hurry, that was Vital telling me he needs more hay. Such a pain, this weather, isn't it? I'll catch you another time.' He almost ran away from me, but I heard his footsteps slowing as he reached further down the stairwell. I scowled, then took a deep breath. I refused to allow myself to fall into the trap of believing his behaviour was about me. Whatever his reaction to me, whatever his rush, was his business. I tried to put it out of my mind, yet couldn't quite. As I walked along the corridor, looking left and right for an open door, I reached out to Oak. He was calm and confident as ever. I breathed in and out deeply, several times. He was always with me. I could do this.

My heart leapt when I found a door wedged ajar, just as Adam had described. I kicked the wedge out of the way, nudged open the door and went inside, closing it firmly behind me. The room was cold, but there was a fire laid in the hearth, next to which was a large basket full of what looked like some sort of fuel bricks. A wide bed was made up with at least two thick quilts atop blankets and sheets, and two plump-looking pillows. The grey flagstone floor had a thick, red rug covering much of it, and a worn but comfortable-looking chair was pulled up close to the fire. A horse that looked very much like Oak was carved into the mantelpiece, instantly making the room feel like mine. I loved it.

I pulled off my cloak and layers of pullovers and undershirts. I removed my boots and socks, then padded in bare feet to the middle of the corridor where there were indeed bathrooms and cupboards full of towels, soap and bath salts. I selected a couple of towels, a bar of soap and a packet of salts and backed into one of the bathrooms with my pile of goodies.

The smell of the salts as I ran a bath of steaming hot water made it too inviting for me to wait until the bath was full. I stripped off and sank into the hot, scented water, grimacing as warmth returned to my hands and feet, but revelling in the feeling of my tired, aching muscles relaxing. As my eyes began to close, I sat up with a start. I didn't have time to fall asleep, I had to get washed and dressed, then go and meet Adam for lunch.

Anxiety flashed through me at the thought of meeting more of the Horse-Bonded, but I pushed it to one side. I'd been fine with everyone I'd met at the villages. I would be fine here, despite Quinta and that man having been a bit strange. Maybe that was what all Horse-Bonded were like? Adam was lovely, but I still suspected he was more than the average Horse-Bonded. Maybe everyone else was always a bit distracted, what with their Bond-Partners counselling them all the time? Maybe I came across as they did, when I stopped to listen to Oak? Yes, that was all it had been with the two I'd just met, I decided as I soaped myself. That, and they were both in a hurry.

I stood up and wrinkled my nose in disgust at the dirty water around my ankles. I couldn't face putting my travelling clothes back on, so I wrapped my towel tightly around myself, opened the door just wide enough to stick my head out, and when I could neither see nor hear anyone, ran down the corridor to my room. I was just pulling on a clean pair of leggings over a thick pair of tights, when a bell sounded. It seemed muffled, and when I peered out of the window and could barely see an arm's length beyond it for the snow billowing past, I understood why. I was glad that Oak and Peace were so well sheltered.

I finished dressing in my usual black attire, then grimaced as I pulled on my cold boots over several pairs of socks. Not knowing what I would be doing after lunch and whether I would have time to return to my room, I added another thick, black pullover before donning my cloak and picking up my hat, gloves and scarf. I tore out of my room, slamming the door behind me, and pulled my garments on as I raced down the stairs. I was the last to join those already at the bottom, chatting and laughing with one another as they hurried along the corridor. I was glad of people to follow, as I wasn't convinced I would easily find the dining hall in the blizzard that raged outside.

I went to take the door from the tall, heavily garbed man who held it open for me, then nodded my thanks as he gestured for me to go through first. I turned to help him pull it shut against the tempest that held it open, but even with our combined efforts, a good deal of snow blew in before we finally felt it click shut.

The man winked at me, a mischievous glint in his hazel eyes. Then he frowned slightly and stood in the blizzard, staring at me. There was no point trying to introduce myself, so I braced myself against the wind until he shrugged, nodded into the blizzard and held out a gloved hand to me, his eyebrows raised in question.

Did he think I was useless? That I couldn't make it through a blizzard on my own? I swallowed, hard. This wasn't who I was anymore, I was just thrown by what had happened earlier. The man was just being friendly and offering help to a stranger.

I nodded and took his gloved hand. It was fortunate for both of us that I did. Twice, I nearly fell and three times, I had to hold tightly to him so that he remained on his feet as we made our way across the square, practically blind in the wind and snow that came at us head on. By the time the man pushed down on a handle

I could barely see, and shouldered open a door, we both practically fell through it. He recovered quickly and poked his head back out to see if anyone else was coming. Then he pushed it shut.

'At least the wind's blowing away from this side,' the man said, pulling off his hat and scarf. 'That was insane, wasn't it?' He held out his hand. 'I'm Shann. And you are?'

I removed my own hat, pulled a glove off and shook his gloved one. 'Rowena. My Bond-Partner and I arrived with Adam and Peace an hour or so ago.'

Why was my heart hammering in my chest? I'd already decided I would be fine here. There was no need to be nervous… and yet there was. I could see it in Shann's eyes, which had suddenly turned serious. The expression didn't suit him, and I had a feeling it wasn't one he adopted very often.

'Spider, now? Really?' Shann muttered to himself, rolling his eyes as he peeled off his cloak and hung it on a nearby peg, along with his scarf and hat. 'Fine,' he muttered. Then he looked back at me. 'So, anyway Rowena, we'll go on in to lunch, shall we?'

'Why is everyone looking at me like they know me, and then behaving as if they can't get away fast enough?' I said.

'Everyone? Who else did? I mean, not that I'm behaving that way, not at all, in fact Spider says…'

'Spider's your Bond-Partner? What did he say?' I took a step closer to Shann as Oak wove his way through my mind. I realised I was scowling and tried to stop.

Shann held his hands up and the cheeky glint I'd seen in his eyes returned. 'Whoa there, you're a bit feisty, aren't you? Spider reminded me that I'm not perfect and everyone tolerates me, and he's right, so anyway, we'll just go on in for lunch, shall we? Before all the best stuff gets swiped?'

'Why does Spider think you need to tolerate me? You've just

met me, you don't know anything about me, we've barely even spoken,' I said. Had I read them all wrong after all? Had the villagers just been kind to me because of Adam? Did I radiate something repulsive that made everyone want to avoid me?

'No, exactly, and I'll make up my own mind,' said Shann. He lifted his arm in the direction of another door, and grinned. 'Shall we?'

'No, we shan't,' I said and stormed past him, pushing through the door.

I was assaulted by a cacophony of voices, cutlery clinking against crockery, and logs spitting loudly in the roaring fires of the hearths that dotted the cavernous dining room into which I'd stepped. I looked back at the door in surprise, wondering how it had held back all the noise from the outer foyer.

Shann appeared at my side. 'Um, sorry, I should have said, you have to leave your outdoor clothes in the lobby. I'll just take them now, and go and hang them up for you, shall I?'

I ignored him as the people sitting at the nearest trestle tables caught sight of me, nudged one another and then one by one, stopped talking. No one smiled. No one moved to greet me, to even talk to me – they just stared. Anger flared in me.

Cloud In The Storm. Our bond.

I shouldn't need our bond, I've been managing without it at the villages. This isn't me imagining things that aren't really there, Oak, they're hostile.

Our bond, Oak repeated. His thought was so kind, so gentle, so in contrast with the scene in front of me, I found I was desperate for the refuge it offered me. I hurled myself into the part of my mind I shared with him, then looked again at those who sat watching me. Where before I saw hostility, now I saw confusion in some faces and compassion in others. A few people looked angry, yet I had the feeling their anger wasn't directed at me. They began to look at one another, as if hoping someone else would speak.

My face softened. Whatever was going on here, it would be okay. A man stood up. He was tall and muscular with slightly greying, black hair and intense, blue eyes. He marched over to me.

'I'm Feryl, the Master of Riding here. Since it seems that no one else is willing to tell you why we're all staring at you, I'll do it.'

The hall was silent apart from the crackling of the fires. Every pair of what must have been several hundred pairs of eyes, bored into me.

I walk by your side. Oak's thought carried far more strength than usual.

I nodded. *I'm still with you. It's okay. I'm okay.*

Feryl appeared to have interpreted my nod as having been in response to his statement. He nodded back and said, 'You're Rowena Harrol, of Clearview.' My mouth dropped open. How could he possibly know that? 'A Herald who goes by the name of Larcen was here a few days ago. He delivered a warning to us all that a thief with your name and description was on her way here, and a request that if and when you showed up here, we pass on a message to you. So, this is the message: Your mother would have you know that you've left your family without the food and resources they need to get through the winter. She expects everything you stole from them to be returned forthwith, and she expects recompense for all of the cloth, fur and thread that you stole from her shop.'

The cavernous dining hall and all of its occupants began to spin around me. It was as if the person Oak had helped me to become just fell away, leaving my worst fear standing there by itself.

My mother. My cold, spiteful, hideous excuse for a mother

had used a loudmouthed, gossiping Herald to spread her poison so that it contaminated every person here. There was nowhere I could go to escape her, nothing I could do to reinvent myself, to be someone other than who she had made me.

I shivered as a white-hot fury crept through me. My surroundings came back into focus. I looked from one face to the next and again saw only hostility. They thought I was a thief. They didn't want me here. No one wanted me anywhere. My mother had won.

Cloud In The... Oak's thought was very faint but I had a sense of the effort it had taken for him to try to reach me through my rage.

Get out! Don't ever try to get in my head again. I never should have believed you, I never should have trusted you, I can't trust anyone. JUST LEAVE ME ALONE.

'Rowena, it's okay...' began Shann, but stopped when I glared at him. I hurled my hat to the floor, turned and stalked from the dining room before he could finish. I wrenched open the outer door and ran into the storm.

Chapter Twenty

The wind was behind me as I tore from the dining hall, colluding with my effort to get as far away from the Horse-Bonded as possible. It blew me past the accommodation block and onto a path that wound up into the hills behind The Gathering. Yes. I would let the storm take me up there, where no one would find me, where I wouldn't have to constantly try to convince myself I could trust people only to find that I'd been right to doubt it all along, and where I wouldn't have to see the big, black horse who had broken down my defences and left me utterly exposed to the agony of rejection.

An image of Oak gazing unblinkingly at me entered my mind. I had a fleeting sense of him throwing himself at the door of his field shelter, and I almost reached out to him. No. I pushed all thoughts of him away. He would only cause me more pain.

The snow deepened rapidly; the path into the hills was little trodden, and the wind was blowing the falling snow against the hillside so that it settled far more deeply than on the flat. My mouth twisted into a rictus of a grin. My flight from The

Gathering was going to be almost impossible. Good. The harder I had to work to keep moving, the less I could feel of anything else.

I soon had to lift my knees up almost to my chin, in order to carry on striding through the drifting snow. I stamped my feet down into it with each step. My mother couldn't have just let me go. She must have been beyond furious when she discovered me missing, and even more angry when she heard that not only had Jewner qualified me as a Tailor in my own right, but that I'd been tugged – that despite her predictions, I was going to make something of myself.

I hadn't taken anything my family needed to get through the winter, and she knew it. She was a liar and… and… she was hurt, a little voice inside me said. Unbidden, a memory surfaced of Oak helping me to see how hard my mother had worked to keep me with her. I'd left her, just as my father had. I'd hurt her all over again.

Thinking of Oak left me with a faint sense of him again. He was struggling through the snow. What was he doing outside? No. I wouldn't be sucked in to caring. Not again – this was where it got me. It was just me against the world.

I fought my way ever upward through the snow, the wind beating at my back, slapping the huge snowflakes against me as it drove me on my way. My mind flew back to the last time I'd been out on my own in conditions like these. Then, I'd been looking for Oak. Now, I was fleeing him.

My mind flew to him briefly. He was in pain as he fought his way through the snow. No, I corrected myself, pushing all thoughts of him aside. That was just me. And it was his fault. If he'd left me where I was, I would have found out that Jewner had qualified me. I would have left Clearview to work as a Tailor with no expectation that people would like or accept me. I would have lived a quiet life, paying my way with my work, but keeping myself to myself. I wouldn't be feeling like this.

I finally reached the top of the hill. The snow bellowed past and away from me, instead of landing in my way. I took a few steps and was relieved to find that up here, the snow was only shin deep. I quickened my pace. I would keep the wind at my back, get as far away as possible and see where I ended up. Maybe I could find somewhere no one knew about me, somewhere that flaming Herald hadn't spread my mother's venom. Maybe then, I could live the only life I had left.

My heart dropped in my chest as I remembered that I'd left my back-sack behind. I had no proof I was qualified as a Tailor. I stopped in my tracks, looked up into the snowy sky, and screamed 'NOOOOOOOOOO!'

I had two choices. I could fight my way back through the storm to The Gathering to fetch my stuff, or I could continue on my way to goodness knew where, in the hope that a Tailor would take me on as an apprentice while I proved my worth all over again.

I turned and faced into the wind. It blew my hair back in a horizontal stream behind me and almost took me with it. I leant into it, my arms outstretched, and gasped as I tried to breathe the air that hurtled past me, but caught only a mouthful of snowflakes. I turned back around. The storm only confirmed what I already knew. Going back would be too hard.

I wrapped my cloak around myself and trudged onward. I ignored the fact that I could barely feel my feet. When I began to shiver, I couldn't find the energy to care. When the wind finally eased, taking the last of the clouds with it before it dropped completely, I barely had the strength to carry on lifting one foot after the other. I began to shiver more violently as the temperature dropped as suddenly as the wind had done. Or was it just my temperature that was plummeting? And what was that noise?

I turned to see a huge, black shape moving towards me. It seemed to be dragging one of its front legs through the snow, and looked as tired as I felt. I dropped to my knees.

Oak, what are you doing here?

I walk by your side.

I don't want you to. Not anymore.

Oak stumbled on his good front leg and almost went down. I felt his agony as he fought to stay on his feet.

What happened to you? I could barely frame the thought.

You are as aware as I.

Immediately, my mind was flooded with sensations and images, one after the other. I felt Oak trying to keep me with him so that I would experience the events in the dining hall through our bond, even as I allowed my mother's message to rip me away from him. When he felt me run from The Gathering, he pushed at the door of his field shelter, trying to follow. It wouldn't budge. He resorted to slamming into it with his shoulder, the point of which had fractured as he burst out into the snow.

He stumbled through the snow to the gate, which was shut. He couldn't jump it, injured as he was, and he felt me drawing ever further away from him, both in body and mind. He hurled himself at the fence, which splintered into his chest as it gave way.

He was bleeding and in agony, but his love for me was all of him. It obliterated his pain as it drove him onward through the storm until I saw myself through his eyes, staggering away from him in the distance. I felt his relief at the sight of his Bond-Partner. His place was with her as her place was with him. They had much to do, much to achieve. She needed him and he would be there for her, whatever it took.

Love for him flooded through me and in an instant, I

wondered at how I could have been so insanely stupid, how I could have let my mother come between us, how something that had been so amazing could have come to this. Where my strength had fled, now it coursed through me. I pushed myself back up onto my feet and staggered towards my big, strong, loyal horse. I flung my arms around him, feeling his pain anew. It almost drove me back down to my knees.

Oak, I'm so, so sorry. What can I do? How can I help you?

It is you who requires assistance. You have moisture that has frozen next to your skin.

My shivering became more violent still and I stumbled and fell. There was a muffled, scrunching sound next to me and Oak grunted in pain as he landed in the snow beside me.

Cloud In The Storm. Assistance approaches. Move close to me and take my body heat so that it does not arrive too late.

I couldn't get my thoughts together enough to reply to him, so I focused on doing as he said. I made it to my hands and knees and crawled through the snow until I felt the warmth of his belly under my hands. He would get cold, lying in the snow. I moved on a little further until I was lying across him, my front to his side.

I need to keep you warm too, I managed to tell him. I could feel his strength, his love for me pulsing through us both. I concentrated on its rhythm, its consistency. It was all there was.

I have no idea how much time passed before footsteps crunched in the snow beside us.

'Flaming lanterns, that's a lot of blood, how did he make it this far?' said a voice that sounded like Shann's.

'Rowena, can you hear me?' Adam's voice sounded by my ear. I couldn't reply and I couldn't bring myself to move. I blinked a few times and hoped that was enough. 'She's conscious, just about, I'm not sure how, she's like ice. We need to get her warmer, and quickly,' he said.

'I can have her up on Spider in front of me and take her back, if you can come back on foot with Oak, Adam? That way she'll have my body heat and Spider'll have us back at The Gathering in no time. Oh, hang on, wait… no. Surely not?'

'Oak wants to carry her back?' Adam said.

'Yep. Spider's pretty insistent it's what Oak wants. Peace told you that?'

'He had no need. There's far more to this than it's our business to understand, I think,' Adam said.

'By the look of him, Oak's going to have trouble getting up, let alone carrying Rowena. Where's all that blood coming from, anyway?'

There was a pause. 'From these wounds in his chest. They're not dreadful, there are just an awful lot of them. I think we'll take Rowena while Oak attempts to right himself, and then we can help her onto his back once he's upright, if I could ask you to assist me?'

'Sure thing.'

I was hauled off of Oak and then strong arms encircled me, holding me close. 'I've got you,' Shann said into my ear. 'We've all got you.'

'Oak,' I managed to whisper. 'Hesshurt.'

'Adam, she's talking, just about. She's slurring her words, but she said Oak's hurt,' Shann said, then whispered to me, 'It's okay, we know, Adam's here, he'll have a closer look once Oak's up.'

I gathered all the love I had for my horse and drew as much strength from it as I could so that I could shake my head against Shann's shoulder. 'Won't up hissown. Pu'me shnow. Hel' him.'

'Adam, I think it's worse than it looks, Rowena doesn't think he can get up on his own, she says we need to help him.'

'His shoulder is fractured,' agreed Adam. 'He needs a Bone-Singer to heal it, but unfortunately, he just has you and me. He's a strong one, though and very determined, judging by his insistence on following Rowena while he's this injured.'

'Spider, get over here, could you?' I was lowered gently to the ground. 'There you go, lean back against Spider's legs for a minute,' Shann told me. 'I can't have you lying in the snow. I'll help Oak and then I'll be right back.'

There was the sound of shuffling in the snow. 'Ready?' Adam said.

'Ready,' Shann agreed.

Oak's agony ripped through me as he reached forward with his front legs in order to heave himself to his feet. Adam and Shann grunted with their efforts to support him, and I could feel them pushing into his back so that all momentum generated by his hind legs would push him forward and up. It wasn't enough.

I wanted to cry for my horse's pain, for my inability to help him, to even open my eyes and see him as he fought to get back on his feet so that he could carry me home.

'We need Spider. Good job you made me go back for the rope,' Shann said. Then, his voice by my ear again, he whispered, 'I'm going to have to lay you back down in the snow. I'm sorry, but we won't be long.'

I was wrapped in another cloak, then another on top of that, and lowered onto my side. 'Draw your knees into your stomach, Rowena,' said Adam, gently and I felt my legs being moved until I was curled up. 'That's it, you'll lose less heat. We'll just be a moment.'

I was back with Oak as I should always have been, as I always would be from now on. I felt the rope being fed around him behind his elbows, his front legs lifting him off of the ground slightly, still stretched out in front of him as they were, still causing him agony as they were. I felt Adam and Shann leaning into his back once more, and I sent all of the love in the world to my horse. I felt him gather our strength and push with his hind legs just as Spider took his weight on the rope and pulled. With a grunt of pain, Oak was on his feet.

'He really is as strong as an oak, isn't he?' said Shann. 'You're a brave lad, Oak, and Rowena's lucky to have you. Are you sure about carrying her, fella?' There was a pause. 'Spider says he's still sure.'

'Then we'd better get her on board, hadn't we? There's really no time to waste,' Adam said.

I was lifted to my feet and then suddenly, I was upside down over what I presumed to be Shann's shoulder, and vaguely mortified that I was in no position to do anything about it. I was hauled through the air before landing on my front over a warm, furry back. Oak's back.

'Do we try to get her upright?' Shann said.

'No, Oak can't carry one of us to hold her up. She's best like that, I think, his body heat will warm her,' said Adam.

Oak waited until I'd finished being thoroughly manhandled, and then took his first lurching steps back to The Gathering. My body wanted to drift into unconsciousness and there was a part of my mind that wanted to let it – but the rest of me fought hard to stay with my horse.

I pushed all my love for him into his body, for I knew because he'd taught me, that from love came resilience, and from resilience came strength.

Chapter Twenty-One

I opened my eyes to see Shann peering down at me. I sat bolt upright and Shann leapt back, holding his nose. I rubbed my forehead where we had connected.

'Oak. Where is he? How is he? What happened, how long have I been out of it? Flaming lanterns, I swore I'd get him back here if it was the last thing I did, is he alright?' I twisted around to sit on the side of the bed. My feet were bandaged and rested on a thick, blue rug that wasn't mine. I looked around, wildly. A fire roared in the fireplace, above which a galloping horse was carved into the mantelpiece. This wasn't my room. 'Where am I?'

'I think you've broken my nose. Adam, take a look, would you?' Shann said, tilting his head back.

Oak? As soon as I reached out to him, I knew he was lying down in a deep straw bed, snoozing. He was tired and his chest wounds were a little sore, but he was otherwise free of pain. *Oh, thank goodness you're alright. I'm so sorry, I must have passed out.*

Yet not before we carried one another back here.

I grinned with relief.

'It's not funny,' Shann said, looking at me out of the corner of his eye while Adam inspected his nose.

'It's not broken, either,' Adam said, and handed him a mug of tea. 'Here, take this. It was for Rowena's pain, but I have a feeling she might appreciate the quiet that should result if you drink it.' He winked at me. 'I'll get you another. In answer to your questions, you did get Oak back here yesterday evening before you passed out completely, and you're in my bed. It was easier to treat you here, with a Tissue-Singer just down the hall in case we needed her to save your toes, and all my supplies just next door. I wasn't sure you were going to live long enough for either of us to help you, mind, but you're a strong one, like that Bond-Partner of yours.'

'I battled storms, kept her warm, helped her horse to get her back here in the coldest temperatures I've ever experienced, spent half the night helping you, Adam, to treat her Bond-Partner and stop her toes falling off from frostbite while she sleeps peacefully, and what does she do? She headbutts me in the nose,' Shann said to Adam's retreating back.

'Weren't you riding Spider for most of that time, while Adam walked?' I said. 'And wasn't it Oak who kept me warm, both before you found me, and afterward, on our way back here?'

'Well I was all for stripping off and wrapping us both in our cloaks so I could warm you with my body heat while riding Spider back, but I was over-ruled,' Shann said, the mischievous glint I'd seen the day before returning to his eyes. I couldn't help but laugh.

Adam handed me a mug of one of his herbal teas. 'I gather you've already met Shann?'

'Thanks. I had the brief misfortune, yes.' The events of the previous day flooded back to me and my smile vanished. I looked down at my bandaged feet. 'That was before I made a mess of everything.'

Adam crouched down in front of me. 'Your feet will recover, and I'm sure you've now checked in with Oak, and know he's doing well. While painful, his fracture wasn't complicated and we have a fine Bone-Singer in residence here at the moment; Holly healed it within a few minutes. As he's already mentioned, Shann was an excellent assistant while I was removing the splinters from Oak's chest, cleaning his wounds and applying the necessary unguents to them.' He smiled. 'In a few days' time, when you're back on your feet, you can start all over.'

I shook my head. 'Everyone thinks I'm a thief, thanks to my mother.'

'None of our horses tend to waste an opportunity to remind us all that each of us has our own challenges to work through, and we have the best chance of doing that if we are left alone to do it,' Adam said.

'But the Herald's message isn't true, not really,' I said. 'I worked in my mother's shop and used offcuts and scraps to make my Tailor's qualification portfolio. When Oak tugged me, I knew my mother would never give me a Quest Ceremony, so I had to take what I'd need to survive long enough to find him.' I began to shiver.

Shann sat down on the bed next to me and threw my cloak around my shoulders. 'You didn't have a Quest Ceremony? Weren't your family proud of you for being tugged? Even if they weren't, surely the rest of your village turned out to wish you well when you left to find Oak? Surely they were proud that one of their own was going to be Horse-Bonded?'

I bit my lip. 'I didn't tell any of them. They wouldn't have been happy, and they wouldn't have been proud. I'm not well regarded in Clearview.'

'But...' Shann began.

'Well, I think that clears that up,' said Adam. 'I will let the truth be known. Please believe, Rowena, that you and Oak are welcome here.' There was something about the way he spoke that left me in no doubt what he said was true.

'Thank you. And you, Shann, I mean I suppose you did help.' I winked at Adam.

'Help? Help? I'm exhausted and so is Spider, and I've only gone and let Justin rope me into helping him fix not only the fence that your horse barged his way through, but the doors to the field shelter that are hanging off their hinges in shreds.'

'You needn't pretend to be outraged when you can't stop the corners of your mouth from smiling,' I said. 'Give Spider a hug from me and tell him thanks for everything he did to help Oak and me, while you're out there helping... Justin, was it?'

Shann stood up. 'That's me dismissed then, is it?'

'You'll be just in time to catch the tail end of breakfast if you bolt for it now, Shann,' Adam said, 'and I think we both need to leave Rowena in peace so she can rest.' He turned to me and chuckled as the door banged shut behind Shann. 'I see you have his measure already.'

I grinned. 'I like him. He makes everything seem lighter, doesn't he?'

'That he does, my dear, that he does. He wasn't exaggerating, though, when he told you of the work he and Justin have ahead of them in order to fix the damage Oak caused. I was just leaving here to go to the dining hall yesterday when I felt Peace's agitation at Oak's attempts to push his way out of their field shelter and paddock. I rushed to let Oak out, but I'm afraid I was too late. By the time I'd made my way there through the storm, he'd gone, leaving a trail of blood and what can only be described as carnage, behind him. Nothing could have kept him from you.' Adam looked straight at me. 'But I think you already know that.'

I did, but his manner drove the knowledge of it in deeper. I felt calm, confident, and at peace with the world. My eyelids began to flutter.

Adam was by my side in an instant. He lifted the sheet and quilts. 'Swing your legs back in. That's it, you need to sleep. I'm going to breakfast now. I'll bring some food back and leave it on the bedside table here for when you wake. If you need anything else, just call out and I'll hear you.'

'Thank you, Adam, for everything,' I said, sleepily.

'Don't worry about anything, Rowena, just rest.'

Oak? He was asleep. I smiled as I drifted off too.

The days that followed were among the happiest of my life. As soon as I was up and about, I was allocated my share of the chores undertaken by all at The Gathering so it could run efficiently. I was initially placed in the kitchen so that I could sit down while my feet continued to recover, but was assured that once I was walking around again, I would be helping to care for the livestock out in the paddocks, chopping wood, taking my turn in the wash rooms, distributing wood and dung bricks to the accommodation blocks, all of which I looked forward to doing in gratitude for being there. In addition, I worked as a Tailor, just as all of us contributed the Trade or Skill in which we qualified before being Horse-Bonded.

The Tailor's workshop was always a happy place to be. Once I'd worked through my share of the day's orders, I was free to experiment with new designs of my own, many of which were soon being made to order once people saw them on the mannequins that were dotted around the workshop.

Much as I loved spending time working, eating and living alongside people whom I liked and who seemed to like me in return, it was when I was with Oak that I was at my most content. I was on his back, exploring the full extent of The Gathering, as soon as my feet were recovered enough for me to spend any length of time outside. He insisted his back had fully recovered from the bruising sustained by my early attempts at riding, and that my body required the reminder of how to move with his before our lessons began in earnest.

The Weather-Singers were predicting a warmer spell, during which hopefully some of the snow would melt and give us all a break from its inconvenience, but I was glad to see that regardless, my riding lessons could begin, thanks to the enormous canopies that stretched over the paddocks put aside for riding practice. As we passed them, Feryl, the Master of Riding, was just coming out through one of the gates.

'Riding bareback? Not advisable for someone with as little experience as you, Rowena. Just hop off, would you, until Oak's saddle is finished and we can begin your lessons properly? That's tomorrow, by the way. The ground is still hard, but for your first lessons, Oak will only be walking. By the time you're ready to ride at increased speed, the warmer weather should be here if the Weather-Singers' forecast is right, and the ground should be a bit softer. Off you get.'

I shook my head. 'We're good, thanks, it was Oak who insisted I ride. My feet are still a bit sore, you see.'

Feryl frowned. 'I disapprove of riding without a saddle too often, even when one is an experienced rider, which quite clearly, you are not.'

'Well happily for me, Oak doesn't disapprove, so we'll be on our way and we'll see you tomorrow, shall we?' I said, cheerfully, and was relieved to be able to maintain my balance as Oak moved on past him.

As long as you...

Stay with you in our bond, I can't lose my balance, yes, darling boy, I know.

Then you are ready. Oak moved to the side of the path so that he walked in previously untrodden snow, and leapt into trot and then into a slow, rocking canter. I whooped and hollered with delight, causing those working in the paddocks to look up, smile and wave. I waved back, completely confident in both my bond and my balance. When the paddocks finally ran out and we burst onto the river bank, Oak slowed to a walk and turned back for the buildings.

Where are you going? I'm not ready to go back, I told him.

We have achieved our purpose.

I sensed that he meant more than just my body remembering what to do. *Feryl? That was for his benefit?*

The time has arrived for the conventions and traditions of the Horse-Bonded to be challenged. You and I are the forerunners of the process.

Challenge tradition and convention? I like it. What do you want me to do?

For now we merely insist on treading our own path when appropriate. That will cause a low level of discomfort to those most resistant to change. There will come a bonded pair capable of causing the far greater degree of disruption necessary for major change. Our efforts will allow them and you to better recognise the way forward.

I'm intrigued. How will I recognise this pair?

They will be unmistakable.

Why is it time for the Horse-Bonded to be challenged? The

communities of The New wouldn't have survived without them passing on their horses' wisdom.

The Horse-Bonded have become too comfortable in their roles. There is so much more they can do but they will not recognise the fact until it becomes impossible to ignore. You will be much needed in the future. To that end there is a task we must undertake to ensure that you are best able to assist when the time comes.

And that is?

We must visit your mother.

A myriad of emotions hit me all at once. My heart leapt at the thought of seeing Heron, Finch, Kestrel, Robin, Swift, Crow, Kite and Wren again, at hugging them all, introducing them to Oak, and hearing about everything they'd been up to. It sank at the thought of all the disapproving looks I would get from the villagers of Clearview – but then leapt again as I envisaged their mouths dropping at the sight of my beautiful horse. And then, when I couldn't avoid thinking about her any longer, a dull pain throbbed in my heart and stomach at the thought of seeing my mother again.

I can't go back there, Oak.

You can. You must refuse to feel that which was only ever her pain. You must hand it back to her. It is the only way forward for both of you. He walked slowly, carefully beneath me.

But we can't go now, surely? I mean, we won't even get there, the snow will have cut them off.

We will remain here until the conditions are more straightforward. You will learn to ride. I will increase my stamina. By the time we leave we will be capable of covering a substantial distance each day.

But I can already ride, I'm doing it now.

You merely follow my movement. You must learn to give my

body signals it can follow so that we can achieve more.

Riding was easy, especially once I had a saddle, I found over the weeks and months that followed. Feryl was complementary about my body's ability to follow Oak's movement, and I soon picked up how to ask my horse to speed up, slow down, and turn, using my legs and seat.

We often rode out with Shann and Spider, Shann's friend, Justin and Justin's Bond-Partner, a tall, chestnut stallion called Gas. Both Spider and Gas were much more lightly built than Oak and fleeter of foot, but Oak gave it his all when the conditions allowed us to move at greater speed. As time went by, the distance the faster horses managed to create between themselves and Oak was less and less.

By the time the snow had turned to slush and the wind had lost its bite, Oak and I were almost as fit, strong and confident in our ridden partnership as we were in our bond. Almost. There were times when Feryl was teaching us that I felt Oak was quieter in his mind than usual, as if he were waiting for Feryl to say more, to push us on further.

There is more to be gained from the ridden interaction, was all he would tell me when I asked him what was going on. When I insisted he elaborate, he would distance himself and I couldn't decide whether it was because he couldn't tell me what he was waiting for, or whether he wouldn't. But each time, I had a sense from him that what he was waiting for would come. That it would be okay. It was how he viewed life in general and he was always right, so I let it slide.

I knew that the snows persisted for longer in the mountains than at The Gathering, but when the slush had melted, the mud had dried, the early bulbs had begun to bloom and the birds swooped overhead with renewed vigour, I knew it would be safe to travel.

'Do you want me and Spider to come with you? It's been a while since we've been out and about to the villages, and I've never been up into the mountains,' Shann told me through a mouthful of vegetables.

I screwed my nose up. 'That's disgusting. Didn't your mother ever tell you not to talk with your mouth full?'

Justin looked from me to Shann and grinned, but kept quiet.

'She may have done,' Shann said. 'What about you, Jus, you and Gas could do with an outing too, couldn't you? How about it, Ro?'

Justin looked up at me and raised his eyebrows, lifting his well-defined brow so that his brown eyes looked a little less serious than usual. He shook his head at Shann. 'Read the signs, mate. Rowena needs to go alone.'

The thought of having them with me was tempting in that I knew they would stop me dwelling on what would happen when I reached Clearview, but the thought of anyone bearing witness to what I would face there was intolerable. And besides, I knew I would need to concentrate on my bond with Oak if I were to have any chance of doing whatever it was he thought I needed to do there.

I shook my head. 'Tempting as it is to be able to see partially chewed food at every mealtime on the way there, Justin's right. I need to go on my own.' When Shann opened his mouth to protest, I shook my head, firmly. 'Thanks, but no thanks. This is something I need to do alone.' My voice wavered slightly and Shann's eyes changed from mischievous to concerned.

He nodded. 'Take care, then. Okay?'

I grinned. 'Oak will be with me. I'll be fine.'

Chapter Twenty-Two

Oak and I left after breakfast the following morning. Shann and Adam appeared at Oak's field shelter as I was saddling him, to see us off.

'Is that slobber in your hair? The green suits you but I'm not sure the slime does, necessarily,' said Shann.

I sighed and turned to where Peace stood just behind me. 'You can't help yourself, can you?' I said to him, and stroked his nose. His soft, brown eyes were bright, but he looked a little thinner and his coat wasn't moulting out like those of the other horses. He wiggled his nose on the top of my head in response.

Adam appeared by my side and handed me a clean handkerchief. 'I'm so sorry, please take this,' he said.

I chuckled. 'What's a bit of slobber between friends? Thanks.' I took the handkerchief and wiped my hair.

'All set, then? You're really sure...'

'Yes, Shann, I'm really sure I don't want you coming with me. I'll see you in a few months. Work on your table manners while

I'm gone?' He chuckled and cupped his hands, ready to give me a leg up onto Oak.

I ignored him and turned to Adam. 'I don't know what Oak and I would have done without you on the way here, when we got here, after we got here… you've done more for me than anyone ever has, and well, thanks.'

Adam enveloped me in a warm hug. 'Whatever you need to do, you can do it,' he whispered.

I gulped. 'Thank you. You'll be here when we get back?'

He winked. 'Maybe, maybe not, I think we'll find that out when you get back, won't we?'

'Ahem?' I turned to see Shann still waiting for me to accept a leg up from him.

I grinned at Adam and rubbed Peace's ear. 'Take care of each other, then. Okay?'

Adam smiled. 'We always do.'

'Seriously, now,' said Shann, still bent over.

I rolled my eyes and put my knee in his hands, ready to jump.

'On three,' he said. I jumped on the count and he almost pitched me over the other side.

'Flaming lanterns, Shann, I'm not that heavy.'

'You're welcome,' he said. 'And for everything else – fighting through a storm to rescue you, getting you back here, saving your horse and your feet, helping you to ride…'

'You're a regular hero, and don't we all know it,' I said. 'Thank you, Shann, for everything you just said. Now just stand aside, if you would, so we can leave?' The glint in his eyes gave him away as he attempted to feign disbelief.

'I'm charming,' he said loudly to Adam as they followed Oak and me to the paddock gate. 'Everyone thinks so, except Rowena.'

'I think Rowena is just a little less easily impressed than the rest of us,' Adam said with a chuckle. 'And that's no bad thing, is it? Sometimes it takes someone with the strength to mount a challenge, in order for us all to move in a different direction.'

I swung around in my saddle. 'Has Peace told you too?' I said to Adam.

'Told me what?' Adam looked up at me, innocently.

I shook my head and laughed. 'You're so frustrating, it's actually funny. I'll miss you.' I sighed at Shann's raised eyebrows. 'Oh, for goodness' sake, and you. Let us go now, before I have to ask Oak to gallop away from you.'

Shann grinned. He and Adam both raised a hand, waved and then headed back to the buildings as Oak and I made for the river. I waved to everyone working in the fields as we passed, and everyone but a group of Earth-Singers – who were intent on combining their voices and intentions to lift a substantial layer of earth above one of the fields while others lay out tiny onions, ready to be covered when the Earth-Singers allowed the soil to fall back down – waved back.

I felt a pang of homesickness. I loved it here. I was leaving acceptance, friendship and happiness to return to the place of misery in which I'd grown up.

Oak increased his presence in my mind.

I know, you're with me. Come on then, let's see what you've got.

I moved effortlessly with Oak as he moved up to a trot and then a canter. The corners of my mouth began to turn up and soon, I was grinning. We were leaving, but we would be back.

The river flew past us but when Oak opened up his stride, we almost matched its pace. I yelled with the joy of spring, of being with my horse, of feeling so alive.

My horse was fit and strong beneath me. He alternated

between walk, trot and canter, eating up the distance without tiring himself. I completely lost track of time. I only noticed how hungry I was and how low the sun was in the sky, when Oak came to a stop by a trickling stream in open pastureland.

We will eat and then rest until the sun rises, Oak informed me.

Right you are.

I dismounted, unsaddled him and rummaged in my back-sack for the grooming kit I'd been given at The Gathering. I selected a stiff-bristled brush and groomed him thoroughly from head to tail, coughing every now and then at all the loose hair, dried sweat and dust I was liberating from his rapidly moulting coat. Where his summer coat was beginning to show through the long winter hairs that stubbornly hung on, it was sleek and an even darker black than his winter coat, if that were possible. I couldn't wait to see the horse who was emerging from underneath all of the insulation that had kept us both alive.

Once I'd removed all of the loose hair, I selected my hoof pick and asked him to lift each of his huge feet in turn, so that I could check them for stones or anything else that might cause him a problem.

When I was satisfied that Oak was clean and comfortable, I removed my cloak and shook it until most of his hair and dirt had been carried away on the breeze. It had been warm all day, especially when the sun had broken through the clouds, but now there was a nip in the air. I glanced around and could see no trees anywhere close. There would be no fire for me tonight. I took my winter hat, several pullovers and a spare pair of leggings from my back-sack and donned them, then put my cloak back on over the top.

I lay a waxed sheet on the ground, arranged my back-sack and saddle on it, draped Oak's thick, sheepskin saddle pad over the top of them both to dry and air, then sat down, leaning back against the underside of the saddle. Oak's warmth still emanated from it, seeping through my clothes and warming my back.

My stomach rumbled loudly. I was out in the open for what promised to be a chilly night, but nestled against my saddle with a lap full of cheese sandwiches and fruit, while my horse munched contentedly nearby and the stream trickled past me, I couldn't have been more content. I fell asleep as soon as the sun went down, after instructing Oak to wake me when he wanted to sleep.

I woke before he needed me to. A restlessness had entered my dreams, a feeling that there was something I should be doing, somewhere else I needed to be; that someone needed me. I came awake with a gasp and sat up in the darkness. 'Oak?'

He lay at my feet. Curled around my feet, actually, his nose resting in the grass. His long, deep breaths caused his crumpled nostrils to flutter. He'd eaten his fill and was content to doze for now while keeping watch over us both. But sleep would be better. I smiled to myself, glad that making our bond a part of me to the extent I had, allowed me to hopefully be as good a partner to him as he was to me.

Sleep, Oak.

He didn't argue or question. Within seconds, he was sound off. I grinned, just able to make him out in the darkness. I crawled over to him and curled up against his belly, revelling in his warmth and companionship. I lay there, listening to his long, even breaths, punctuated every now and then by the rustling and calling of night animals going about their business nearby. There were no sounds that gave me cause for concern. Oak slept soundly on, confident that his trust in me was well placed.

I was almost disappointed when the sky began to lighten and Oak, who had been lying flat out in the grass for some time, jerked and heaved his head and neck off the ground so that his weight now rested on his elbows.

Welcome back, sleepy, I teased. I felt a little sleepy again myself, but I'd enjoyed being awake, savouring the night and Oak's trust in me.

I would eat. You should eat and rest further. Then we will continue.

Nothing like receiving orders to ruin the moment, but fine, I'll get out of your way. I grinned as I crawled back to nestle into the underside of Oak's saddle, its flaps curling around me.

I shivered. A heavy dew had settled over us and I missed Oak's heat. I pulled a food parcel from my back-sack and munched on its contents while watching Oak grazing in the light of the early dawn. Then I stood and walked around a bit until I felt warmer, before curling back up against the saddle and closing my eyes.

I woke to warm breath on my face and Oak's nose right in front of my eyes. He removed it, and I blinked at the sunlight that took its place. The morning was well in progress. I sat up and leapt to my feet with a start. *Sorry, you should have woken me before.*

There was no need.

But the morning's almost half gone.

We move when we move. We rest when we rest. His thought was as matter of fact as always, and I found myself nodding.

Fair enough.

I brushed him down and saddled him, packed my extra clothes and waxed sheet into my back-sack, which I donned before putting a foot into one of my stirrups and swinging easily onto Oak's back.

∼

Our fast pace and direct line took us to Mountainlee in less than a week. Goats roaming freely, their bells tinkling, told me that we were nearly there long before I saw the smoke unfurling from its chimneys.

Oak walked carefully over the short grass interspersed with rocks, as the cottages came into sight.

I'll dismount to make it easier for you, I told him.

Neither your weight nor your balance disturbs me.

You think if I ride you, I'll find it easier to stay with you in my mind. I don't need to deal with the villagers here through our bond, Oak. I've got this.

As do I. He really did mean the rocky ground. Thunder and lightning, I'd stepped away from the place I shared with him in my mind without even realising it; I'd seen the cottages that housed those at whom I'd shouted the last time I was here, and immediately assumed that he doubted me as, I realised by my attempt to convince both him and me, I clearly doubted myself. He would have been right to.

Yet I do not. Your lapse in concentration was brief and your return to our bond immediate. You have nothing to prove. Our visit here will merely allow us to provide the help that we were unable to when last we were here.

Sudden movement caught my eye. Someone was standing, waving with both arms, on the hillside between the village and the barns. I grinned. It could only be Gert or Hilva. I waved back, and as Oak continued to pick his way closer to Mountainlee, I watched the figure run down to the village and reappear a few minutes later with another. As they hurried towards Oak and me, they soon indeed resolved into my friends. I leapt down from Oak's back and rushed to meet them.

'You and Oak are a sight for sore eyes, look at you, Rowena, riding as if you were born to it,' Hilva said, pulling me into a warm hug.

'Let her go, Hilv, you'll pull her over,' Gert said and when his wife obliged, drew me into a hug of his own. Then they both rushed to Oak, marvelling over how handsome he was now that they could see him without the thick covering of fur he'd had in the winter.

Oak nuzzled them both as they stroked him and spoke to him as if he were a long-lost son. I couldn't stop smiling.

I put an arm around each of them. 'You'll never know what you did for us both, taking us in when you did. If there's anything we can do for you while we're here, please don't hesitate to ask.'

They both turned to look at me, Gert with his eyebrows raised and Hilva with a warm smile.

'Your voice is different,' Hilva said. 'You're happy.' She reached a hand up to squeeze mine as it clasped her shoulder. 'And I'm happy for you. You and Oak will of course stay with us.'

I smiled as I released them. 'We'd love to, thank you.'

Hilva reached up and tugged my chin. 'Smiling suits you. Look how beautiful you are.'

'I feel a celebration coming on, looks like I'll be needing to fetch another barrel of homebrew from the cellar,' Gert said. 'Come on, let's get you both settled in.'

We turned to walk to the village, Gert and Hilva either side of me, and Oak walking behind. 'Would you mind if I invite anyone who wants Oak's counsel to come and see him in your barn?' I asked.

'If... um, if anyone wants to see you both, then yes, of course,' Hilva said.

'Thank you. Then, if there's homebrew on offer, it would be rude of me to turn it down.'

Gert chuckled. 'That's my girl.'

I glanced over my shoulder to check that Oak was alright. He was walking more easily now, the rocks fewer in the immediate vicinity of the village. I should remount, I decided suddenly. From my place in my bond with him, I knew I could stay there without being mounted, regardless of what the villagers threw at me – but they would feel more confident asking us for help if I arrived on horseback, my training from The Gathering obvious, my bond with Oak clearly established. We were here for them and together, we would do what I'd prevented us from doing last time.

Oak's eye met mine and I felt his love, his pride in me. I smiled and rubbed his wide, black forehead, then leapt up onto his back.

Gert and Hilva both looked up at me. Hilva smiled and Gert nodded. They waited until Oak was between them and then walked either side of him. By the time we reached the cobbles of Mountainlee, some of the villagers were there to meet us. I didn't recognise any of them now that they weren't covered from head to toe in winter clothing, but they clearly recognised me. I saw their anger, disappointment and disapproval. I'd let them down. I'd made a mistake. I would put it right.

'If I may, I'd like to say a few words,' I called out to them. 'When Oak and I were here last, I was newly bonded and finding it difficult to adjust to my new situation. I took that out on you, and I'm sorry. We're back here so I can make that right. I've changed a lot during the winter, and it's all down to this wise, beautiful, patient, amazing horse.' I leant forward and rubbed Oak's neck. 'I'm sure all of the horses give good advice, but take it from me, you won't get better than from this one, he's one in a million.' My voice broke slightly and I bit my lip. Hilva put a hand to my leg and I smiled down at her. Then I looked back at those who had gathered to listen to me. 'Oak will be staying in Gert and Hilva's barn, and I'll be staying at their cottage. Please pass the word around that anyone wanting his counsel can knock for me there.'

Oak turned for the barns.

'Can I come now?' a tall, heavily-built woman called out behind us.

I smiled at her over my shoulder. 'Of course. Oak's pretty good at counselling while he's eating, he does it for me all the time.' I winked and she hurried after us.

'What about you, Rowena? Don't you need to rest and eat?' Hilva whispered up to me.

'I need to do this more, I think.'

'Well I'll bring a hot meal out to you, then. It may not be as cold as when you were last here, but it isn't warm, and sitting in the barn, you'll be shivering in no time.'

'That would be very welcome, thank you.'

The rest of the afternoon blurred into the evening as villager after villager came to ask Oak for his advice. As I'd come to expect, he never told anyone what to do or say, but gave a similar message to all of them in a hundred different ways. Each and every time, he encouraged them to view their concerns and disputes from an angle other than that which they were currently adopting. And each and every time, just as when he counselled me, the exact meaning of at least part of his advice wasn't immediately easy to grasp hold of. Villagers who had arrived full of opinion and emotion left nodding thoughtfully to themselves, often with a slight frown, as if they recognised his advice was good, but couldn't immediately discern what they should do with it.

It's to slow them down, isn't it? I asked Oak whilst watching the last of the day's visitors scratching his head as he wandered out of the barn, bumping into the doorframe then looking at it in surprise. He was a different man from when he'd arrived at the barn at a purposeful march, full of the perceived wrong against him. *You tell them what they need to change in themselves so they don't see their problem in the same way and it stops being a problem, but if you just did that alone, they wouldn't fully accept it. So you slow them down. In their heads. Their thoughts. You get them thinking and wondering, so their minds have time to accept your advice.* I grinned as I thought back over the day, to the looks of surprise and respect as I relayed Oak's advice, followed by those of confusion. *So that's what I look like when you do it to me.*

Oak merely lifted his head from the huge pile of hay I'd shaken up for him, and watched me, his jaw grinding rhythmically from side to side.

It's simple, really, isn't it? I observed. *If humans just stepped back and saw things the way horses do, we wouldn't have half the problems we do.*

Yet the human tendency to create discord is equal to the opportunity created by the discord.

Opportunity? For what?

For learning. For advancement. He continued to stare at me.

You're saying that problems are necessary so we can learn from them? Wouldn't it just be nicer to be happy all the time?

Human happiness is precarious so long as it relies for its existence on the meeting of expectations.

You once told me that feeling rejected is really just the unfulfillment of expectations.

The same mistake can have many guises. Oak dropped his head and selected more hay.

I shifted on the straw bale upon which I was perched, and frowned thoughtfully. Then I grinned. *I'll just leave the way everyone else did, shall I? I've been Oaked – that's my new word for those who come into your presence feeling entirely themselves and leave feeling like they don't know anything, but are somehow better for it. I need some of Gert's homebrew.* I hugged him, checked his water trough was full, then made my way through the darkness to Gert and Hilva's cottage.

Chapter Twenty-Three

I sat at the kitchen table with my head in my hands. I was sure it hadn't pounded this much last time. There was a thud on the chair opposite me and the table juddered. I winced, then swallowed in an attempt to persuade the contents of my stomach to stay there.

'Sorry, I banged my knee. You look how I feel,' groaned Gert.

There was a crash from the pantry, as if two saucepans had been banged together on purpose. 'Well that will teach you not to make it so strong next time, won't it?' Hilva called out. Footsteps approached, then her voice sounded softly in my ear. 'Sorry for the noise, dear, you couldn't have known this batch was so much stronger than the last. I didn't know myself until Gert admitted it during the night, in between heaving his guts up.' Her voice strengthened again. 'Thank goodness I didn't partake, eh Gert? There'd be no one fit to get porridge down the two of you, would there?'

My stomach lurched at the thought. 'I'm never drinking anything, ever again.'

'You see? Rowena has sense. You, on the other hand, will do this over and over.' A pan banged down on the stove and pain exploded in my head. 'Will you be up to seeing anyone today, Rowena, dear?'

'I'm hoping everyone who needed to, came to see us yesterday but if anyone knocks, I'm available as long as they speak quietly,' I whispered, unable to bear the sound of my voice in my head. 'Thank goodness Oak doesn't speak out loud.'

I'd barely managed to get my breakfast down when the first knock sounded on the front door.

'I'm not sure we've ever had a Horse-Bonded with a hangover before.' Gert chuckled and then stopped suddenly, one hand going to his forehead, the other to his stomach.

'That's because none of them have had the misfortune to stay with us,' said Hilva. 'I'll get the door. Shall I tell whoever it is that you'll meet them up at the barn, Rowena? You'll feel better for the walk up there in the fresh air.'

I nodded and got slowly to my feet. 'Thanks. What are you up to today, Gert?'

'I'm going back to bed.'

I banged my chair against the table. 'Oooops, sorry. See you later, then.' I grinned at his scowl, which turned into a weak grin of his own.

I stepped out onto the front step, breathed in the cold, mountain air, and immediately felt better. The clear, spring sky was an almost startling shade of blue through which birds soared, chirruping merrily. The wild mountain flowers were a mass of colour either side of the path to the barn, and up towards the mountains themselves, as far as I could see.

By the time I reached the barn, I was whistling, softly. Hilva's porridge had settled my stomach, the air had, as she said, cleared my head, and I was going to spend another day with my wise, beautiful horse. There were four people standing, chatting between themselves as they waited at the paddock gate.

I smiled. 'Morning, who's first?'

It took a further two days for Oak to make his way through everyone who wanted his counsel. When, late in the afternoon of the second day, several hours passed with no sign of anyone else coming to see him, I began to reconcile myself with the fact that the following morning, we would move on towards Clearview.

Over dinner that evening, Gert tried to persuade me to join him in another evening of homebrew, and Hilva tried to induce me to stay for a few days longer "just to relax a bit before you go home". Neither succeeded. When smiling and politely shaking my head failed to stop either of them from continuing in their efforts, I finally raised my hands.

'Gert, thank you for teaching me my limits when it comes to alcohol. Hilva, thank you for teaching me how to manage a hangover, although I don't intend needing to do it again. And thank you both for showing me what it's like to have parents. I'm not your daughter, but in the short time I've spent with you, you've treated me as if I am, and I'll never forget it.'

Hilva rushed around to where I sat, and hugged me. 'You're always welcome here, you and Oak. Promise me you won't be a stranger? You'll come back whenever you can?'

'I promise.'

Gert cleared his throat. When I looked up at him, he raised his glass of water to me and took a sip. 'Always welcome,' he repeated. He got up and went into the pantry, then reappeared with Kerk's back-sack and hunting gear. 'You'll be wanting to return these.' He looked into my eyes with sorrow in his own.

Pain stabbed through my heart. 'You know, don't you?' I breathed. Hilva sat down next to me and took my hand.

Gert nodded. 'A Herald passed through the village the day after you left. I didn't believe you were a thief, neither did Hilva. We tried to stop him telling anyone else, but you know what Heralds are like, take themselves a bit too seriously sometimes, if you ask me. Everyone here believed him, but they don't now.'

I suddenly felt very tired and overwhelmingly sad. 'He took a direct route to The Gathering. He'd been and gone by the time Oak and I got there.'

Hilva gasped. 'So everyone at The Gathering thought you were a thief when you arrived there?'

I nodded. 'And it's true. I took the food and hunting gear I needed in order to go looking for Oak, without asking.'

Hilva stood up suddenly, her chair crashing to the floor behind her, and put her hands on her hips. 'But you shouldn't have needed to ask. You should have been given everything you needed for your trip during your Quest Ceremony... ohhhh. You didn't have one? What sort of mother doesn't give her child a Quest Ceremony when they've been chosen by a horse? She would have let you go without the means to feed yourself, to keep yourself alive? You could have starved to death, frozen to death, in fact you almost did, anyway.'

'I didn't tell her I was being tugged. She wouldn't have believed me, she would have tried to stop me and she would never have given me what I needed, so I took it and left during the night. And now I'm going back to face her. To face them all. Thanks, Gert, I will indeed be needing to return those.'

Hilva's voice shook. 'We'll come with you, won't we Gert?' She looked to her husband, who nodded. 'I'll give that woman a piece of my mind, just see if I don't, you shouldn't have to go back and face her alone.'

I smiled sadly. 'Thank you, both of you, but I won't be alone. Oak will be with me.'

Gert and Hilva both looked in the direction of the barn, and then back to me.

Hilva sat back down with a sigh. 'Are you sure he'll be enough?'

My smile was stronger this time. 'I'm sure.'

I was up at sunrise the following morning. I packed my back-sack, attached the hunting gear and extra back-sack to it and left it by the front door. Hilva and Gert were already in the kitchen eating porridge and drinking tea. A steaming bowl of the former and a mug of the latter sat on the table awaiting me. I smiled and sat down. 'Morning.'

'Sleep well?' Gert said.

I nodded. 'You didn't though, you look tired. And you, Hilva. Are you alright? Are you going down with something?'

Hilva shot a look at Gert and smiled at me. 'We're fine, dear. You just get that little lot down you, and if you want more, help yourself.'

'Okay, thank you.' They were strangely silent as I ate my breakfast and drank my tea. I swallowed my last mouthful of porridge and asked, 'Are you sure you're alright?'

Gert nodded. 'We're fine, just a little worried about you.'

Hilva bent down and heaved two large, bulging saddlebags onto the table. 'I know it won't take Oak long to get you to Clearview, but, well, it's still cold and you might not get a good reception. I couldn't think of you going hungry, so I packed these for you.'

My mouth dropped. 'What's all that? It's not for me?'

'It's food. I know you have enough clothes, being a Tailor and all, but you might not have enough food. And if you do, then you give this to that mother of yours and tell her I won't have anyone calling you a thief. With that, the hunting gear and the back-sack, you'll be returning most of what she accused you of stealing, so she can wind that poisonous tongue of hers back in and...'

'Hilv,' Gert warned, and Hilva quietened.

I shook my head. 'You must have been up since the early hours, preparing this for me. Did you make the bags too?' I looked between them.

Gert smiled. 'Nope, that was Jeddin. Thanks to you and Oak, he and his wife are now happier than they've been in years. It took him half the night, what with him having to go up to the barn to measure your saddle and Oak's back to make sure they'll sit comfortably on him, and then decide how to make them – he's never had call to make saddlebags before – but he dropped them off a few hours ago.'

'What? Why didn't I hear him? Why didn't you wake me? I need to thank him. Where does he live? And you both, I always seem to be doing it, but, well you know, thank you. Again.'

Hilva smiled, warmly. 'Let's get you ready to travel, and then we'll all go and thank him together, shall we?' She glanced at Gert, who winked.

'Okaaaaay, well I have my stuff by the door. I'll get my cloak and boots on, then we'll have a group outing to Jeddin's, shall we?'

I donned my outdoor clothes and Gert practically put my arms through the straps of my back-sack for me. When I stared at him, he grinned and carried on. 'All set?' he said.

'Yep. Here, Hilva, you're not lugging those, I'll carry them.' I hugged her as I relieved her of the saddlebags. 'And yet again, thank you.'

She giggled. 'You're welcome, dear. Go on, out you go, we'll follow.'

I opened the door and stepped back in shock as cheering erupted outside. The villagers of Mountainlee stood in two rows, forming a corridor that stretched down the path and, as far as I could make out, around the corner and up towards the barns.

Jeddin stood on the doorstep. He held out his hand and when I took it, said, 'Thank you for coming back here to see us, it must have been hard for you, but you and Oak have helped us all tremendously. Gert and Hilva told us you didn't have a Quest Ceremony when you left to find Oak, and it's clearly a bit late now, but we just wanted to send our love and good wishes with you as you go on your way.'

I looked behind me to where Gert stood grinning while Hilva wrung her hands together, smiling but looking nervous. 'I hope you don't mind us telling everyone, it just seemed so unfair and we wanted to put the record straight, and well,' she waved her hand at the queue of people outside, 'this is the result.'

I flung my arms around her and Gert. 'I can never thank you enough.' I turned back to everyone waiting outside and cupped my hands to my mouth. 'I CAN NEVER THANK YOU ENOUGH,' I shouted to them all, and their cheering increased.

I hugged Jeddin. 'Thank you for the saddlebags, I'll treasure them. Honestly, I will.'

He waved me past him. 'It was nothing compared to what you and Oak have done for me. Farewell, love.'

I was hugged and wished well by each and every villager as I made my way past them, to the barn. By the time I left the human corridor behind, I was covered in flower petals, and tiny horseshoes made from metal or fabric hung in my hair and from my clothes, carrying the best wishes of everyone who had showered them on me. Everyone cheered again and followed me up to the barn, where Oak waited at the paddock gate, massive as ever, his black ears pricked, his eyes shining. He stood patiently accepting strokes and hugs while I went to fetch his saddle from its place atop a straw bale in the barn. When I returned, he, like me, was covered in petals, and more of the tiny horseshoes hung in his forelock, mane and tail.

I couldn't help laughing aloud, both in delight and at the sight of my huge, powerful horse standing stoically as ever, neither delighting in his adornments, nor deeming them of sufficient bother to shake off. He blinked a flower petal off the eyelashes of one of his eyes, and I laughed even harder.

Oak, I'm sorry, it's just that – well, look at you. Look at us both!

He just blinked again. There was no sense of displeasure from him, no sense that he felt one way or another, actually. He was just waiting for me to saddle him and mount, and then we would be on our way.

I waited until everyone had stroked, hugged and kissed him goodbye, then cleared the petals from the saddle area of his back. Once his saddle was in place and Jeddin had shown me how to attach the saddlebags, I climbed onto the fence and mounted. Cheering erupted again.

I looked around for Gert and Hilva, and saw them standing together, arm in arm, at the back of the crowd. I blew them each a kiss, which they returned. As soon as I looked up at the mountainside, Oak walked towards it.

I turned and waved to the villagers of Mountainlee. 'THANK YOU!' They all waved and cheered.

Oak picked his way through the rocks, up the slope. When we reached the trees, I looked back down to the village. I made out two dots where the crowd had been, and waved with both arms, hoping that Gert and Hilva could see me. I thought my eye caught a little movement, and hoped they were waving back. Then we were in the forest.

The trees grew closely and their lower branches, although leafless and apparently dead, were too low for me to get under whilst on Oak's back. I stopped following my horse's movement and he stopped beneath me. I landed on the forest floor with a thud, and ran my stirrups up their leathers so they wouldn't bang his sides. As soon as I was by his head, he strode onward.

My stomach fluttered. *To Clearview, then.*

I walk by your side.

I breathed in and out, slowly. I was with Oak. He was my horse, my partner, my strength. My stomach calmed.

Chapter Twenty-Four

*O*ur trek back to the pass between Highpasture and Clearview was a slow one. Oak wanted me to ride him, but I refused to entertain the idea. There was little for him to eat whilst we climbed up the mountainside through the trees, and, although I was relieved to see grass lining either side of the track along the ridge, it was sparse and tough. What little nutrition Oak could gain from it was for him to use to keep himself going, without the burden of carrying me.

I was relieved when we reached the turning to Highpasture. The village was named for the rocky grasslands that surrounded it, gradually tapering to wide swathes both sides of the track that met the one on which Oak and I had been walking. Immediately, he dropped his head to graze. Relieved beyond measure, I unsaddled him and brushed him down, then sat down at the edge of the track and leant back against a rock, enjoying the feel of the warm sunshine on my face even as the spring air nipped at my nose and ears.

There was just the mountain pass to go before Clearview

would be in sight. My stomach flipped, and then settled as the sound of Oak's steady munching calmed me. I supposed I should eat too. I found some smoked meat sandwiches and some dried fruit in one of my saddlebags, and forced them down. Then I closed my eyes and snoozed the hours away until Oak was ready to move on.

When I felt him divert his attention from selecting which blades of grass to eat and which to discard, I sat up and stretched. *We'll be there before dark. I'm not sure if anyone will put us up in Clearview, but there'll be plenty of grass by the lake for you to eat, and water, obviously.* I smiled. The thought of camping out by the lake appealed to me. I had food, water, clothes... and Oak. That was all I needed.

Oak wandered over and stood patiently while I saddled him, making sure his saddlebags rested comfortably against his sides. I moved to his head, ready to walk with him.

You should ride to your home village, Oak informed me.

I don't think it will have the same effect as when we arrived in Mountainlee. I'm not coming back here as a Horse-Bonded, to help, I'm returning as the embarrassment of the family, of the village, to try to make amends.

Yet you are Horse-Bonded. You cannot be otherwise. Be true to who you are and that is who they will see.

So I just act as if the past didn't happen? I arrive as any other Horse-Bonded would, and offer your counsel to anyone who wants it?

If you allow yourself to be drawn back to the past then you will make it the present. Focus on who you are. We are Bond-Partners and we will behave as such. He was as solid in my mind as he was in his body.

I stroked his neck as I stood on the rock against which I'd been leaning. *I'm so glad you're here with me.*

I would be nowhere else.

I mounted and as soon as I had my feet in my stirrups, Oak headed for the pass. He walked purposefully, confidently, and I was glad he'd insisted I ride. My body moved with his and my mind settled into his. I could do this.

Oak's footsteps echoed as he trotted through the pass, bouncing back and forth between the walls so that it sounded as if there were hundreds of horses instead of just one. When we reached the far end, the sun was low in the sky, its rays skimming the water and then dancing off towards our destination.

As soon as we reached the bank of the lake, Oak leapt into canter, overjoyed to be free of the rocks and stones that had slowed our journey from Mountainlee. I laughed, delighting in his speed and power.

We were upon Clearview in no time. Those out attending to chores in the paddocks that adjoined the cottages stood staring, and some waved. My heart fluttered. No one here had ever waved to me before.

You are Cloud In The Storm. Oak's use of the name that only he called me brought the tiny part of my mind that had strayed from him, bounding back.

I looked around us both as he slowed to a trot, his hooves clattering on the cobbles, and then to a walk. People flung open windows and ran out of cottages, smiles on their faces – until they recognised me. Those who hung out of windows stared, those who had been running stopped in their tracks. I could feel my mind separating from Oak's again as I recognised each in turn, and remembered.

I shook myself. That was then. *I'm Horse-Bonded,* I told my horse, *and I'm with you.* We halted as one.

I looked around at everyone who was staring at me. 'You all know who I was, but I'm not that person anymore,' I called out, my voice clear and strong. 'This is my Bond-Partner, Oak. He's helped me to see all the mistakes I've made, and to move past them. He's wise and patient and I'm trying to be more like him.'

'You? Rowena Harrol? Wise and patient? Ignorant, arrogant and aggressive, more like,' someone called from a window. My breath caught in my throat.

Cloud In The Storm.

I was back with him. His strength was mine. 'I'm Rowena of the Horse-Bonded. If anyone would like Oak's counsel, I'm more than happy to pass it on to you. We're going to visit my family and then I imagine we'll be camping down by the lake, if any of you would like to come and see us there. We've come here from Mountainlee, where a lot of people are a whole lot happier for having received Oak's advice. Please, don't let the past be the present. I apologise for any wrongs I've done here; I didn't know any better. Now, thanks to Oak, I do. He's helped me, and he can help you all too.'

There was silence. Everyone stared at me, some with their mouths open. Oak took a step forward, then another. I gently squeezed my heels to his sides in agreement to move on. I smiled to everyone who watched us, and more mouths dropped open.

Footsteps sounded on the cobbles behind us and I turned to see that those who had been outside their cottages were following us.

'As I said, Oak and I are going to see my family. If you'd like his counsel, we'll be available for that once we're down by the lake,' I said to them.

'I'm not missing the look on your mum's face when she sees you,' said a boy I recognised as a friend of Finch's. The mention of my mother was almost enough to shake me loose from Oak. Almost.

Oak spun around to face the boy, who stepped backwards.

'Tarry Swinson,' I said firmly. 'Your parents didn't bring you up to delight in the pain of others. Go. Home.'

Tarry looked from Oak to me, then nodded and did as he was told. Those who were behind him turned and walked away too, but not before a couple of them nodded to me, one with the ghost of a smile. I slowly breathed out as Oak turned back the way we'd been going.

I nodded and smiled at those we passed on our way to Harrolhouse, occasionally stopping to repeat my earlier apology and offer of help, and once to ask another small crowd who had decided it would be entertaining to see my mother's reaction to my return, to leave us be. Everyone did as I asked. I was Rowena of the Horse-Bonded, I reminded myself over and over.

We reached Harrolhouse just as the last rays of sunshine were fading, one by one. I knew that my family would be preparing to sit down to dinner at this time, with Heron and Finch in charge of herding the others to the bathroom to wash their hands, and then back down the stairs to sit at the table before their food got cold. I looked up and down the street, which was empty. Curtains twitched at a few windows, though. I sighed.

The front door was flung open. Heron peered out, her eyes wide. 'Ro? Is it really you? When I heard hooves on the cobbles, I hoped it was, but I can't believe it.'

Finch pushed past her. 'Of course it's her,' he said, grinning, and tore down the path. I dismounted just in time for him to throw himself at me. 'I knew you'd come back, I knew it,' he said, hugging me tightly.

I laughed as I hugged him back, but soon stopped as I felt his shoulders shuddering. I stroked his hair and whispered, 'I'm sorry I left the way I did, I'm so sorry. Don't cry Finch, there's no need to cry, everything's okay.'

He stepped back from me, frantically wiping his face with his hands. 'I'm not crying. I don't cry. I just... missed you, that's all.'

'We all did,' Heron said, sidestepping her brother and putting her arms around me. 'When that Pedlar brought word about why you left, we understood why you did it the way you did, but we were so worried about you when the snows came,' she whispered.

'You know me, tough as old leather,' I said with a grin, stepping back from her as Kite and Robin came tearing down the path. 'This is Oak,' I said to Heron and Finch, nodding to where Oak stood watching my newly-arrived, crying brothers wrapping themselves around my waist and back as if it were a scene he saw every day. He lowered his head and blew gently on the top of Kite's head. My four-year-old brother stopped crying and looked up at the big, black giant above him, his eyes wide.

'He's beautiful, isn't he, Kite?' Heron said, crouching down next to my youngest brother and hugging him even as he still clung to me.

Shouts and screams announced that the rest of my brothers and sisters had heard of my arrival. I was kissed and hugged, Oak was kissed and hugged, and there was squealing and laughter all around, until suddenly, everyone was silent except for two-year-old Wren.

'Lift me, Weena, lift me,' she begged. I hoisted her onto my hip, where she giggled as Oak began to nuzzle her shoulder. Movement caught my eye and I looked over my siblings' heads to the front step, on which now stood my step-father and my mother. My step-father smiled. I knew the look my mother wore, from long experience. She was furious.

Chapter Twenty-Five

𝓜y mother glared at me, her blue eyes cold and penetrating. That one look from her was all it took for me to forget everything except that I was disliked, unwanted and unloved.

Anger unfurled within me, spreading rapidly until I could see no way past it. How dare she look at me that way? How dare she be angry? She'd made my life a misery. She'd given me no choice but to leave the way I did, and then she'd poisoned the world against me. I thought back to what had happened at The Gathering and felt anew the pain she'd caused me. But then I remembered turning in the snow to see Oak dragging himself towards me. My anger melted like butter in a hot pan. My horse loved me. I reached for him where I knew he would be – where I knew he would always be.

You once more absorbed her pain and felt it as your own, he told me gently. *You have already lived it. Acted on it. In so doing you have protected her from having to feel the full force of it for herself. Cloud In The Storm we are the love and the strength you*

*saw in me when you gave me my name. Use what we are. Refuse
to adopt your mother's pain as your own so that you can both
begin to heal.*

Through our bond, I saw my mother clinging to Kerk whilst
continuing to glare at me. Where I'd seen dislike, disapproval and
rejection in her eyes, now I just saw the pain of someone who had
been left by her first love and then, twenty years later, by her
second. My heart went out to her. She felt so much pain because
she felt so much love. The two had become so twisted together
where my father and I were concerned, she couldn't separate them
back out.

'I just need to talk to Mummy. I'm going to pass you to Heron,
so you can carry on stroking Oak. Okay?' I whispered to Wren.

She nodded happily, barely pausing her gentle strokes of Oak's
nose as Heron took her from me. My brothers and sisters parted to
let me through, most of them looking nervously between my
mother and me. Then their eyes widened and Wren let out a
disappointed shriek.

I walk by your side. Oak appeared next to me, crushing my
mother's plants under his enormous feet.

I put a hand to his neck. *I love you, Oak.*

My mother pushed Kerk away slightly as Oak and I stopped in
front of them. She stood straight and put her hands on her hips.
She didn't look at Oak. Not once. 'So, you've finally decided to
grace us with your presence, have you? There's no room for you
here. We don't welcome thieves into our home.'

I flinched, but Oak's massive presence held on to me. I
shrugged off my back-sack, untied Kerk's hunting gear and back-
sack and handed them to him. 'I apologise for taking these, Kerk,
but I didn't know how long it would take me to find Oak, and I
knew you wouldn't need them until spring...'

'Which arrived some time ago. How do you think Kerk felt,

having to ask Kerry to make him a new bow, because his had been stolen by a member of his family? STOLEN!' screamed my mother. She grabbed the bow and arrows and shoved them back at me. 'You wanted them so badly that you stole them and slipped away into the night? You keep them.'

I heard Wren and Kite begin to cry and turned briefly to see Heron and Kestrel trying to get them to smile and skip as they lead them away.

'You asked Larcen to make sure your message reached me, and I received it. You said you wanted everything returned that I took. So here is Kerk's gear.' I handed it to Kerk, who took it and mouthed, 'Thank you.'

With trembling fingers, I undid the buckles that held Oak's saddlebags in place, and put them both down on the step. 'And here is food to replace what I took. If it's not enough, I have more in my back-sack.'

'Of course it's not enough. You took off without a word to anyone, leaving me to look after the children and see to the shop by myself, and you think that turning up months later, when it's too late, makes everything alright, do you? You always were selfish. You always had to have everything your own way. I should never have trusted you. I should never have loved you.'

I stared into her eyes. She was looking at me, but seeing my father. That was how it had always been, I could see that now. I felt the pain I'd always felt when my mother looked at me that way, but I felt removed from it, as if it weren't really mine. Oak stood unmoving beside me, his slow, deep breaths inviting mine to stay slow and deep beside him, reminding me of our bond. Our strength.

'I love you, Mum. I've made your life difficult, I know that. Every time I saw the pain in your eyes when you looked at me, I thought you didn't love me, so I pretended I didn't love you either. But I do. And I know you love me too.'

Her eyes softened and for a moment, she looked at me the way she looked at Heron, Finch, Kestrel, Robin, Swift, Crow, Kite and Wren. But then her eyes hardened again. 'You aren't capable of love. I had to stand here, on my own front doorstep, and listen to Jewner telling me how proud I should be of you, how talented a Tailor you are. When I told him you'd passed my work off as your own, he had the gall to tell me you couldn't possibly have done, that it was the highest quality workmanship he'd ever seen! As if that didn't make it mine!' She narrowed her eyes. 'You did that to me. You made me look like the fool you've always been. And then you left, as I always knew you would. You left without a backward glance, for something better. As if I'm not good enough, as if I could never be good enough.'

What would once have been a shooting, lancing pain in my heart at her words, was a dull ache that merely passed through it, immediately dissipated by the love I felt from my horse. I glanced at him as he stood beside me, composed as ever, his ears pricked forward towards my mother, his eyes bright, as if she were all he hoped to see. I looked back at my mother, whose eyes were now wild. The contrast between the one who had shaped my life up until a few months ago and the one whose lead I now followed, couldn't have been greater.

'It doesn't matter what you say to me, Mum. I love you. I hope that one day, you'll let yourself believe me.'

'People who love other people don't leave them,' she spat.

'People who love other people let them go,' I said softly. 'Oak and I will be camping down by the lake for a few days, so maybe we'll see you again before we leave. I love you, Mum. And you, Kerk.' I attempted to smile at him. He gave a half smile back, and nodded.

Oak and I turned and walked back down the path. Finch had an arm around Crow, and Robin and Swift were hugging each other. All four were crying, although Finch was biting his lip and rubbing his sleeve against his face as he tried not to. 'It's okay, everything's okay,' I said, hugging each of them in turn.

Finch shook his head. 'No it's not. We had plenty of food to last us the winter, you only took what you needed. And you were tugged. You had to go and you had to do it the way you did, we all know that, except her. She's a cow to you, she always has been and now she's even worse. It's never going to be the same again, is it? You're never going to live in Clearview again, are you?'

'No, I'm not. My place is with Oak, now, but that doesn't mean I won't visit, and it doesn't mean I don't love you all. Finch?'

He nodded and tried to smile. 'I love you too, Weena.'

I laughed. 'You were the first one to call me that. Look at you now, fourteen, handsome and pretty flipping amazing. I'm proud of you, Finch, and you three.' I looked at Crow, Robin and Swift. 'You look after your mum, okay?'

They all nodded, and Finch reached for my hand. 'We're proud of you too. So's mum. She'll never admit it, but I see her smile when people talk about you being Horse-Bonded. She can't look at you, but she loves you.'

I smiled. 'I know. See you tomorrow?'

'You're really going to camp down by the lake? In the cold?' said Robin.

'Yes, I am. Don't worry, I'm used to it and anyway, it's never cold when Oak's with me.'

'Does he keep you warm?' Swift said, her eyes full of concern.

'He does. He lies down next to me, and I snuggle up to him. He's so big and warm, it's like cuddling up in front of the fire.

Come and put your hand on his shoulder, and you'll see what I mean.'

Swift, Robin and Crow all rushed to do as I said.

'Can we come and camp with you? Can we snuggle up to Oak too?' Crow said.

'I don't think Mum will like that,' Finch said, scowling towards where my mother and Kerk still stood on the doorstep. My mother was crying.

'No, she won't and she's right not to. You four run on inside, now. Heron and Kestrel will be back soon with Wren and Kite, and I bet your dinner's getting cold. I'll see you tomorrow, okay?'

Crow's eyes filled with tears and he wrapped his arms tightly around me. 'You promise you'll be there? You won't leave in the night again?'

I crouched down to him. 'Did you find the crow I left for you on your pillow?'

He nodded.

'When I stitched it together, I put a little bit of myself into it. So you see, I never really left you, because that little piece of me was always with you. But yes, I promise Oak and I will be by the lake in the morning, and for a few mornings after that, I should think. Go on in now, and I'll see you tomorrow.'

I hugged them all, then repeated my promise to Heron and Kestrel as they arrived back with Kite and Wren. Heron sent our youngest two siblings running up the path to dinner, then lingered with Kestrel.

'You're different,' Kestrel said, stroking Oak's nose. 'Happy. I'm glad for you, Ro.'

'You found your letter and certificate from Jewner?' Heron said.

I nodded. 'I'm so sorry I didn't wake you. I couldn't risk

anyone making a noise and waking Crow, you know what would have happened if Mum had woken up.'

'I told you, we get it. We all do,' Heron said. 'I don't suppose you need to be qualified as a Tailor now, though? Now you're Horse-Bonded?'

I smiled. 'I do. I have a place in the Tailor's workshop at The Gathering. I love it.'

Heron smiled back. 'What's it like?'

'Heron, Kestrel, come on now, please, dinner's already cold thanks to your sister, I need your help heating it back up,' my mother called from the step.

My sisters looked at her and then back at me, their brows creased, their eyes sad.

'It's fine, go. We can catch up tomorrow. Come and see me and Oak whenever you have time.'

They both nodded, then obediently headed for the house. I smiled and waved as they shut the front door. My stomach began to ache as I stood out on the street, looking at the building that housed those I loved, but in which I wasn't welcome.

I didn't do anything wrong. I said the right things, I know it, I can feel it through our bond. But it still hurts, Oak.

It will hurt for some time yet. During your life you have absorbed more pain than you have been able to express. The difference is lodged within your body. You will feel it whenever events cause it to rise to the surface. Then you will release it a little at a time until there is nothing that can cause you to forget who you really are.

Oak and I walked the streets of Clearview, silent now that the temperature was falling as rapidly as the darkness. I felt a strange sort of contentment. I was back where I'd formed so many unhappy memories, and as it stood, things weren't a whole load different; I was out in the cold, literally, while everyone else was warm in both their houses and the companionship of their families. Yet I felt distanced from the life I'd lived here, as if its hard edges had softened, as if the sharp points of its corners had been rounded off – as if it weren't as bad as I remembered it after all.

Chapter Twenty-Six

*O*ak and I spent four days in Clearview, most of it at our lakeside camp, and much of it in the company of my brothers and sisters.

I was always warned of their imminent arrival by the laughing and shrieking of the younger ones as they tore up to Oak, who would raise his head from grazing and calmly watch their approach, then patiently endure the kissing and hugging of whichever parts of his body they could reach.

I loved my horse for not moving a muscle as Wren hugged his knees, Kite hugged his hocks, Crow hugged his belly and the others took it in turns to hug his head and neck. He blew over them, nuzzled them and conceded to every request from each and every sibling, to be allowed to sit on his back. He took to going back to his grazing while one or two, sometimes three of my younger sisters and brothers sat astride him, stroking his neck and back as they chattered away to him and to one another.

'He looks so massive and scary, but he's so gentle, isn't he?' Finch said as he, Kestrel, Heron and I sat together, playing with

Wren whilst watching Crow and Kite sitting facing one another on Oak's back, playing a clapping game. Robin was brushing Oak's thick, black tail while Swift was jumping up and down, trying and failing to brush Oak's rump.

'He's gentle, he's patient, he's loving and he's wise,' I said.

'So he's just like you,' Kestrel said. 'You can be scary on the outside, but inside, you're all of those things.'

I reached across and squeezed her hand. 'Thanks, Kes, I'm trying to be. I really am.'

I wish Mum would see it,' said Kestrel. 'It doesn't matter how much we stick up for you, she just won't believe us, even now you're Horse-Bonded.'

I sighed. 'It's not really me she can't stand, it's my father. She loves your dad, you know that, but mine is like a thorn wedged in so deeply, she doesn't know how to get it out. In wanting to be rid of it, she drives it in deeper. What she needs is a poultice to draw it out.' In an instant, Oak was with me in my mind, observing, waiting. I remembered the change in my mother's eyes when I told her I loved her, and gasped. 'I know what the poultice is.' I stood up. 'Come on, you lot need to come with me.'

Heron stood up. 'Where? I promised I'd have this lot back in time for dinner. Even then, Mum didn't want us to come. She won't let us come again if we're late.'

'You won't be late.'

There was a shriek as Oak slowly, carefully, made his way over to us so as to not dislodge Kite and Crow, who clasped hold of one another and began to giggle.

'Right you two, off you get, Robin and Swift can take a turn after they've worked so hard making Oak gleam like that,' I said. Kestrel and Finch each dragged a laughing child from Oak's back, and Heron and I gave ten-year-old Robin and eight-year-old Swift a leg up, as I'd shown them the previous day. Robin wrapped his arms around his sister, who held on to a clump of Oak's mane. 'Sit loosely and follow his movement, like I showed you yesterday, okay?' I said and they both nodded eagerly. 'Thanks mate,' I whispered to Oak. Oak barely registered my thought; my gratitude was unnecessary.

My heart swelled with love for him. I knew he sensed how much it meant to me to leave my brothers and sisters with happy memories of us both for when we couldn't be with them.

We walked around the lake until we were no longer between it and the village, then headed up behind the village, to the woods. Oak had picked up from me where we were going and walked on ahead, carrying a quiet, concentrating Robin and Swift. The rest of us followed, Heron carrying Wren on her hip, me with Crow on my shoulders and Finch with Kite on his back.

'Has Oak been here before? He seems to know where we're going,' Finch said.

'He knows everything, but at the moment he's following the sense he has from me of what we're heading for. You'll see why when we get there.'

'I've only been in these woods once, when Finch and I were little kids and you ran away,' Heron said. 'But you kept coming back here after that. Are we going to your hiding place?'

Oak stopped in front of us. Robin and Swift stared up at the massive tree that stood proud and strong in its clearing.

'We're here. This is the tree I used to come to when I needed to get away from Mum. I used to climb into its branches and I felt... actually, never mind that, you climb it for yourself and see how you feel. Go on, it's really easy, there are handholds and footholds everywhere. I'll wait here with Kite and Wren.'

Finch and Crow needed no encouraging. By the time Heron and Kestrel had helped Robin and Swift down from Oak's back, the first two of my brothers to reach the tree were already up past the lower branches. Robin and Swift were quick to follow, and as I lifted Wren and Kite back up onto my ever patient Oak, Heron and Kestrel also began to climb. As they disappeared from sight, there were excited shouts from higher up in the branches.

'This is amaaaaaaaaazing,' called Crow.

'We can see for miiiiiiiiles,' agreed Robin.

'Why haven't we ever done this before?' Heron's voice wafted down to me. 'This is such good fun.'

'Find a branch to sit on, and then just be still and quiet for a few minutes, see how you feel,' I called up.

There was rustling and the odd crack as twigs were removed for easier passage, then all was silent.

'Are they awight?' four-year-old Kite asked me.

'They're fine. They've gone quiet because it's very peaceful up there. When you're bigger, Finch will bring you up here and you can find out for yourself. Let's watch really carefully and see who's the first to spot one of them, shall we?'

Kite and Wren stared up into the branches. None of our siblings moved.

Eventually, I called up to them all. 'Okay, you lot, you're going to have to come on down now, or you'll be late for dinner.'

'I could stay up here all night,' Kestrel's voice wafted down dreamily.

'And me,' Swift replied.

There was a rustling of leaves and Heron's foot appeared, searching for a foothold.

'There.' Kite pointed. 'It's Hewon, I won, I saw her first.'

'Well done Kite,' Heron said. 'Come on you lot, it's harder coming down than going up. We don't want to be late home, because Ro'll get the blame.' Branches shook and leaves rustled as the others obeyed her.

Wren pointed her tiny finger at high up in the tree. 'Crow.'

'Finch, are you up there with Crow?' I yelled.

'Yep,' Finch yelled back breathlessly. 'We're on our way down now, if I can keep up with him. You'd think he was born up here, the way he's leaping around.'

I smiled. Of all my brothers and sisters, Crow was the most sensitive. He slept lightly and woke at the slightest sound. He panicked easily and was usually the last to do anything new, preferring to wait until he'd seen everyone else go first. The ease he'd taken to being around and sitting on Oak had amazed me, so I guessed I shouldn't have been surprised the tree had the same effect on him. It wasn't just my mother who would benefit from coming here regularly.

Thanks, Adam and Peace, I thought to my friends, wishing I could let Adam know the effect his tree was having on my brother.

He knows.

How? Can he connect with my mind the way you can?

Not yet. He knows what he left behind. He knows the effect it has.

Adam infused the tree with love. Why?

That is for him to tell you if he so chooses. He left it here for whoever requires it. You were wise to bring your family here. You have set in motion a sequence of events that will lead to the healing you wish for them. For you. We should be on our way soon.

Why do we need to go? My brothers and sisters will bring my mother here. Could I not wait to see if she'll accept me once the tree starts working its magic on her?

You likened your father to a thorn that must be drawn out of her. Your presence here will hold that thorn in place even as the love within the tree works to draw it out.

The ache in my stomach returned.

And you must have the time and space to release the pain you have stored within you, Oak told me.

The only way we can both heal is if we're apart from one another?

Even then it will take time and it will not be easy. Yet you will both emerge from the lessons you have taught one another with knowledge you could not otherwise have gained. That which causes pain in one instant can be viewed in another as that which was necessary for greater understanding.

You're always right, I know that, it's just that... it's just...

When you need respite from the pain of the situation you have only to take sanctuary in our bond.

Our bond. Immediately, the pain in my stomach eased, and peace and strength returned. I smiled as Finch reached up and picked Crow off the tree trunk, tickling him as he put him on the ground.

'I take it you all enjoyed that?' I said.

Crow, Finch, Swift and Robin all nodded, avidly, their eyes bright.

'I can see why you spent so much time up there.' Heron nodded up at the huge branches that stretched over our heads. 'It's like the rest of the world is far away and nothing can upset you, isn't it?'

I smiled as I nodded to her. 'It is. What about you, Kes?' I turned to my fourteen-year-old sister.

'I didn't want to come down. I felt like I used to when I was little and Mum used to sing me to sleep. Thanks for bringing us here, Ro, I'll definitely be coming back. I think we all will.'

'And you'll bring Mum? She might not want to climb the tree, but that doesn't matter. Just being near it will help. It's the poultice we were talking about.' I glanced quickly at Heron,

Kestrel and Finch, all three of whom nodded. 'Right then, let's get you back.'

The sight of Wren and Kite riding Oak bareback through the streets of Clearview brought people running to their front gates, waving and smiling at my youngest brother and sister, who giggled and waved back delightedly. When we reached Harrolhouse, I lifted them both down and hugged them, then Swift, Robin and Crow.

'Take Mum to the tree as soon as possible, and after that, try to get her up there as often as you can. Okay?' I murmured to Heron.

She nodded. 'We'll be down to see you again tomorrow.'

'Only if there's time. Taking Mum to the tree is more important. I think you'll have your hands full keeping Crow away from it, anyway.'

She laughed. 'He was a different boy when he was near it, wasn't he? Okay, fine, I'll make sure we all go up there. But I'm seeing you too, even if I have to come down to the lake after dinner, in the dark.'

I grinned and hugged her. 'Love you. And you, Kes.' I grabbed Kestrel and drew her into our hug. 'And you, Finch.' I grabbed my brother, who yelled in protest at being hugged by three sisters at once, out in the street. 'Now get gone.'

They all grinned before following the younger ones, who were already yelling about their experiences at the tree, to Kerk, who stood just inside the front door, hugging each as he propelled them inside. He waved to me and grinned. I waved back and then turned to walk away with Oak at my side, as always.

'Um, Rowena?' I turned to see one of my old schoolteachers standing at the gate of her cottage, diagonally opposite

Harrolhouse. Maila was retired now. Her lined face was as kind as I remembered it; she had always been very fair with me, even when my behaviour was at its worst. 'I have a question for Oak. Is this a good time to ask him, or shall I come down to the lakeside after dinner? Or I can bring dinner for you and me down to the lakeside, and we can eat it together?'

I smiled at her. 'This is an excellent time for you to ask him. He's hungry, so I need to get him back to where he can graze, but you're welcome to walk with us?' She smiled back warmly, and fell in beside me.

It was as if everyone else in the village had been waiting for the first to approach me before following suit. By the time Maila and I had reached the grazing between Clearview and the lake, a crowd of people trailed behind us.

'Please thank Oak for his advice,' Maila said as my horse dropped his head down to graze. She looked back at those who followed in our wake. 'It looks as though you have a long evening ahead of you. I'll be back in an hour with your dinner; that's one job less for you to do. And then you and Oak are welcome to come and lodge with me for the remainder of your stay in Clearview? There's plenty of room in my paddock for him now I only have chickens, and plenty of grass. I would have asked before, but with living so close to your family and, well, with your mother...'

I lifted a hand. 'Maila, it's okay, I understand. Dinner would be lovely. Thank you for your invitation, but as you said, you live close to my family, and it's easier on my mother if she doesn't have to see me, so regretfully, I'll decline your invitation to stay.'

'It's so cold at night, though.'

'I don't really feel it with Oak to snuggle up to. Don't worry, I'm fine. I'd better get on and sort this lot.'

She nodded. 'Okay, well I'll be back in an hour, then.

Rowena,' she said as I turned to the crowd. I turned back to her. 'You had a rough time, I know that. I did what I could, but I never felt as if it was enough. Despite it all, you've grown into a young woman any mother should be proud of. In any case, I'm proud of you. We all are.'

The ache in my stomach returned. I reached for Oak and it disappeared again. 'Thank you.'

Maila nodded and hurried away.

I turned back to the people now crowding around Oak. 'Right you lot, lovely as it is that you want Oak's advice, we'll never get through you all this evening. You guys,' I made a slicing motion with my arm, cutting off the two thirds of the crowd to my right, 'will need to come back in the morning, I'm afraid. An hour after dawn will be fine. The rest of you, if you could just hang back a bit so that whoever is with Oak and me has a bit of privacy... that's it, great. Okay, Simon, I think you were first, come on over.'

The following day saw one villager after another coming to see Oak for his counsel. Some of them were awkward to begin with – mostly those with whom I'd had the biggest fights and quarrels – but as soon as I began to relay Oak's counsel to them, their faces relaxed into the now familiar expression of one trying to understand and absorb what they were hearing.

I had many offers of lodging, all of which were gratefully received but refused. The hot food that was brought at regular intervals was welcome, however. I'd just finished one such meal when Heron appeared out of the darkness.

'I waited until everyone else had gone,' she said. 'Was it that busy all day?'

'Pretty much,' I said, motioning for her to sit down by the fire that crackled merrily as it fended off the cold mist settling over the lake. 'Good day?'

She nodded. 'Strange day, starting with the fact that Crow slept the whole night through for the first time ever. He's been full of how amazing the tree is, and kept on and on at Mum until she and Dad both agreed to come with us after the kids got home from school. Dad didn't seem affected by it much, but as soon as Mum saw the tree, she pretty much ran up to it and put her hands on its trunk. She didn't even notice Crow climbing it as fast as a squirrel, right next to her. I thought Dad was going to faint. He only just grabbed hold of Kite before he followed Crow. Then Mum just sat down on the ground, leant back against the tree, and cried. Not loudly, in fact only Dad and I noticed, but it was like a blister popping, you know when all the goo inside just oozes out?'

I nodded.

'Like that. When it was time to go home, she stood up, hugged Dad and then all of us, and didn't talk until we were back at the house. Then she flicked back into being Mum again, you know, saying who had to help her with dinner, who had homework to do. What is it about that tree? Why does sitting in it feel like sitting on Oak?'

'They're both made of the same stuff,' I said. 'Remember that when we're gone.'

'You're going tomorrow, aren't you?' Heron said, a tremble in her voice.

'Yes, I think so. By all accounts, there are only a few people left wanting Oak's counsel, so we'll be on our way.'

'Back to The Gathering?'

I considered. 'Eventually. We'll take our time getting back there, I have some villages to visit on the way.'

'It must be amazing, being Horse-Bonded.'

'It's challenging, and scary at times, but yes, it's amazing.

You'll bring the others to see us off? We won't leave until lunchtime.'

'I wish you didn't have to go. We'll all miss you and Oak so much.'

'I'll miss you too, but I'll write as often as I can. Let me know how Mum gets on? Letters sent to The Gathering will always reach me sooner or later.'

She nodded and hugged me. 'I will. I'd better get back. I'll see you tomorrow.' She disappeared into the night.

I couldn't have known that it would be four years before I would return to Clearview – four years of turmoil and upheaval for the Horse-Bonded; four years of challenge and hardship from which we and the rest of the human race would emerge unrecognisable from who we were now; four years before my mother would be ready to see me, to welcome me home, to pull me into her arms and cry at all that had happened between us, all the time we had lost. But through my bond with Oak, I knew that everything would be okay, eventually.

It was a tearful farewell all round. Each of my brothers and sisters presented me with a drawing they had done of Oak and me. They ranged from Wren's, which was little more than a black squiggle, to Kestrel's, which portrayed my horse and me as one giant black beast with two faces, one pale with dark eyes, the other dark with white, ethereal eyes. It was mesmerising. Heron's drawing was in charcoal and depicted me as tall and beautiful, sitting gracefully astride the powerful majesty that was Oak. A lump rose in my throat at each and every depiction of my Bond-Partner and me, so different but so personal, so touching.

I hugged and kissed them all, staying slightly longer with

Finch than the others so that he had time to wipe his tears before turning back towards where the rest of the village waited, further along the bank of the lake. Then I swung up into my saddle and waved at everyone gathered there.

I almost did a double take at the sight of Kerk and my mother standing right at the back of the crowd, only just past the cobbles of Clearview. I raised my hand higher and waved at them specifically. Kerk waved back and my heart leapt as my mother's hand began to lift from her side. The pain in my stomach returned, accompanied by a stabbing in my heart as her hand dropped back down.

Our bond, I remembered as my beautiful horse gathered himself beneath me and powered us both away along the bank of the lake. I immersed myself within it until the pain faded away to nothing. As long as I had the love of my horse, nothing could hurt me. As long as I remembered our bond, I had the strength of Oak.

You are ready for that which lies ahead, Oak informed me.

Which is?

You will recognise it when it comes.

You're referring to what's going to happen at The Gathering? The change for which we're the forerunners?

I felt his assent. Our strength surged through me.

Epilogue

*O*ak and I made our way slowly back to The Gathering, stopping off at Tallwood, Mountainlee, Mettletown and a host of other villages on the way.

In Tallwood, I sought out the elderly couple whose offer of hospitality I rejected whilst on my way to find Oak. In Mountainlee, I stayed with Gert and Hilva, who were delighted to welcome me back again so soon. When Oak and I arrived in Mettletown, we kept moving until we were outside Shirlee and Rudi's front door, from which wafted the most amazing smell of bread, baked, I subsequently learnt, by Shirlee.

We arrived back at The Gathering during the summer. As soon as Oak was settled into the paddock of his choice, I made for Adam's rooms. His things were all there so he was definitely in residence, but there was no sign of him anywhere and no one seemed to know where he was.

I will take you to He Who Is Peace, Oak informed me.

He Who Is Peace? You've never called him that before. I

hurried to fetch Oak's saddle from the tack room, where I'd only just left it.

It would not have been appropriate before. You should bring equipment that will allow me to move that which is heavy.

I saddled Oak and as soon as I was mounted, a long coil of rope tied around my waist, he took off at a canter down the path to the river. *Oak, you're scaring me. What's happened to Adam? And where's Peace? I don't see him in any of the paddocks.*

They Who Are Peace are well. They merely have need of our assistance.

As soon as Oak was clear of the paddocks, he tore along the river bank for a stretch before veering off of it, up into the hills. He didn't slow down until we reached the brow of one of them... upon which lay Peace.

Adam crouched by his horse's side, his hand on Peace's shoulder as it so often was when they were together. He looked up as Oak, sweating and blowing, halted the same distance from Peace as that upon which the old skewbald horse had insisted when they first met. Peace didn't move. Some of the white hairs of his mane lifted in the gentle summer breeze, then fell back down, as lifeless as he was.

Tears poured down Adam's face, yet he was smiling.

'Adam, I'm so sorry,' I said. I dismounted and began to run to him, then slowed to a respectful walk, unsure what to do, how to be. Losing Oak was something I couldn't bear to even contemplate, so I had no idea how to comfort someone who must surely be in the worst pain imaginable – yet Adam continued to smile at me. 'He Who Is Peace,' I murmured.

He nodded, still smiling. 'Don't be sorry for me, or for Peace. He and I are both fine.'

'But he's... gone.'

'He hasn't, not really. He just wanted to leave this old body of his. He was tired, you see. I'm glad you're here, I'm going to need some help burying him.'

We sat side by side, Adam and I, looking over the mound of earth that we had taken turns piling over Peace once Oak had slowly, gently, pulled him into the hole that Adam had insisted on digging by himself with a shovel he'd brought with him; clearly, he and Peace had come here knowing what they were about.

The river sparkled below us in the afternoon sunshine. The sound of Oak grazing nearby soothed me even as I wanted to scream with the pain that Adam had to be feeling as he sat with one hand on the soil of his horse's grave – yet he was still smiling. It wasn't the manic smile of someone who has yet to accept what has happened, or the smile of someone pretending they're okay when they aren't. It was a smile I could feel as well as see. It came from deep inside him and oozed with... peace.

'I'm Cloud In The Storm. You're He Who Is Peace,' I said.

Adam nodded, still looking towards the river. 'I am. Finally, I'm the person Peace always knew I could be, even when I didn't believe it was possible. He never gave up on me. He stayed in his body well past his time until at last, I managed it.' He looked at me. 'Cloud In The Storm, eh? Yet not quite so much as you were, I think. You've had a productive trip.'

I nodded. 'And now we're back. Apparently, I'm ready for what lies ahead of us all.'

Adam's smile was broader than ever. 'I see I'm in formidable company.'

'Do you know what's going to happen? Oak says I have to

challenge opinions and traditions where necessary, which is fine by me, obviously…'

'Naturally,' agreed Adam.

'…because we're the forerunners for a bonded pair who will turn everything upside down. Peace said the same to you?'

'Not exactly. It would make sense for us to all have different roles according to our strengths, though, wouldn't it?' He winked at me.

'Are you ever going to tell me who you are, Adam? I mean, really?'

He shrugged. 'I'm exactly who you think I am.'

'Don't fob me off. You changed that oak tree and it had a huge effect on me, just as it's now affecting my whole family. How is it that my whole life has been connected to you, from when I was a child growing up hundreds of miles away, to now?'

'Everything is connected. It always has been and always will be, sometimes in ways that are obvious, more often in ways that aren't. It seems that, to use Oak's terminology, I've been the forerunner of the forerunners. Don't waste your energy wondering about me. Focus on doing whatever Oak tells you to do, and know that when whatever is coming gets here, I'll be there for you if you need me.'

'What will you do until then? Will you stay on here without Peace?'

Adam put his hand back to the mound of soil. 'It isn't possible for me to be without Peace, not now. Nevertheless, I think I need to be somewhere else while I adjust to the loss of his physical presence.'

'But what if everything blows up while you're gone?'

Adam was quiet for a while. Then he said, 'I don't think it will. I think we have a little time yet. Regardless, you can be confident that if Oak has told you that you're ready for what's coming, then you are.'

I looked over to where Oak grazed, the image of vitality, power and strength. I nodded. 'I'm ready.'

Other books by Lynn Mann

**Humankind is ready for change and
Rowena has a part to play...**

The Horses Know Trilogy

The Horses Know

Amarilla is one of those chosen by a horse as a Bond-Partner. She looks forward to a lifetime of learning from her horse and of passing on the mare's wisdom to those seeking help. But then she discovers that she is the one for whom the horses have all been waiting. The one who can help them in return.

In order to give the horses the help they need, Amarilla will have to achieve that which has never been attempted before. Only her beloved mare can give her the motivation, the courage and the strength to believe she can succeed. If she does, a new era will dawn for horses and humans alike...

The Horses Rejoice (The Horses Know Book 2)

Amarilla and Infinity have been the catalysts for change that they agreed to be, but they know there is more to be done. If they can befriend the Woeful and persuade the rest of humankind to do the same, then the destructive ways of The Old will forever be in the past.

Amarilla, Infinity and their friends set out on a journey to find the Woeful but their search becomes something so much more due to a courageous chestnut mare, a lone Woeful youngling and numerous herds of wild horses who seek their help along the way. But the friends never forget what they agreed to do. They must reach the heart of the Woeful community. And then they must be willing to risk losing everything...

The Horses Return (The Horses Know Book 3)

It has been more than twenty years since the Kindred came to live in Rockwood. Most of the villagers have embraced the Kindred and all that they have to teach, but there are those who fear the Kindreds' influence, and so have drifted away to live as outcasts. The outcasts suffer, living as they do, but they refuse help, even from the Horse-Bonded.

Will is adamant that he can succeed where the Horse-Bonded have failed, and bring the outcasts home. But his forceful personality constantly gets in his way. He is the key to the future, but if he is to play his part, he must allow a herd of wild horses to show him how to be the person he needs to be. Only then will he fully understand the lengths to which Amarilla and Infinity have gone to ensure that he can fulfil his destiny and reunite the human race...

In Search Of Peace (A Prequel to The Horses Know Trilogy)

Adam is on the verge of grief-induced insanity when a horse chooses him as a Bond-Partner and refuses to leave his side. He tries to rid himself of his unwanted companion as he has everyone else, but finds it more difficult than he could have imagined.

Just when it seems as though the horse has managed to find a way through Adam's grief and bring him back to himself, Adam rejects him in the worst possible way, resulting in catastrophe. In order to save the Bond-Partner who has tried so hard to save him, Adam must remember what his would-be saviour tried to teach him. And he must do it soon, before it is too late for both of them…

In Search Of Peace, like The Strength Of Oak, is a prequel to The Horses Know Trilogy and can be read before, alongside or after the other books.

Tales Of The Horse-Bonded
(Companion Stories to The Horses Know Trilogy)

A collection of short companion stories to The Horses Know Trilogy, Tales Of The Horse-Bonded is available to download free. To find out more, please visit www.lynnmann.co.uk.

Did you enjoy The Strength Of Oak?
I'd be extremely grateful if you could spare a few minutes to leave
a review where you purchased your copy. Reviews really do help
my books to reach a wider audience, which means that
I can keep on writing!
Thank you very much.

I love to hear from you!
Get in touch and receive news of future releases at the following:

www.lynnmann.co.uk

www.facebook.com/lynnmann.author

Acknowledgments

Special thanks to Caroline Macintosh for sharing the antics and wisdom of her horse, Miley, with me. He was the inspiration for a significant part of Oak's character and outlook, and a very special horse about whom to write.

Thanks as always to my editorial team: Fern Sherry, Leonard Palmer, Rebecca Walters and Caroline Macintosh – I'd be lost without you all – and to Amanda Horan for her cover design; I get so excited when it's cover reveal time and she never disappoints!

Lastly, massive thanks to you for having read this book – I love spending time in the world of the Horse-Bonded and their horses, and having readers who indulge me by reading my books allows me to do exactly that!